The Complete Fables of La Fontaine

The Complete Fables of La Fontaine

A New Translation in Verse

Translated from the French by Craig Hill
Illustrations by Edward Sorel

Arcade Publishing • New York

For Heather

FIRST EDITION

Library of Congress Cataloging-in-Publication Data

La Fontaine, Jean de, 1621–1695.
  [Fables. English]
  The complete fables of La Fontaine : a new translation in verse / translated from the French by Craig Hill ; illustrations by Edward Sorel. –1st ed.
      p. cm.
  ISBN 978-1-55970-896-8
  I. Hill, Craig. II. Sorel, Edward, 1929– III. Title.
  PQ1811.E3H55 2008
  398.2–dc22   2008031190

Published in the United States by Arcade Publishing, Inc., New York
Distributed by Hachette Book Group USA

Visit our Web site at www.arcadepub.com

10 9 8 7 6 5 4 3 2 1

Designed by API

EB

PRINTED IN THE UNITED STATES OF AMERICA

Contents

BOOK I

Contents

Contents

Contents

BOOK V

BOOK VI

Contents

BOOK VII

Contents

BOOK VIII

Contents

Contents

Contents

List of Illustrations

Translator's Note

When I began these translations, now more than half a century ago, I had no idea what I was getting into. In 1952, five years out of university and imagining that writing poetry was my destined métier, I had left San Antonio for Boston. Once there, I settled in the (long since demolished) West End, on Milton Street – the address seemed an ideal one for practicing my profession.

Among the elder poets of the day whom I read devotedly, one I especially revered was Marianne Moore. But when I began seeing in magazines several of her translations of fables by a seventeenth-century French poet, Jean de La Fontaine, I was puzzled. Though I knew little French at the time, Moore's versions of his work seemed oddly wrong.

These were simple tales, after all, Aesop's fables, transformed by La Fontaine – so critics said – into great works of French poetry. But Moore's English versions of them came across to me as awkward and humorless, with none of the brilliance of language and wit that had made the originals so enduringly famous. (Many years later, when the letters of her friend, Elizabeth Bishop, were published, I learned that Moore's fellow poets had felt as I had at the time but couldn't bring themselves to tell her.)

So it seemed a perfect coincidence when, the following year, on a family visit to San Antonio, among a lot of books that had belonged to a beloved grandmother, I discovered a French edition of the fables, published by Librairie Hachette in 1929, with a rather tattered French–English dictionary sitting on the shelf beside it. It was an irresistible challenge. I took the two books back with me to Boston to see just how difficult it might be to translate such simple-looking poems.

As I said at the beginning, I didn't realize what I was getting into. Though I did not intend at the start to produce a complete translation and indeed ended up doing other things than writing poetry of my own, I kept on translating fables and putting them in the drawer. And though the effort of translation in time became a central thread of my life, both poetically and intellectually, I never worked systematically or sequentially at the task. Admittedly, I skipped around, often trying the fables that looked easiest to do – but still finding it difficult to get them right – and sometimes even stopping altogether for a time as I went through the stages of an ordinary life.

Thus, it is somewhat accidental that you, reader, whoever you may be, now find this volume in your hands, because it was not until much later, when I was in my sixties, that it finally occurred to me that if I kept at it, tortoise–like, I might yet come up with a complete translation. I began to work on fables I had skipped over earlier, filling in the gaps and, one by one, checking off the twelve books into which La Fontaine had divided his extraordinary work. Finally, in August 2006, I had finished translating "The Judge, the Physician, and the Hermit," the fable with which La Fontaine brought Book XII to a close. I had begun translating the fables when I was, quite possibly, younger than La Fontaine when he started composing them and had finished the job when I was older than he was when he died.

As one might expect, my notions about translation changed as I went along. Though my first impulse was to do without rhyme, I soon saw the error of that and began, quite happily, using rhymes of all sorts, perfect and less than perfect, and, like the originals, hardly ever in any formal scheme. (I have, however, retained a few unrhymed or partially rhymed early translations, such as "The Man Who Ran After Fortune and The Man Who Waited for Her in Bed," "Baggage," and "Death and the Dying.")

As to whether I should convert the original hexameter of the fables into iambic pentameter, a question that often comes up in French–to–English translation, I well knew the argument for doing so: hexameter, especially in its alexandrine form, is not a particu-larly comfortable meter for English poetry. But as I thought about the question, torn both ways, I began to see that hexameter's supposed unsuitability was actually a splendid reason to use it: I wanted La Fontaine to "'sound" French, after all, not English.

And so I came down generally on the side of using La Fontaine's own choices of meters: fables he wrote in pentameter I have translated in pentameter; where he used his unique "free verse" mixture of hexameters and tetrameters I have followed suit, not line by line but in each poem as a whole. And the same for fables written in trimeter or in lines of seven syllables, where one must tread a bit carefully so as not to sound like some latter-day Longfellow. Many of the earlier fables, those in the first six books, were clearly meant for reading aloud, and I have paid some attention to that, hoping to give readers at least a hint of the aural pleasure, as well as the wit, that the French have for centuries enjoyed, giving voice to the words La Fontaine wrote.

Craig Hill

Introduction

Since their publication in the seventeenth century, Jean de La Fontaine's fables have sometimes been mistaken for poems for children. But though children learning French have often been made to memorize and recite "Le corbeau et le renard" or one of the other deceptively simple poems with which *Selected Fables* begins, La Fontaine's great book is no more a work for children than are George Orwell's *Animal Farm* or William Blake's *Songs of Innocence*.

Clearly, much of the blame for the confusion lies with La Fontaine himself, because it was to two children that he dedicated the first and last of the twelve books finally making up the complete work. Book I, published in 1668, was dedicated to Louis XIV's son, the seven-year-old dauphin, and Book XII, twenty-six years later, to Louis's grandson, the Duke of Burgundy, the former dauphin's twelve-year-old son.

All of which should serve to confirm the truism that it is best to be cautious in believing what poets say about their work, especially poets who live under tyrants, more especially the satirists among them. Like Stalin in our modern era, Louis XIV was an art lover with a vengeance, not so lethal as Stalin but nonetheless casting a gigantic shadow over all the arts of his own time.

La Fontaine and Louis XIV were very much aware of each other, though the poet would have been at most a speck in the broad landscape of the monarch's long reign, a minor annoyance, while for La Fontaine the king was always a threatening presence, needing to be placated, never to be trusted. The two men, as they say, had a history.

After La Fontaine's early education, he made several false starts at finding a career, first spending two inconclusive years at the Faculty of Law in Paris and then a year as a novice in a seminary, the Oratoire – where, as he later admitted, he found he preferred reading novels to studying religious texts. At last, over the course of another year in Paris, having concluded that he lacked a vocation either for the law or for the religious life, he fell in with a crowd of aspiring young *littérateurs* who gathered at a tavern, La Table Ronde, and realized he had found his life's occupation. But lacking any prospect for supporting himself as a writer at age twenty-five, he returned in 1647 to his parental home in the small town of Château-Thierry, a few miles east of Paris.

Over the next thirteen years, he worked for his father, a minor government official, married a fourteen-year-old local girl from a wealthy family, and fathered a son. He must also have begun to write in earnest, for in 1654, a year after the birth of his only child, he self-published a play, *The Eunuch*, based on a comedy by the ancient Roman dramatist Terence. It did not make a splash.

Three years later, La Fontaine submitted his first major poem, *Adonis*, to France's superintendent of finance, Nicolas Foucquet. Based on the same Greek myth as Shakespeare's *Venus and Adonis*, the effort brought him his first taste of success. His profession was settled: poet. La Fontaine was invited into Foucquet's entourage and offered a generous stipend in return for producing a few suitably entertaining verses each year for his patron's pleasure. By now he was thirty-eight.

La Fontaine had been rescued from oblivion in the provinces. He found himself an equal among a group of the most talented younger poets, dramatists, artists, and intellectuals in France – most notably Molière, a year younger than he but already beginning to be known. One can imagine the deep gratitude he must have felt toward Foucquet. His career as a poet was to be immensely affected over the next several years as he watched the unfolding of his patron's tragic fate.

Politically astute, Foucquet had made himself wealthy in office during the years of the regency following the five-year-old Louis XIV's coronation in 1643. That he would have used his office to enrich himself was perhaps only to have been expected by the standards of the day. Yet he had wanted more than wealth. He seems to have envisioned himself as a Medici prince, a generous patron of all the arts. As such, he needed to build himself a commensurate setting, a palace.

By the time La Fontaine joined his entourage, Foucquet had already begun building his château at Vaux-le-Vicomte. It was to be an architectural masterpiece in the new Palladian style, designed, constructed, and furnished to the last detail by the brilliant trio Foucquet had assembled: the architect Louis Le Vau, the painter Charles Le Brun, and the landscape architect André Le Nôtre. As he watched the building take shape, La Fontaine composed a poem, *The Dream of Vaux*, describing for his patron the beauty of the château and its garden at their completion.

By then permanently separated from his wife, La Fontaine may well have anticipated living in this aesthetic paradise, a happy conjunction of all the arts and social graces. But like other paradises it was soon lost. What Foucquet had failed to consider was that over the preceding eighteen years Louis XIV, crowned at the age of five, had grown to maturity.

In 1661, with his dream château at last complete, Foucquet held a grand celebration. For the three days of the occasion, Molière wrote a delicious one-act comedy; the fountains were turned on; swans were released to swim in the reflecting pools and long water avenues; there were fireworks; girls dressed as dryads – tree nymphs – emerged from papier-mâché tree trunks on cue to greet the guests. The superb gardens, inhabited by marble gods and goddesses, seemed to extend to the horizon in geometric perfection. La Fontaine was among those attending, surely pleased to be taking part, if only as a bit player.

Louis XIV was the guest of honor. He had spent his childhood under the governance of Cardinal Mazarin and the regency of his mother the queen, Anne of Austria. But now the cardinal was dead and Louis, a year married and a new father, was at last king in fact. Accompanied by his mother and his retinue, he came trundling over from nearby Fontainebleau.

Instead of feeling delighted by the symmetric perfection of the château and its grounds, the king was enraged, consumed with jealousy. The effrontery! Louis was not stupid, and he was not forgiving. Foucquet had stolen from him, the king, to produce this monument to his own audacity. Within three weeks, once the party was over and the guests had gone home, Foucquet was under arrest for embezzlement. After a trial lasting three years, the panel of judges proposed banishment for Foucquet, permanent exile, but Louis was not satisfied. On the monarch's insistence a far harsher sentence was imposed: life imprisonment. Foucquet's château was stripped of its furniture and its Gobelin tapestries, all sent to Versailles and soon to be followed by Le Nôtre, Le Brun, and Le Vau, commissioned by Louis to begin the transformation of the old royal hunting lodge into something along the lines of Foucquet's Vaux–le–Vicomte but on an immensely magnified scale, one that would demonstrate the superior power of the monarch many times over.

In the aftermath of Foucquet's arrest, as most of the other members of his entourage slid easily into the orbit of the king – Molière's repertory group soon became the King's Players – La Fontaine had the bad judgment, or the simple loyalty, to stick by his fallen patron. He sent poems to the king, pleading him to forgive Foucquet, to no avail. Foucquet was to remain in prison until his death sixteen years later. La Fontaine seems genuinely to have grieved for his lost patron, while at the same time he must have seen the king as practically godlike in his power, an implacable force, a merciless despoiler of beautiful things.

After Foucquet's downfall, La Fontaine would find other patrons to support and protect him, noblewomen who offered a refuge from the king's possible displeasure. Even so, the poet, neither a brave man nor a social reformer – nor a fool – would henceforth take care to cultivate the king.

In dedicating his first volume of fables to the young dauphin, La Fontaine claimed his guiding purpose in writing it had been merely to assist in the prince's education by turning Aesop's stiff fables into poetry. Using an educational sales pitch hardly unfamiliar to parents in the present century, the poet suggested in the preface to his book that as the boy listened, delighted by Aesop transformed into amusing verse, he would at the same time unconsciously be absorbing the wisdom he would need someday as ruler of the nation.

La Fontaine's explanation of his motive could well have sounded reasonable to the king, so long as he did not bother reading past the flattering dedication. If he had done so, as seems unlikely, he would soon have come to the second fable in Book I, "The Crow and the Fox," warning of the stupidity of believing flatterers. As his readers well understood at the time, La Fontaine's versions of Aesop satirized the monarch, along with his court and contemporary society, with a wit that spared no one.

In the fables one sees numerous personifications, or animalizations, of kings and, by extension, of Louis XIV himself – as King Lion, ferociously demanding all as his lion's share; as a rutting bull that chases from his turf a rival for a heifer's favors; as a voracious crane the god Jupiter sends to rule over the frogs when they complain once too often about the harmless log king he had sent them previously; and as many other avatars. But of course, La Fontaine could never be accused of any disrespect for His Majesty: he was merely adding rhyme and meter to the moral tales told in ancient Greece by the wise Phrygian slave, Aesop.

It would be a mistake, however, to imagine that skewering the king was all that La Fontaine had in mind. Had that been so, his poetic fables would perhaps be seen now only as charming period pieces. Far from it, they have long been recognized as among the greatest lyric poetry written in the seventeenth century – or any century – and they have an immediacy about them, at times even a topicality, that has not lessened since the publication of the first six books of selected fables in 1668.

How can this be? After all, La Fontaine lived under an absolute monarchy that was, at first glance, utterly unlike our turbulent era of mass democracy. But despite the deep differences, his age, like ours, was dominated by images of spectacular wealth and hollow celebrity; of struggles for power, political and financial, at the top of society; of endless wars that wasted resources on a staggering scale It was an age in which the question of what was owed, if anything, to the needy in the way of help for their plight was frequently answered, with great moral superiority, in the negative.

Then as now, the strong could, and frequently did, brutalize the weak with little fear of the consequences. Women were hardly guaranteed lives free of abusive treatment, and the exercise of great political power seemed irresistibly equated with comparable sexual power. La Fontaine had witnessed at close range how the acquisition of power and wealth was no guarantee against their being rapidly and devastatingly lost, and more than one of the fables portrays just such an outcome to a promising career.

The moral satirist was hardly a prig – in his lifetime he was perhaps as notorious for his several popular books of bawdy erotic tales, the *Contes*, as he was famous for his fables – nor did he lead an exemplary life. Though he preceded two of the eventual twelve books of *Fables* with flowery dedications to royal children, it seems hard to believe that he cared greatly for children in general, certainly not on the evidence of his apparent lack of interest in his own son, Charles. Because his marriage had almost without question been an arranged one, it is not surprising that his failed – he was bitter about marriage as an institution – or that he is said to have had many casual liaisons, not an unfamiliar story nowadays.

And though he based many of his fables on those of Aesop and other Greek or Roman fabulists, his interests and his sources broadened as he continued writing. By 1695, the last year of his life, he had published the 236 poems – not all of them fables, by any definition – translated in this book. They comment on a multitude of subjects familiar to us even now, from statecraft to astrology, from financial panics to animal intelligence. Like Shakespeare, though on a far smaller scale, La Fontaine transformed prosaic materials into great poetry. Borrowing not only from Aesop and the Roman fabulists Phaedrus and Avienus and other European sources, but also in later fables from yet more ancient Hindu and Persian storytellers, he set out his own vision of humanity, in all its imperfections, with an art that is timeless.

La Fontaine essentially invented the idea of giving witty dialogue to the animal – and vegetable – characters in the fables, and in the process, surely not having intended to do so, he unwittingly had invented the whole genre of children's literature from *The Wind in the Willows* to Dr. Seuss and the animated talking cartoons that began with Disney. In his own (translated) words, from his dedication to M.C.L.D.B. with which Book V begins, he portrayed a cast of characters

> *who in a hundred acts rehearse*
> *A comedy of manners endlessly passing by*
> *Upon this stage, the universe.*

Chronology

La Fontaine's era, essentially the last three quarters of the seventeenth century, was, like ours, a period of turmoil and almost continuous warfare among nations and between religious groups. And like ours, it was also a period of revolutionary breakthroughs in scientific thought. Galileo, Descartes, and Newton flourished in La Fontaine's lifetime. Harvey solved the mystery of the circulation of the blood. In 1660, Leeuwenhoek invented the microscope, which La Fontaine mentioned in fable IX.1, "The Faithless Trustee," published in 1678. The following chronology gives a partial idea of some of the actors and political events of the time:

1608	John Milton born
1613	Galileo's *Lectures on the Solar Spots* published
1616	Shakespeare dies.
1621	La Fontaine born
1622	Molière born
1628	Harvey describes circulation of blood.
1637	Descartes's *Discourse on Method* published
1638	Louis XIV born
1639	Racine born
1642	Galileo's work on solar system published
	Isaac Newton born
1643	Louis XIV crowned at age 5
1648	Charles I beheaded. Oliver Cromwell becomes Lord Protector.
	Charles II, 18, flees to Paris, with philosopher William Hobbes as tutor.
1658	La Fontaine, 37, submits *Adonis*, to Nicolas Foucquet, 43, who becomes his patron.
	In England, Cromwell dies.
	Foucquet begins building château Vaux–le–Vicomte.

1660	Charles II regains English throne.
	In Holland, Antony van Leeuwenhoek invents microscope.
1661	Louis XIV, 23, assumes full regnal power.
	Vaux–le–Vicomte completed. Great celebratory dedication, with play by Molière and fireworks. Louis XIV, guest of honor, has Foucquet arrested three weeks later. His trial lasts three years. La Fontaine finds new patron.
1664	Foucquet is convicted and sentenced, at Louis XIV's order, to life imprisonment.
1665	*Contes et Nouvelles* published
1666	Sequel to *Contes* published
1668	Publication, in March, of *Fables Choisies, mises en vers*, (*Selected Fables, Put into Verse*), Books I–VI, in 2 volumes. A second edition appears in October.
	Newton invents reflecting telescope.
1678	Books VII–XI published
1685	Edict of Nantes revoked. Protestant Huguenots forced to flee France.
1687	Newton's *Principia* published
1694	Book XII published, dedicated to Louis, Duke of Burgundy (1682–1712), grandson of Louis XIV, twelve–year–old son of the dauphin (now grand dauphin) to whom the first collection of fables was dedicated.
1695	La Fontaine dies, age 73.

La Fontaine's Preface

The indulgence that has been shown for some of my fables gives me hope that these may be as generously received. This is not to ignore the fact that one of our leading men of letters has from the start been opposed to the very idea of putting them into poetic form, for he contends that the principal ornament of fable is in having none; besides which, the demands of rhyme and meter, together with the severity of our language, would often so hamper my efforts that most of these tales would lose that brevity which may very well be called their soul and without which they become lifeless. That is the opinion of a man of undeniably excellent taste; I ask of him now only that he should be a little less rigid in his judgment and concede that the Spartan graces and the French muses are not such born enemies that they might not at times go along agreeably together.

After all, I have not embarked on my effort without a guiding example – not that of the Ancients, who are of no concern to me, but that of the Moderns. In every age and among all peoples who practice the art of poetry, the gods of Parnassus have always claimed fable among their dominions. Indeed, the fables attributed to Aesop had scarcely appeared before Socrates found it a worthwhile project to clothe them in the robes of the muses. Plato's account of this is so compelling that I cannot resist including it as one of the ornaments of this preface.

He tells that when Socrates was comdemned to die, his execution was delayed because of a religious festival. When Cebes went to visit him on the day of his death, Socrates told him that the gods had frequently sent him a message in his sleep, advising him that before he died he should devote his talents to music. At first he had had no idea what the dream might mean; for, since music hardly made humans more virtuous, what was the good of it? There had to be some underlying meaning concealed here, for the gods kept sending the same dream. It had continued to recur during the time of their festival, and with such insistency that as he pondered what the gods were asking of him it came to him that music and poetry were so closely related that it was perhaps the latter of which they were speaking. There is no good poetry without its accompanying music, nor for that matter is there any without its accompanying fiction – and Socrates spoke only the truth. At last he saw how to resolve the matter: he would choose fables that contained some intrinsic truth, such as those of Aesop. And during the final hours of his life he was attempting to put some of them into verse.

Socrates was not the only one to regard poetry and fable as sisters. Phaedrus showed himself in agreement, and by the excellence of his work we may judge that of Socrates, the prince of philosophers. After Phaedrus, Avienus took up the same subject. The Moderns followed them. We have many examples of their work, not only from other nations but from our own, though in the days of our forebears the language was so unlike ours now that they too seem foreign to us. This has not in the least deterred me in my attempt; on the contrary, I flatter myself with the hope that if I do not finish the journey I shall at least win fame for having shown the way.

It is possible that my effort will encourage others to carry the project still further. The material is so far from being exhausted that many more fables remain to be put into verse than I have done. I have undoubtedly chosen the best of them, or at least those that seem so to me; but, beyond that, given that I may have made bad choices, someone else can easily take a different approach even to the ones I have selected; and should that difference result in poems shorter than mine they will undoubtedly win greater approval. But whatever the case, all will be in my debt, whether because my impulse had happy consequences and I was not forced to swerve too far from the path I had to follow or whether I did no more than motivate others to do better still.

I believe I have sufficiently justified my project; as to my success in accomplishing it, the public must judge. They will find here neither the elegance nor the extreme brevity for which Phaedrus was renowned: these are gifts above my talent. But since it was impossible for me to imitate him in this way, I concluded that it would be necessary to make my versions of the fables more amusing than his. Not that I criticize him for having kept within the limits of his tradition. The Latin language demanded nothing more. Indeed, if one considers the matter, one finds in this author the true character and spirit of Terence.

Great authors share a magnificent simplicity; but as I did not possess their perfect command of language, I could never have risen to their level. I saw that I had to remedy that deficiency by some other means, which I have been encouraged even more boldly to attempt, in light of Quintilian's pronouncement that there is no such thing as making a story too amusing. I don't really need to prove this, of course: it is enough that Quintilian said it.

Nevertheless, I would also have to take into account the fact that everybody knows these fables, and if I did not make them new by adding some fresh ingredients that restored their taste, I would have accomplished nothing. That is what people want these days: novelty and amusement. And by amusement I do not mean that which simply makes one laugh, but rather a certain charm, an agreeable quality that may be given to subjects of every kind, even the most serious.

But it is not so much by the form I have given this work that it can be evaluated as by its practical utility and by its subject matter, for what worthy qualities can be found in any work of the imagination that are not found in the genre of apologue: the fable? Fable has such an air of divine origin that many in ancient times attributed most of those in this book to Socrates himself, considering as their author the one mortal who was in closest communication with the gods. Indeed, I cannot understand why the gods did not simply send these same fables directly down to us or why they did not assign some one god among them to be their heavenly patron, just as they had done for poetry and oratory.

What I am saying is not entirely nonsensical, for – if I may be permitted to mingle our most sacred beliefs with the errors of pagan thought – we see that Truth has always spoken to humanity through parables, and is parable any different than fable in entering the mind with all the more ease, the more common and familiar the tale it tells? Anyone who would tell us to take as our models only the wisest men provides us with an easy excuse: but there is no such excuse if even ants and bees are capable of doing what is asked of us.

It is for these reasons that Plato, having banished Homer from his republic, gave Aesop a very honorable place in it. He wanted children to drink in fables with their mothers' milk; he advised their nurses to use fables to teach them, for one can never begin too early to acquire familiarity with wisdom and virtue. Rather than having to reform bad habits, one must work at making children good while they as yet lack any idea of either right or wrong. And what better way is there to accomplish this than through fables?

Tell a child that Crassus, at war with the Parthians, invaded their lands without planning how he would leave again and that as a result he and his army perished, despite all their attempts to withdraw. Tell the same child that the Fox and the Ram jumped into a well to slake their thirst; that the Fox got out again by using his comrade's shoulders and horns as a ladder, but that the Ram, on the contrary, had to remain there, stuck at the bottom, because he had gone in without forethought – teaching that one must always think of the end result. I ask, which of these two examples would make the greater impression on the child? Would he not be drawn to the latter, as better attuned and less out of proportion than the former to the immaturity of his mind? Do not tell me that children's minds are by nature already childish enough, without filling them with more such trivialities. For they are trivial only at first glance: in the final analysis they hold a very untrivial meaning. Just as, by learning the definition of a point, a line, a plane, and other well-known principles, we gain the competence to measure the skies and the earth, in much the same way, from the arguments and conclusions that may be drawn from the fables, we learn judgment and moral sense, we become capable of great actions.

The fables are not merely sources of moral understanding, they provide other kinds of knowledge as well. They set forth the innate proclivities and diversity of characters of the animals and consequently of humans as well, for we are the summation of all that is good or evil in those unreasoning creatures. When Prometheus wished to create human beings he took the dominant quality of each type of animal: from these utterly different materials, he put to‑ gether our species, he created that work we call the Microcosm, the human animal. Thus all of us will find our portraits painted here. And by the likenesses each sees, those of mature years will find con‑ firmation of the lessons life has taught them, and the young will learn what they will need to know. As the latter are still new to the world, they will not yet be familiar with its other inhabitants, nor will they know themselves. They must not be left in their ignorance any longer than necessary: they must learn what lions are like, and foxes, and all the others; and why one man in particular might be compared to this fox or that lion. That is what the fables seek to do: furnish the elementary understanding of such things.

My preface is already longer than is customary; nevertheless, I have not yet fully explained the rationale of my work. The apologue consists of two parts, one of which might be called its body, the other its soul. Its body is the fable; its soul the moral. Aristotle admits only animals into fables. He excludes both humans and plants. However, that rule is less a necessity than a matter of taste, since neither Aesop, nor Phaedrus, nor any of the early fabulists observed it, in complete contrast to the moral, which none of them ever omitted. If at times it happens that I do so, it is only in those instances where a moral cannot gracefully be introduced into the tale but can easily be sup‑ plied by the reader. In France, the only consideration is whether a thing is pleasing: that is the primary rule, not to say the only one. Thus I have thought it no crime not to employ the traditional forms if I could not use them without doing them harm.

In Aesop's time, the fable was told quite in the simplest way, separate from the moral and invariably preceding it. Later, Phaedrus did not consider himself bound by that scheme: he would embellish the tale and sometimes begin with the moral. When I have had to find a place for it, I have ignored the original precept only in follow‑ ing one of no less authority: that of Horace. He wanted no writer to struggle against the limits imposed either by his talents or his genre. According to him, anyone who wants to succeed must never do that. He will give up trying to do anything he knows he cannot do well:

> *And those things*
> *At which he despairs of shining he relinquishes trying.*

And that is what I have done with regard to some of the morals I felt I had little hope of expressing well.

All that remains is to give an account of Aesop's life. I do not know anyone who does not suppose that the one left us by Planude is itself fabulous. It is generally assumed that this author wanted to give his hero a character and adventures that echoed his fables. At first, I thought this was plausible, but in the end I grew less convinced of it, partly based as it is on what went on between Xanthus and Aesop: a lot of foolishness, it would seem. But is there any famous man to whom such things have never happened? Socrates had his less serious moments. What confirms me in my belief is that the character Planude gives Aesop resembles the one Plutarch portrayed in his *Banquet of the Seven Sages*, which is to say that of a clever man who lets nothing escape him. I have been told that the banquet of the seven sages is also a fiction. It is easy to cast doubts on everything, but as for myself I cannot readily see why Plutarch would have wished to impose on posterity in that one work, when in all his others he sought to be truthful and to describe all his characters faithfully. If in this case he did not, my own account of Aesop would lie only because it was founded on someone else's falsehood: would I be any less believable if it were solely my invention? For all I can do is to weave a tissue of my own conjectures and call it *The Life of Aesop*. However plausible-sounding I made it, fable for fable, readers would always prefer Planude's version to mine.

To Monseigneur the Dauphin

MONSEIGNEUR,

If there is any one accomplishment in all literature that can be called ingenious, it is surely the way in which Aesop imparted his moral observations concerning human behavior. Undoubtedly, it would have been far preferable if other hands than mine had given them the ornament of poetic form, for the wisest soul of antiquity considered that to be no frivolous task.

I now dare, MONSEIGNEUR, to present you with some efforts of my own in that regard. It is a mode of instruction suitable to your early years. You are at an age when princes can properly indulge in play, yet at the same time you must devote some of your attention to serious matters. Both of these possibilities we find in the fables we owe to Aesop. At first glance, they seem childish, I must admit; but these childish qualities serve to frame important truths.

I have no doubt, MONSEIGNEUR, that you will look favorably upon tales that are so instructive and at the same time so entertaining, for what more could one ask of any work than that it should offer both of these qualities? It is they that have introduced knowledge to humanity. Aesop discovered a unique way of joining the two together.

Reading his fables is to sow the mind imperceptibly with the seeds of virtue and at the same time teach it to seek self-knowledge, all the while unaware that it is so engaged and supposing itself to be doing something else entirely.

It is a way of teaching that will very enjoyably complement the studies to which His Majesty has till now turned his eyes for instruction. It will allow you to learn painlessly – or, better said, pleasurably – all that which is needful for a royal prince to know. We have great hopes of that knowledge. But, in truth, there are things from which we expect infinitely more: these, MONSEIGNEUR, are those talents given you at birth by our invincible monarch. It is the example that at all times he sets before you.

When one sees him give shape to such great plans; when you see how he proceeds unperturbed in the face of the turbulence across Europe and the plots set in motion to frustrate his efforts; when with his first sortie he penetrates clear to the heart of one province, faced at every step by seemingly unbreachable barriers, and in a week's time conquers another – this, in the most difficult season for military campaigns, a time when in the courts of other kings the reigning mood is one of indolence and indulgence; when, not content with conquering men, he triumphs over the elements as well, and when, on returning from that expedition like a victorious Alexander, you see him govern his people like an Augustus, you must recognize the truth, MONSEIGNEUR: you aspire to glory with an ardor equal to his, despite the lesser power of your early years; you wait impatiently for the time to come when you can declare yourself his rival in the affections of that divine mistress. You do not simply await it, MONSEIGNEUR, you preordain it. I need no other proof of this than that noble energy, that vivacity, that ardor, those marks of spirit, of courage, and of grandeur of soul that you demonstrate at every moment.

Undoubtedly this is a source of immense joy for our king; but it is at the same time a wonderful thing for all the world to watch thus growing to maturity a young tree that will one day give its protective shade to so many people and nations. I could expand at length on this subject, but as my purpose, that of entertaining you, is more within my competence than that of praising you, I hasten to the fables, and to the truths I have uttered I have nothing to add but this, MONSEIGNEUR: that, with happy respect, I am

Your most humble, most obedient, and most faithful servant,

DE LA FONTAINE

To Monseigneur the Dauphin

I sing the heroes who were Father Aesop's brood,
A troop whose histories admittedly are lies,
But lies, I say, from which great truths may be construed.
All speak through me, the beasts, the birds, the fish likewise,
Who could not say a word before – but now they can:
They speak to teach us what we are, the species man.
ILLUSTRIOUS SCION OF A PRINCE to whom the eyes
Of all the world are turned and whom the very skies
Regard with favor – he, who having lately made
The proudest bow their heads, may henceforth count his years
By numbering his conquests, a warrior with no peers –
Though others with more ringing voices have portrayed
Your royal forebears and set out a monarch's powers,
My modest hope is rather to amuse your hours
With lesser deeds I've lightly sketched and versified,
Or earn, if I should fail, the honor to have tried.

Book One

The Cicada and the Ant

The Cicada, having sung
All summer long,
Was in want and starving thin
Once the winter wind set in.
With no slightest scrap put by,
Bit of worm or bite of fly,
She approached her neighbor, Ant,
Pleading for a loan, a scant
Seed or two to live upon,
Just till these hard times had gone.
She'd repay, no need to dun her,
Swore upon her insect's honor,
Principal and interest both.
But the ant to lend was loath:
Stinginess was her least blot.
"What did you do when it was hot?"
She asked the one who begged for aid.
"Please you, ma'am, I did the thing
I liked best, which was to sing
Night and day at any chance."
"You sang, you say? Well, you have made
My answer easy – now, go dance!"

I. 1

The Crow and the Fox

Perched in a treetop, old Mister Crow
Was holding a cheese in his beak.
Drawn by the smell, Mister Fox, down below,
Peered up, then proceeded to speak.
"Why, hello, fair Sir Crow! Lovely day!

3

How you dazzle my eyes! How rare your display!
Not to lie, if your voice when you sing
Is as fine as the cut of your wing
I'll know you're the Phoenix reborn in these woods!"
At these words the old crow became giddy with pleasure
And, thinking to prove his voice a treasure,
He opened his big beak – and promptly dropped the goods.
Fox pounced upon his prize, then said, "My dear, dear sir,
Learn now that every flatterer
Lives at the cost of those who give him credit.
That lesson's worth a cheese no doubt, so don't forget it!"
The crow, in shame and deep chagrin,
Swore, a bit late, never again to be taken in.

I. 2

The Frog Who Wished to Be as Big as the Ox

A frog sees an ox, says, "Love his size!"
And then, although no bigger than an egg, he tries,
With envy goading him, to grow to be as gross
In bulk as the enormous beast. He delegates
Frog Two, his sister, to watch close
As he inhales, expands, swells up, fills out, inflates!
Says, "Sis, how's this?" "No good." "So does this do it?" "Nope."
"This?" "Too small." "–iss?" "Nohow."
Until, with one more gasp, the little pipsqueak dope
Gets so puffed up he bursts – KAPOW!

The world is full of types without one whit more brain.
Each bourgeois yearns to build a palace of his own,
Each minor king sends envoys from his little throne,
Each marquis dreams of pages, carrying his train.

I. 3

The Two Mules

Two mules came down the pike, one lugging oats in sacks,
One, heavy chests of coins from some new tax.
The second mule was proud of his important load
And, wishing it no lighter, not a single pound,
He pranced his way along the road,
Making the bells on his harness sound.
Then out jumped bandits from the ditch,
Looking for treasure to make them rich,
And set on the mule with the seal of the crown.
They seized his reins, he reared and bit –
But they had knives, his throat was slit.
He whinnied loudly, gasping then as he went down,
"Is this the fine reward I get for all my trying?
The mule behind me had no cause to be afraid,
But I have fallen, I am dying!"
"Old pal," his former partner brayed,
"It's risky doing jobs for great prestige or wealth.
If you, like me, had plodded in some humble trade,
You might not feel in such poor health!"

I. 4

The Wolf and the Dog

The Wolf grew gaunt – his bones stuck out –
Because for once the watchdogs never shut their eyes.
At last he took a drowsy mastiff by surprise,
A gorgeous, glossy-coated, oxlike layabout.
Sir Wolf would happily have set upon this giant
And ripped him all to shreds, but seeing his huge size
And his stout means of self-defense,
To challenge him to combat simply made no sense,
And so instead he groveled, winningly compliant,
And told him how he envied him his plump physique.

5

"Dear boy, if being fat as I is what you seek,
It is entirely up to you," the mastiff said.
"Just leave the woods and you'll improve your lot –
For there the only close associates you've got
Are stupid, ragged and ill–fed,
They live half–dead from hunger, just a bunch
Of desperate losers. Why? They've no free lunch,
No real security. There, all live by the knife.
But follow me and find the way to better life."
"What must I do?" the wolf replied.
"Not much at all," the mastiff said. "You wait outside
And chase off beggars from the door
And old lame types with walking sticks,
You lick your master's hand and fawn before
The family, and in return you get a mix
Of lovely leavings, bones of chicken or of squab,
And they will pat your head and scratch behind your ears."
Picturing all this, the wolf's delight was such
Emotion overwhelmed him, and he began to sob.
But as they walked along together, through his tears
He saw the mastiff's neck looked raw and bare.
The wolf inquired, "What happened there?"
"Oh, nothing." "That is nothing?" "Nothing much."
"But, what?" "The collar they attach me with may be
What caused the little spot of soreness that you see."
"Attach?" the wolf replied. "You mean you are not free
To go just where you want?" "Well, not always, no –
But does that matter?" "Matter! Yes, it matters so
That I refuse to touch one bite of your fine swill.
For even a treasure, that price would be too high for me!"
That said, the wolf ran off, and he is running still.

I. 5

The Heifer, the She-goat, and the Ewe in Partnership with the Lion

Three gentle sisters, the heifer, the she-goat, the ewe,
Started a company. They asked to join their board
A fierce lion who was the local overlord.
They'd share the profits equally, the losses too.
A stag was captured when the she-goat set a snare,
And she told them all they should assemble there.
When all were met, the lion counted on his claws:
"I make it four," he roared, "to split this prize."
And having ripped the carcass into quarters
He claimed the first of them because, for starters,
He was the king. He said, "It's mion
For the simple reason that my name is Lion."
If anyone objected, nobody said a word.
"This second part," he said, "is mine by right, of course.
That right is known as the Right of Superior Force.
As the most aggressive here, I also claim the third.
And that fourth part – if any dares so much as sniff,
She'll get her silly little head torn off."

I. 6

Baggage

Jupiter said one day: "Let all that live and breathe
Be summoned. Gather, ye, around my mighty feet!
If anyone perceives some flaw in how he's made,
Step forward fearlessly and speak.
I will repair my least mistake.
Come, Ape, you may speak first – and one can well see why.
Regard these animals. Compare the beauties of
Their features with your own.
Are you well satisfied?" "Who, me?" the ape replied.
"Why wouldn't I be? Don't I have four legs, just like them?

Till now, my portrait's given me no cause for shame.
But, take poor brother Bear, he's very crudely sketched –
He'd have to be upset to see himself in paint."
The bear came next, and all expected some complaint.
But they were wrong. He was in love with his own shape.
And yet he criticised the elephant: his tail
Did not hang right, his ears should be pruned back,
He was a mass devoid of elegance and form.
Then, in his turn, the elephant,
Despite his fabled wisdom, spoke the very same.
According to his lights, Dame Whale
Was very grossly out of scale.
Dame Ant dismissed the mite as being much too small,
Though she herself was just colossal.
"Meeting adjourned!" said Jupiter. "You see defects
In everyone except yourselves." In this parade,
Our species led the rest, for in our hearts we are
Lynx-eyed to others, mole-blind to ourselves,
Forgiving our own trespasses, not our fellow man's:
We see our neighbors and ourselves with different eyes.
The sovereign fabricator
Has made us each two bags to carry through the world –
The style today is just as it has always been.
The one behind we use to pack our faults away,
The one in front we carry other people's in.

                                                        I. 7

The Swallow and the Little Birds

From flying far, a swallow grew
To know a lot, for those who've seen a lot well may
Have learned a lot along the way.
She had a gift for sensing winds before they blew
And when a storm was hatching she
Would warn the sailors out at sea.
One year, at planting time for hemp, she saw below

A farmer in his furrows, seeding row on row.
To all the smaller birds she cried, "Oh, now beware!
I see great danger coming, but for you, not me:
I know a place to hide, I have swift wings to flee.
But do you see that hand go whirling through the air?
The day is coming, all too soon,
When ruin springs from every seed that it has strewn.
For from those seeds wide nets will grow to catch your wings,
And hidden snares with strangling strings,
And many and many a cruel machine
That will in its due season mean
Your lives are lost, your freedom done.
Beware both cage and cooking pan!
To save yourselves you now must plan
To peck those seeds up, every one.
Listen to me! Heed my words!"
But she was twitted by the birds,
Who said too many seeds already had been sown.
Then, when the hemp was showing green,
The swallow once more urged them, "Peck up every sprout
That pokes its evil tendril out,
Or you will reap perdition soon!"
"You babblebeak," they said, "false prophet, crazy loon,
A fine task you have set for us!
The fields are wide. To pluck them clean
It would take myriads more of us."
Then when the hemp was growing tall
The swallow warned again, "Now no good can befall:
The bad seed ripens all too fast.
And since you have not listened to one word I say
You soon will come to realise
That once the seeding time is past
And harvest is still months away,
Then idle men will war on every bird that flies.
And then, since when their traps are set
It is the small birds that they get,
You must no longer dart and flit

9

But keep within your nests or fly to other lands.
Whir off like woodcocks, emulate the cranes in flight –
But as your wings allow you neither speed nor height
You cannot cross the waves and desert sands
To search as we for worlds where man has never been.
Your only sure salvation now must be to find
The hidden chinks in walls and seal yourselves within."
The little birds, who had no mind
For any enterprise so daft,
Began to chitter noisily,
Much like the people of the Trojan state
Who never listened, only laughed,
Whenever crazed Cassandra made a prophecy:
They also met a Trojan fate,
And many a little bird went into slavery.

Because we listen to no promptings but our own
We fail to hear the warnings till the missile's flown.

I. 8

City Rat and Country Rat

City Rat in days gone by
Sent Country Rat a note that read:
"Dear friend, tonight do come and try
Urban luxury instead."

Only picture, if you can,
The delights they had in store:
Dainty scraps of ortolan,
Turkish carpet on the floor.

Nothing lacked, not in the least,
Of soup or meat or sweet or wine,
But someone upset their feast
As the pair prepared to dine.

At the doorway to the hall
They heard noises! City Rat
Scuttled back inside the wall,
Closely tailed by Country Rat.

Silence again. "Now is our chance!"
Said City Rat. "Our gracious host
Has departed. Quick! Advance!
Seize the cheese, mop up the roast!"

"I've had my fill," said Country Rat.
"Next time you must visit me.
Understand, it isn't that
I don't like some luxury,

"But where I come from life is quiet,
I eat at leisure when I wish.
Fie! I say, on any diet
Where fear contaminates each dish!"

I. 9

The Wolf and the Lamb

Might makes right. That's true and always was –
Now let us see just how it does.

A thirsty lamb bent down her head
To sip at a clear-running brook.
A wolf was watching, with a growling stomach,
Drawn by hunger out to prowl the neighborhood.
"How dare you have the gall to foul my drinking water!"
He snarled in utter fury at her.
"A punishment must follow such audacity."
"Sire," replied the lamb, "His Gracious Majesty
Ought not to get so mad at me,
For if he would consider first

That as I stand to slake my thirst
I'm twenty paces, at the least,
Downstream of His Highness, he would see
There is no way that I could foul his drinking water."
"You foul it anywhere you stand," replied the beast.
"And last year you insulted me. I don't forget."
"But no," replied the lamb. "I wasn't born as yet.
I'm small, and I still suckle at my mother."
"Well, if not you it was your brother."
"But I don't have one." "Then it was another
Just like you. None of your race
Speaks well of me, not you, your shepherds or your dogs!
So, since you are not nice
To me you have to pay the price."
And thereupon he drags
Her off into the forest, there to chaw
And swallow her, without restraint by any law.

I. 10

The Man and His Image

FOR THE DUKE DE LA ROCHEFOUCAULD

A man who loved himself so much that no one else
Came close believed he was the handsomest of men.
If mirrors showed him otherwise they must be false,
And in this error he lived happily. But then
Officious Fate, to cure this self–deception, placed
At every turn he took one more
Of those unspeaking judges women plead before:
Mirrors set in bedrooms, mirrors found in shops,
Mirrors in the hands of fops,
Mirrors spangling every skirt and top and waist.
What does our poor Narcissus do? He goes and hides
In some far region where he hopes no glass will show
Some aspect of himself he does not dare to know.

But he encounters here a stream whose current glides
From some pure source far down below.
For once he sees himself and his offended eyes
Perceive a shadow man, as vacant as a dream.
He wishes to avert his glance but, though he tries,
It is not easy doing so –
There is such beauty in the stream.

What I am getting at seems plain.
I speak to all, for this gross error of the mind
Is an affliction all are pleased to entertain.
The man so smitten with himself: in him I find
An image of our soul. And all those mirrors mean
The follies of our time, in which our sins are seen.
And as to that clear stream, why, look,
Dear friend, it is the *Maxims* in your book.

I. 11

The Dragon of Many Heads
and
The Dragon of Many Tails

An envoy of the Turkish Porte,
So history says, once dared to claim
Before the Holy Roman court
That his great sultan's forces put to shame
The armies of their emperor.
At which a shaggy Teuton knight was heard to roar
That this false was. Had not the emperor vassals
Who each, besides his several castles,
Had wealth enough to field an army of his own?
At which the subtle Asian said, "I have long known
That each elector's strength is held to be immense.
And knowing this brings to my mind

A strange yet true experience.
In a frontier garrison, once, encamped behind
The timbers of a palisade,
I felt the very blood within my veins run thin –
A hundred-headed dragon was trying to get in!
And yet there was no cause for me to be afraid.
The heads came thrusting in between the pales – but then
The single body they conjoined could not get through.
Then on the following day we were attacked anew
By yet another dragon – this one with a single head
But a vast plethora of tails.
First, the head pierced through, and then the writhing tails,
Their smaller strengths united by the one that led.
I would suggest that these two dragons show the powers
Of your great emperor, compared to ours."

I. 12

The Thieves and the Mule

Two thieves scuffled. They had stolen a mule.
One wished to keep him, the other to sell.
But while they were exchanging blows,
Lefts to the body, rights to the nose,
A third mule rustler came
And stole what each had tried to claim.

The mule can stand for some poor province,
The thieves being each some royal prince,
As of Transylvania, Hungary or the Turks –
Of whom one knows that when two fight, the third one lurks.
A little of their statesmanship is still too much.
And which one wins the province? Seldom one of these:
A fourth thief enters, engineers a peace
And in the process grabs full title to the beast.

I. 13

Simonides Preserved by the Gods

Three sorts of beings one can never praise too much:
The gods, one's mistress and one's king.
A hoary jest, but still I find it has the ring
Of truth about it – praise is a feather's touch
That captivates all spirits with its pleasuring.
Many a beauty's favors yield to flattering.
Now see how gods rewarded it in ancient times.

Simonides agreed to cobble up some rhymes
To puff an athlete but he found the going hard.
The fellow spouted pointless stories by the yard;
His family was an absolutely boring one,
His father a bourgeois boor and he his father's son,
Small stuff as inspiration.
"Our hero's deeds I sing," the laboring poet began,
But when he soon exhausted the little he had to say
He cast that theme aside and tried a different plan.
Castor and Pollux were invoked. He wrote that they
Eternally inspired all pugilists,
He eulogized their greatest bouts and reeled off lists
Of cities honored, victims flattened by their fists,
Until, of all this heap of words,
Castor and Pollux had two thirds.
The man had promised to pay the poet one gold talent
But after reading the piece the gallant
Reduced it to one third. He stressed
That Castor and Pollux should pay the rest.
"They're good for it because they're gods, those two!
But no hard feelings, man, alright?
Come and have dinner. I'm planning a bash tonight
For just a very special few,
Including my family and all my closest friends.
Who knows? If you recite, it might pay dividends."
Simonides accepted, possibly because
He feared to lose not just his fee but the applause.

When he arrived he found the crowd in festive mood,
All laughing and drinking and swilling food.
A servant rushed in. "Oh, please, Simonides, come out!"
He said. "Two strangers pound upon our gates and shout
That they must see the poet!" As he rose, all chewed
As usual. There at the door, straight from the starry sky,
He found the heroes of his ode, the Gemini.
Both thanked him, said they loved his poem and, as proof,
Warned him to get out of there, because the roof
Was imminently due to fall.
And so it did. A post gave way, the ceiling crashed
Upon the banquet and broke all
The flagons, cups and plates,
And bashed
Not just the serving platters but the servers' pates.
And then what iced the cake, poetic-justice-wise,
Was that a falling slab broke both the athlete's thighs
And most of the guests were badly maimed.
Of course, the incident was widely publicized –
A miracle, all said. The poet grew famed
And doubled his fee, as one divinely recognized.
Now members of the better class
Descended on the poet en masse
Offering any sum he'd please
To versify their family trees.

Which leads me back to my original text –
First, that it is wise to praise in every way
The gods and those most like them. Next,
The Muse need not be held in any less regard
For asking, having labored hard,
That she be given proper pay;
And, lastly, that we poets should know our art's high worth:
The great do themselves honor acknowledging our own –
Olympus and Parnassus, every age has shown,
Stand friends and brothers on this earth.

I. 14

Death and the Luckless Man

A luckless man, a loser every time,
Kept asking death to come.
"Oh, Death," he'd say, "you're beautiful!
Come quick and finish off my lousy life!"
So Death decided she would pay a call.
She knocked at his door, came in and showed herself.
"What do I see?" he cried. "I hate the sight!
You're hideous! Meeting you face to face
Fills me with disgust and fright."

Mecaenas was a man of an uncommon grace.
He said once, "Though I should become a slack,
Pain-ridden, one-armed thing, lame and confined,
If life somehow remains in me, I am resigned."
Oh, Death, don't ever come! says all of humankind.

I. 15

Death and the Woodcutter

Invisible beneath his bale of branches, bent
As much by years as by the weight upon his back,
A poor woodcutter hobbled, groaning as he went
Along the pathway winding to his wretched shack.
At last, when pain and effort had exhausted him,
He let his burden fall and, standing there, began
To catalogue his miseries. In all his time,
What pleasures had he ever known? Had any man
Been half so poor, so lacking bread, with never rest
From landlord's jobs and crying brats, demanding swarms
Of tax collectors, usurers, thieving men-at-arms:
A picture of despair that left him so depressed
That he called out for Death. And there at once she stood,

17

To ask what she might do for him today.
"Just help," he said, "lift back this wood
Upon my shoulders, then be gone without delay."

Heaven puts all pains to rest –
Still, we prefer this earth instead.
The motto on our human crest
Says, "Better to suffer than be dead."

I. 16

The Man Between Two Ages and Two Mistresses

A man of a middleish age,
With white hair starting to spread,
Supposed he had reached the stage
For finding a wife to wed.
And, since he was rich,
The question was: which?
For myriads of women vied to share his bed –
Which made our lover even slower to decide:
It is no simple matter, taking on a bride!
At last two widows led the contest for his heart,
One fresh and green, one just a trifle past her prime,
Yet able to restore by art
The wreck of nature caused by time.
With laughter, joking, sweetly smiling,
Each of the widows, all in fun,
Sought to give him a restyling –
That is, each played with his coiffure.
The older, wanting him more mature,
Plucked out his black hairs one by one;
The younger, not to be outdone,
Yanked all the white that she could find,
Until of hair our man had none

Of either sort, but now was of a clearer mind.
"Lovelies," he said, "a thousand compliments to both
For harvesting my overgrowth.
My gain exceeds my loss, however,
For now there'll be no wedding, ever.
I would have lived, as you have shown,
After your fashion, not my own.
My head, though bald, is mine alone.
Thank you, darlings, for the lesson."

I. 17

The Fox and the Stork

Slick Brother Fox once got to acting generous,
Invited Sister Stork to dine at his expense –
She found a chinchwad's feast, short on ingredients.
The gentleman, quite parsimonious,
Served just clear broth, more nearly water,
Dished out so thinly on a platter
That long–beaked Stork could neither sip nor sup,
While Tricky instantly lapped every smidgeon up.
To pay him back for that rascality,
The stork soon afterward in turn invited
The fox to dine with her. "I'll be delighted,"
Fox said. "With friends, I totally eschew formality."
He came to her door with perfect punctuality,
For foxes are never tardy when it's time to eat.
He flattered his hostess's savoir faire,
Told her he knew the meal would be a splendid treat,
Cooked to perfection, not overdone yet not too rare.
He found delightful the aroma of roast meat
Minced in miniature morsels. How tasty they would be!
But the banquet was presented – inconveniently,
In a tall, narrow vase with a neck so thin
That only the stork's long beak went in –

For the gentleman's muzzle was too broad-gauged,
And he had to slink homeward unassuaged,
Looking mortified as if he'd been caught skipping town
With a stolen hen, his tail adroop, his ears bent down.

Swindlers, I've written this for you:
Just wait – your turn is coming too!

I. 18

The Boy and the Schoolmaster

In this next tale I use a fool as model
To show how stern remonstrance may be twaddle.

A little boy at play beside the Seine
Fell in and seemed about to perish when –
Thanks be to God – he found a willow tree
Just there, its branches trailing down where he
Could cling. Well, as he held on, terrified,
There came that way along the riverside
A schoolmaster. The boy cried, "Help! I'm drowning!"
The pedant turned to see whence came the noise,
Then gave not help but scolding. Gravely frowning,
He said, "Now see what comes of foolish boys
Who act like young baboons. Henceforth, my lad,
You'll know there is a cost to being bad.
Unfortunate the parents of a child
Forever into mischief, running wild.
I weep for them. What trials they have in store!"
His lecture over, then he hauled the boy ashore.

The targets here for my disapprobation
Are lecturing pedants, moralising preachers:
Let them look here and see their silly features.
Their number passes all imagination,
God having blessed their powers of procreation.

Whatever situation might arise
Serves only to give their tongues brisk exercise.
Friend, save me from the danger first,
Then preach your sermon – do your worst.

I. 19

The Cock and the Pearl

A cock one day scratched up
A pearl, which he gave to
A jeweler who
Chanced by. He said, "Well, I sup–
pose it's nice, but I'd consider
The smallest grain of millet nicer."

An ignorant dunce fell heir
To a manuscript, which he sold
To a neighboring bookseller.
He said, "It's nice, I'm told,
But I'd consider
The smallest coin of gold much nicer."

I. 20

The Hornets and the Honeybees

Know the workman by the work.

Who owned some honeycombs was in dispute.
Some hornets claimed that they were theirs,
A swarm of bees brought counter suit.
A wasp, expert in such affairs,
Agreed to judge. He soon discovered
It was not easy to adjudicate.
Witnesses told that as of late

They had observed the said combs covered
By certain creatures, winged, buzzing, elongate,
With tawny markings – like bees, to be exact.
Then the rebuttal: don't hornets look like bees, in fact?
The wasp, uncertain how to judge the evidence,
Subpoenaed a nest of ants nearby –
But found their testimony didn't clarify.
"So please the court, but all this makes no sense!"
A very prudent bee objected.
"In six more months of judgement pending
We'll be no closer to the ending,
And while we wait the honey sits there unprotected!
The judge must reach a decision at last –
Hasn't this bear cub nursed enough to be a bear?
The time for these maneuverings is past.
Have done with all this gibble gabble legalese!
Let both groups work, hornets and bees,
And soon enough we'll see how they will fare
At building perfect cells which each must fill
With sweetest honey made from nectar that they gather."
The hornets by refusing proved they lacked the skill
For such creation, and thus not they but rather
The bees as rightful makers were adjudged entitled.
Would God all suits were just as simply settled,
That we might follow those Caucasian tribes
Whose code of law is just plain common sense:
There would not then be such expense
That eats us up, that grinds us down,
That wears us out with its delays,
That leaves at last the lawyers dining on the oysters
And leaves the claimants sucking on the shells.

I. 21

22

The Oak and the Reed

One time the oak said, "Reed, let's talk.
I see how you might say that nature is unfair.
Even a wren must be a burden on your stalk
And any passing puff of air
That scarcely marks the water's face
Makes you bow down. Yet in my case
My brow, unyielding as a granite mountainside,
Not only stops those rays the sun shoots far and wide
But it defies huge tempests, too.
Life is a breeze for me, a hurricane for you.
If you could spring up here beneath my leafage, spread
To shelter everything around,
No storm could ever touch your head
For I would guard you night and day,
And yet you seem confined to ground
That borders marshy kingdoms where the winds hold sway.
No, nature is not fair to you, I have to say."
"Old oak," the reed replied, "your sentiments betray
A natural goodness. But leave off worrying for me;
Far less than you am I endangered by the wind –
I never break, I merely bend.
And though till now your back has weathered every blow
The wind has struck, we never know
How things will end, we always have to wait and see."
Just then, through the horizon's crack, the worst
Of all the Northwind's awful offspring burst
In fury from that howling pack and battered both.
The reed bowed low, the oak stood fast.
Then doubly hard the wind drew breath
And raged and roared till one came down –
The one that had well-nigh brushed heaven at its crown,
But at its base was rooted in the realm of death.

I. 22

23

Book Two

Against the Hard to Please

Had I at birth received from muse Calliope
Those promised gifts that she proverbially showers
On her best-loved, I still would have employed my powers
On Aesop's truthful fictions, for though poetry
Has always fancied telling tales, I never deemed
Myself so loved by all nine sisters as to know
How to bejewel all their forms. At most, it seemed
That I might give some one of them new luster – so,
That's what I've tried. A greater could have done far more,
But, nonetheless, since then, in a new language, I
Have taught the wolf to speak and made the lamb reply.
And, harder yet to do – and never done before –
I've given plants and trees their voices. Who would not see
In all of this at least a touch of sorcery?
The critics tell me, "It is true – you have created
Some five or six splendid little tales that should endure
As nursery-story literature."
So what do you carpers want? Something more elevated?
More approved of? Listen!

After ten years of war
Outside their walls, the Trojans had worn out the Greeks,
Who with a thousand sharp attacks,
A thousand tricks, a hundred battles, had yet failed
To bring their haughty city to an end – until
With matchless artifice and skill,
Athena crafted a wooden horse, whose girth concealed
The wily Ulysses, brave Diomedes, the rash Ajax
And their phalanxes with them, eager to deploy,
When that colossus on its tracks
Had brought their fury in, to ravage and destroy
The altars of the very gods who guarded Troy:
A stratagem till then unknown, but that repaid

27

The plotters' patience and the game they played.
"Enough! Much, much too long!" one of my experts chides.
"You'd better catch your breath. Besides,
A tale of a wooden horse that held a whole phalanx
Of warriors crammed inside it ranks
As even more outlandish than the one where, thanks
To flattery, the fox outwits the crow. Then, too,
A high style doesn't suit you." So, I'll try a low:

For her Alcippus yearning, Amaryllis, burning,
Supposed she was alone,
With but her flock and sheepdog nigh to hear her moan.
But, wandering through the willow grove
Shepherd Thyrsis spied her and as he followed after
Heard her imploring Zephyr with his soft breath to waft her
Words to her dear love.

"Stop that bad verse," my censor says. "I find it flawed.
Such wretched stuff should be outlawed.
Send both these pieces to the font to be recast."
Damned critic, have you done at last?
Will you not let me tell my tale?
You are too hard to please. However much one tries,
One knows that one is bound to fail
With precious types like you, whom nothing satisfies.

II. 1

The Congress of the Rats

A cat called Genghis Caligula Jaws
Did things to rats that were not nice
And now quite few were left because
He'd sent so many to paradise.
The poor survivors, scared to leave their holes to forage,
With nothing in their larder now but northwind porridge,
Starved. And Genghis in their eyes became

28

Not merely a cat but Satan by another name.
But then one day Old Tom felt siren passion calling
And off he went to search the alleys for a bride,
And while he and his fiancée were caterwauling
True love duets and otherwise preoccupied,
The rats surviving caucused in a manger
To take some action on their present danger.
The oldest, wisest rat, an eloquent debater,
Urged that they must – and sooner, preferable to later –
Suspend a bell around the neck of their huge foe
So when he stealthily attacked them it would sound
A tocsin, giving them time to scamper underground –
How else, when he came creeping, could they know?
His statesmanly advice went over very well.
All said the plan was great, terrific, cool!
But there was just one problem: who would attach the bell?
One said, "I'm not about to try it. I'm no fool."
Another, "Never, me." Till each in turn had spurned
The task and, having done nothing, they adjourned.

Many's the committee, synod, congress, that's
No more effective than a gathering of rats.
Wisdom abounds, they reach a binding resolution –
But not a soul will bring the thing to execution.

II. 2

Wolf vs. Fox before Judge Ape

The wolf claimed that a thief had robbed his lair.
The fox next door, he lied, who had a sordid name,
Had done it. This dishonest pair,
Proceeding without lawyers, came
Before the ape in robes assigned to the affair.
In simian memory it had been many a day
Since Justice had been given such a load to weigh.
The magistrate grew sweaty sitting on his throne.

29

At last, when each had testified,
Denied, replied, and raged and cried,
The judge, to whom their knavery was too well known,
Said, "Friends, you have stood here so many times
That now you both must pay the price for all your crimes.
For, Wolf, you always howl although all know you're faking
And, Fox, you always prowl and take what's there for taking."
The judge maintained that one cannot go too far wrong
In punishing ill-doers – just make the sentence strong.

II. 3

The Two Bulls and the Frog

Two bulls began a fight to see which would possess
A heifer – and the empire, too.
A frog made noises of distress.
"But what have they to do with you?"
Inquired the croaker's croaking friend.
Replied the first, "But, can't you guess?
It's all too clear how this will end:
The loser trotting off to exile from the fields,
The victor chasing after him until he yields
All claims of being king upon the grassy plain.
And then when he comes here among our reeds to reign,
We will be trampled in the muck before he's done!
This war that lust for Madam Heifer has begun
Will end by crushing all our nation, one by one."
His apprehension was correct.
The losing bull ran off to cower
Down in the swamp, with the effect
Of squashing twenty frogs per hour.

Alas! All ages demonstrate
That small folk are destroyed by passions of the great.

II. 4

The Bat and the Two Weasels

Swooping, flittering, flying blind, a bat
Nosedived into a weasel's bailiwick.
The weasel, a confirmed mouse–hater, seized him quick
And went to eat him, just like that.
He said, "How dare you show me your unpleasant face
After the dirty tricks I've suffered from your race?
Surely, you're a mouse? I want a straight confession.
If you're no mouse, I'm not a weasel, that's for sure!"
"Oh, la!" the captive said. "My dear monsieur,
You are mistaken. Mouse was never my profession.
Some scandal monger spreads these lies.
Thanks to the One who made all things,
I am a bird. You see my wings?
Hurrah for those who sail the skies!"
The logic worked, the facts were clear,
The argument was so sincere
The captive was released again.
And then a few days after that
Our dizzy, blindfold acrobat
Crashed in a second weasel's den –
But this one hated birds, not mice.
So here he was again, about to pay the price
Because the longnosed lady of the house inferred
Since he had wings he was a bird.
He lodged a protest. "Madam, it is evident
That you are unobservant altogether.
How can I be a bird? Have I one single feather?
No, of course not. Why? Because I am a rodent.
Let's hear it for the rats!
May Jupiter confound all cats!"
By fancy footwork, artful jive,
He'd managed twice to stay alive.
Just so, in crises, many a man proves able
To save his skin by altering his party label.

So wise ones sing, when faced with execution,
"Long live the King! Long live the Revolution!"

II. 5

The Bird Wounded by an Arrow

Pierced by a feathered arrow, dying fast, a bird
Lamented its sad fate. "Absurd, absurd, absurd,"
It sang in mortal agony, "that anyone
Should from himself provide means for his own destruction.
Cruel humankind! You pilfer from our wings
The very vanes that guide these deathly flying things.
But do not pride yourselves, you race without compassion,
For many of you yet will fall in just this fashion,
Since, of the sons of Japheth, each to each a brother,
The one half always arms the other.

II. 6

The Hound-bitch and Her Friend

A pregnant bitch, about to whelp,
And needing a refuge for the birth,
Persuaded her close friend to help
By lending her the den she'd scrabbled in the earth.
Then when her benefactor asked to have it back
She whined to be allowed to stay a few weeks more –
Her pups were small and blind, too weak as yet to walk.
Her plea was granted, as before.
A further time went by, the owner asked again
To have returned to her her house, her room, her bed.
The bitch bared all her teeth and said,
"My pack and I will leave here when
You drive us out by force!"
Her pups by now were hounds, fiery-eyed and fierce.

32

Kindness done ill-doers always ends in sorrow.
In order to recover what they beg to borrow
You will be forced to prove your mettle.
First you must plead, then you must battle.
The single step you let them get on you today
Becomes four steps tomorrow.

II. 7

The Eagle and the Scarab

The eagle, gliding over, saw the rabbit, Jack,
And swooped to catch him. Jack, in fear, hopped off – zag zig,
Zig zag, the eagle's talons close above his back.
Just then, he saw a scarab's hole, not very big,
Yet offering perhaps a refuge. He crouched low,
But soon was seized, despite his cries of sanctuary.
And now the scarab tried to intercede.
"Great Queen of birds, although you easily could carry
This poor creature off," it said, "you *must* not. No!
You hear Jack Rabbit begging for his life. I plead
That you should show him mercy, or you will offend
On two accounts: he is my neighbor, and my friend."
The bird of Jupiter, not saying anything,
Just flicked the scarab with her wing,
Leaving it stunned, too dazed for speech,
Then carried Jack away. Offended by this breach
Of civil conduct, in its turn the scarab flew
Up to the eagle's nest and in her absence broke
Her eggs, her precious eggs, the dearest things she knew,
All gone, destroyed in one swift stroke.
When she came home at last and saw the havoc there
The eagle's screaming filled the air,
Her rage made worse by lack of anyone to blame.
But still the wind that blows carried her cries away,
She knew a mother's mourning all the year that came.

33

Next year she chose a higher peak where she might lay
Her eggs in safety, but again the scarab tossed
Them out, once more repaying Jack's demise.
Her second grief was such that for six months at least
The forests echoed with her cries.
The bird that carried Ganymede,
Compelled at last to go to Jupiter for aid,
Now nested in his lap, imagining
This spot was safe, since if it were attacked the king
Of all the gods would surely come to her defense:
No thief would dare give such offense!
And she was right – for no one did.
But her small foe was not yet stopped;
It flew above great Jupiter, took aim and dropped
Its dungball on his robe, at which the god so flapped
And flailed that he dislodged the eagle's nest, which slid
Below and smashed. The angry bird
Made threats at Jupiter. She raged
At his incompetence, said she preferred
Some god–forsaken desert to his stupid court,
Said he was crazy if he tried to keep her caged
One second longer – and other ravings of the sort.
Poor Jupiter just acted dumb.
But now the scarab had to come
Before a grave tribunal in the sky
To offer charges, make defenses, testify.
It was established that the eagle was at fault,
But since not even Jupiter can bring a halt
To ancient feuds, he changed the time when eagles mate
To coincide with that when scarabs keep
In winter quarters, sound asleep
Like groundhogs when they hibernate,
With paws curled up and eyes shut tight,
For six months keeping from the light.

II. 8

The Lion and the Gnat

"Begone, ignoble insect! Speck of excrement!"
The lion one day told the gnat,
Or roared to this effect, whereat
The gnat immediately went
To war. "King, sweetie, thinkest thou
Your royal title makes me get cold feet?
A mean old bull is twice as strong as you
And I make him do any tricks I want him to,
So when I see you, baby, all I see is meat!"
No sooner was this spoken than
With his small trumpet he began
To sound the charge, this one–gnat band
And street guerilla both combined.
He mobilised, struck tail and mane,
And drove the lion near insane.
The quadruped began to froth, his eyes glowed red.
He roared! Small creatures hid and great ones fled:
A scene of universal dread
Accomplished by one tiny gnat.
This dwarfish fly zoomed all about,
He stung the lion's rump, he stung the lion's snout,
Then flew inside of that and stung.
The lion's mounting fury reached its topmost rung:
His unseen foe was winning, gleeful as it saw
How in his rampant fury every tooth and claw
Performed the butcher's job for which it was designed –
The lion bled from many a self-inflicted wound.
He lashed his tail along his flanks,
But only struck thin air; his mane fell out in hanks,
Until frustrated rage so weakened him he swooned!
The insect left the field with oak leaves on his brow;
As earlier the charge, he sounded victory now!
But soon thereafter, going through the world to tell
His glorious feat, proceeding down a road he fell
Into a spider's ambush – and met his end as well.

Is there perhaps a lesson to be drawn from this?
Well, I see two. The first: if one has enemies
The ones to fear the most are often least in size.
And, second: one may come through holocausts untouched
Then choke upon a grain of rice.

II. 9

The Ass Who Carried Sponges
and
The Ass Who Carried Salt

Every inch the Roman emperor,
A drover of asses, waving his scepter,
Marshalled his splendid two-ass train.
The first, bearing sponges, tripped lightly as a courier,
The second trudged with signs of strain –
As if he carried millstones, one would say,
But sacks of salt in fact. Our pilgrims wended
Up hill, down dale and over the way
Until they reached a river they would have to ford.
And here their journey might have ended,
But having made the crossing many another day
The drover simply caught Old Sponge and got aboard,
Prodding Old Salt along ahead,
As he loved leading. But now instead
He stepped in a hole and sank from sight.
He thrashed around, came up, went down, at last emerged,
Because his load of salt by being long submerged,
Was finally dissolved,
Which left his load at last so light
That nothing could hold that jackass down.
Comrade Old Sponge, not one to deviate, resolved
To follow his leader like a sheep to slaughter:
See the ass go, launched out upon the water –

In which he promptly plunges
Over his head, along with his rider and his sponges.
Both ass and rider now become engrossed
Contesting with the sponges which can absorb the most.
The sponges win. They gain such weight
The drowning ass can't possibly regain the shore,
And the man, arms locked around his beast, seems sure
To share, quite soon, his watery fate.
Don't worry, someone saved them, it doesn't matter who.
The main thing is to see that the following is true:
All must not try to act the same –
Which is what I set out to claim.

II. 10

The Lion and the Rat

Treat all, to the extent you can, with deeds
That tie their loyalties to you,
For often there come times when even the strongest needs
Those not as strong. That this is true
The next two fables show – as, often, life does too.

A lion once caught a rat that popped up blindly
Between his paws from its nest in the earth below.
The king of beasts (on this occasion) acted kindly
And, showing his kingly nature, spared it and let it go.
His kindness was not in vain, although who would have bet
That there might come a day
The lion would need the rodent to repay his debt?
But so it did. Outside the forest for a foray
In cattle country, the lion fell in a trapper's net
That, loudly though he roared, would not release its grip.
But now Sir Rat appeared – how rapidly he traveled!
And with his big front teeth began to gnaw and snip
Until one knot was cut, and all the rest unraveled.

37

Persistence and passing time will in their course
Accomplish more than rage and brutal force.

II. 11

The Dove and the Ant

A dove sat drinking at a brook and, as it sipped,
An ant came teetering along the edge and tripped
And tumbled in. And since for it the stream was wide
As the Pacific, although with its whole strength it tried
To save itself, it couldn't – as the dove soon saw –
Without some help have managed to regain the shore.
At which the bird kindheartedly flung out a straw
That like a floating causeway bore
The ant's small weight and let it get to land once more.
But now, just moseying along, barefoot and slow,
Here came a ragtail country boy, holding a bow,
Who seeing Venus' favorite bird, decided she'd
Taste excellent, baked, stewed or fricaseed.
He drew, took aim, got set to let an arrow go,
But, just before, the ant climbed up and stung his toe.
He turned his head to see what could be happening.
The dove perceived its peril and was on the wing!
His dinner had flown away, he wasn't to have any:
You cannot buy a pigeon if you've got no penny.

II. 12

The Astrologer Who Blundered into a Well

When an astrologer once
Fell down a well, somebody said,
"If you can't see what's underneath your feet, poor dunce,
How can you hope to read the sky above your head?"
This simple tale, without the least elaboration,

38

Can be a lesson to the bulk of humankind,
For in our earthly population
I see but few who aren't inclined,
Without the slightest thought, to state
That mortal men can read what's in the Book of Fate.
Yet, anciently, in books of epic circumstance
By Homer and his like, men saw fate born of chance –
As in our day of Providence.
Well, of the future, none has knowledge in advance,
And if one did, then what would be the sense
Of using words like 'chance', or 'luck' or 'Fortune'
Concerning outcomes that are notably uncertain?
And as to the sublime intent
Of Him who made all things, and nothing without plan,
Who may know that but He alone? How may mere man
Read what is in his heart? Could he have meant
To plainly print with stars upon the firmament,
What time's dark night keeps veiled within its element?
What would that serve? To busy those whose speculations
Link this globe's life to that great sphere of constellations?
To put us so in dread of evils sure to come
That present pleasures leave us numb,
And any future good whose coming we foresee
Is turned by this to ill before it comes to be?
One would be wrong, or sacrilegious, thinking so.
The firmament is moving; the stars, unswerving, go
On their fixed paths; the sun lights all our days
And all our days its brightness comes at last to night –
And if this were not so, why, only then, one might
Think it was not necessity but other needs
That made it shine, temper the seasons, ripen seeds,
And touch all living beings with its light.
That said, how can the steady march of stars relate
To fortune, with its evermore erratic gait?
You, charlatans, casters of horoscopes,
Begone from courts of kings and popes,
Along with alchemists and their bellows, puffing fires –
You no more merit our belief than those great liars!

39

But I'm becoming too worked up. Let us resume
In re that cloudy theorist who met his doom
In drinking water. Surely, more than just portraying
The uselessness of this false science, he typifies
Those credulous souls who, as they gaze into the skies
At dim chimeras, never see they may be straying
On dangerous paths, both for themselves and all they prize.

II. 13

The Hare and the Frogs

Down in his hole a hare sat brooding –
In a hole, after all, what else is there to do?
He felt depressed, grim thoughts kept intruding,
For hares are forever feeling apprehensive and blue.
"Those who are consumed by dread
Suffer awfully," he said.
"They cannot eat a bite that isn't wasted on them.
All of their joys are spoiled by fears that prey upon them.
Just look at how I live: this hellish sense of dread
Will never let me sleep except with open eyes.
And if some genius says my fears are in my head,
Is that a thing my fears somehow must recognize?
And men, so far as I can see,
Are plagued by fears the same as me."
Philosophising thus, our hare
Came creeping up to peer outside,
Trembling as he sniffed the air,
Where shadows, breezes, dust–motes, left him terrified.
Where is it safe? He cannot think.
The world's too dangerous to face.
What is that noise? A shot? Quick as a wink,
He bounds away to seek a better hiding place.
He scampers in his panic past a pond where frogs
Are sunning. Splash! They vanish from their logs
In mass retreat to grottoes down below.

"Wow!" says he. "I see that I can do to others
What others do to me. What do you know –
I scared them! Yes! I frightened those green brothers!
How have I grown so fierce, who never was before?
By seeing other creatures shake in fear of me,
I've turned into a conqueror.
There's not a soul on earth who is so cowardly
He couldn't find a soul more cowardly than he."

II. 14

The Old Cock

Upon a tree limb, keeping ever-watchful guard,
An ancient cock was perched, a wise and crafty bird.
"Brother," the fox called up – he made his voice go sweet –
"No more quarreling for us.
This time, it's universal peace.
I had to tell you first. Come down and get a hug.
But please don't keep me standing here, for goodness sake,
Because I must have twenty other stops to make.
You and yours can just relax.
You're free at last from all attacks.
The two of us are brothers now.
Tonight let bonfires celebrate
The dawning of an age of bliss –
Meanwhile, come down and let us kiss
A kiss of peace and brotherhood!"
"My friend," the cock replied, "I have not heard such good,
Such happy, such amazing news in all my years
As yours
About this peace.
And hearing it from you will just increase
The joy I feel by two. Doubtlessly, the pair
Of greyhounds I see racing toward us there
Are couriers with more good news to bear.
How fast they run! They're almost here!

41

I'll be right down. No doubt they'll join the kissing, too."
"Goodbye now," said the fox. "It seems I have to dash.
We must postpone the celebration banquet till
Some future date." At which point, in a flash,
The gentleman hitched up his socks and hit the road,
Unhappy with the way his plot turned out,
While, up above, the old cock crowed
In victory. He'd put the fox to rout!

The pleasure is increased by six
When the trickster is caught by his own tricks.

II. 15

The Crow Who Wished to Imitate the Eagle

Jupiter's favorite bird once carried off a mutton.
A crow who saw the deed, though not
One half so strong, was equally a glutton
And it decided on the spot
To do the same. Circling the pasture in the air,
It chose the fattest sheep of all the hundred there,
A creature raised for sacrifice,
Meant for immortal mouths to taste in paradise.
But Crow, a hungry-eyed rapscallion, cawed,
"I don't know who your mama was, but, hey!
She must have nursed you well for you to grow so broad,
And now your body is my prey!"
With that, it swooped upon the bleating creature.
The sheep, in common with its sheepish genus,
Outweighed a cheese, and it possessed another feature
Cheeses lack – a thick and curly coat of wool
As dense and wiry as the beard
Of that old Cyclops, Polyphemus.
Once it had sunk its claws in this, the bird
Found getting them out again impossible.

The shepherd caught it, gave it to his brats to do
Anything with it they might have wanted to.

The message is clear: you'd better know your proper size,
Because the eagle has powers denied the crow,
And, tempting though it is to fantasize
That you can soar off in the skies,
The chances are you're stuck below.
There's an old saying that applies –
Big wasps aren't caught in spider webs, just little flies.

II. 16

Juno and the Peacock

The peacock shrieked at Juno.
"Goddess," he said, "don't think I make this fuss,
This loud complaint, for nothing. I know you know
This voice you gave me sounds horrendous.
All nature hates to hear my call;
And yet the nightingale, the drabbest of us all,
Forms sounds so brilliantly mellifluous
That it is she who wins the honors of the spring."
Juno replied – oh, she was furious! –
"You jealous bird, you'd best not say one thing!
It's scandalous that you should grudge the nightingale
Her voice, when all can see you carry round your neck
A shimmering rainbow of a hundred shades of silk,
And when you strut and fan your tail
A dazzlement is spread before our eyes
Such as a jewel case displays.
Is there another bird beneath the skies
So gifted as you are to please?
No creature has all qualities.
To some there falls the gift of strength and size,
The falcon is swift, the eagle brave,
The crow has powers of prophecy.

So has the rook, but for catastrophe.
Each one accepts the voice I gave.
Now, cease complaining, or as punishment
I'll pluck off all your feathered ornament."

II. 17

The Cat Who Became a Woman

A man adored his cat to an insane degree:
How delicate, how darling, how delightful, she!
Her mew made such a melting music in his ears
That finally, by prayers and tears,
By sorcery, spells and magic charms
He wheedled Fate to bend its laws
And change a cat with fur and claws
Into a woman with legs and arms –
Whom then, Sir Fool personified,
That very day he made his bride,
For love had driven him as mad
As, earlier, affection had.
No beauty celebrated for
The amorous career she led
Ever pleased a lover more
Than this new bride her groom, new wed.
He sweet-talked her, she called him honey,
And so the two – hey, nonny, nonny!
He found in her no trace of cat,
Certain, as his delusion grew,
She was pure woman, through and through.
But when one night soon after that
Some mice made noises gnawing underneath their bed
Then instantly the wife assumed
A cattish crouch: the mice all fled.
The mice returned. Now she resumed
Her feline posture, as before,
And this time pounced upon her prey,

For since she'd metamorphosed they
Were less inclined to fear her anymore –
While they to her proved bait, whose source
Of power over her was nature's shaping force
That mocks at any change once time enough has passed.
Emptied, the vessel smells; once made, the crease will last,
The wheel stays in its rutted track,
What's done grows past undoing, nothing will change it back.

Strike nature with your pitchforks, take your whips to it,
You won't reform it, not one bit.
Advance together, sticks in hand,
It won't obey though you command.
Slam your door in its face when nature comes to knock –
And it will climb through windows you forgot to lock.

II. 18

The Lion and the Ass Go Hunting

The King of Beasts had an idea one day!
He'd hold a hunt, to be his birthday celebration.
Of course, it's not small sparrows that are lions' prey
But lordly boars and stags of an exalted station.
The lion appointed the ass to be his aide – a choice
Inspired by his stentorian voice,
For 'Royal Hunting Horn' describes the job precisely.
The lion stationed him, in branches hidden nicely,
And ordered him to bray, knowing the awful blare
Would bring the bravest quarry bolting from its lair,
Since none of the beasts as yet had known
The loud *heehhaww* of his trombone.
The air resounded with a rude reverberation
That panicked every creature in the whole creation.
All fled – and all ran straight into the fatal snare,
To find the lion waiting there.
"Well, wasn't I great! Shouldn't I feel proud?"

The ass exclaimed, presuming he had been the star.
"Oh, yes," the lion replied, "you were immensely loud.
Had I not known beforehand what an ass you are,
I would myself have been quite scared!"
The ass would have resented this, had he but dared,
Although he well deserved to be put down,
For who can bear to hear the bragging of a clown?
It doesn't befit their character.

II. 19

Aesop Explains a Will

If we can believe the legend, Aesop's single mind
Surpassed in power Athens's wisest heads combined.
He was the oracle of Greece,
As will be seen in this next piece,
A very pleasant tale which those who read may find
Not only instructive but delicious.

An Athenian had three daughters, all pernicious:
One was a drinker, one a coquette,
The third completely avaricious.
He made a will by which this trio was to get
All of his worldly goods, divided
Precisely into thirds – yet, oddly, it provided
The mother also was a full and equal heir
Who would receive her portion when and only when
Not one of the three daughters still possessed her share.
The fellow died, the women ran
To open the precious document,
But having read it end to end
Had no idea what it meant.
Impossible! There was no way
To pay their mother's share if none had means to do it.
They read it once again. How were they to construe it?
What did their father mean to say?

They asked the Areopagus to help decide,
But its wise judges, after endless consultations
And myriads of futile, worthless explanations,
Threw off their wigs, confessing they were mystified.
Yet, finally, they counseled: "It is this courts's decision
That legatees may now proceed with the division
According to the first, entirely clear, provision
Of legator, and just not bother with the other.
Each daughter, on the mother's sole volition,
Shall undertake to pay her mother
One third said daughter's portion under this partition,
Unless the widow should prefer
That interest on the principal be paid to her
For a term deemed to have started
With the decease of the departed."
By this decree, three lots were made of goods and chattels.
The first contained all that pertained to drinking wine –
A pergola for sipping it beneath a vine,
Tall sideboards holding ranks of bottles
In which it was decanted, and golden bowls and vessels
From which to quaff the vintage Malmsey, and the vassals
Whose task it was to fetch and pour when duly roused;
In short, the whole machinery for getting soused.
The next lot held such props as a coquette employs –
The townhouse graced
With furnishings of just the most exquisite taste,
The staff of maids to coiff her hair, the eunuch boys
To bring the jewels she enjoys,
And women to sew the gowns that show her tiny waist.
In the last lot went the farms, their croplands and their woods
And pastures, farm equipment, household goods,
Their well-filled granaries and grazing flocks and divers
Field slaves, shepherds, teams of oxen and their drivers.
All Athens cheered the court's decision,
For nothing was left to chance by its inspired division:
Each sister was afforded just what was her druthers.
Each chose accordingly, as did the others.
It was in Athens long ago

That all this happened. Now, although
The citizens, both high and low
Agreed with both the judges' and each sister's choice,
They soon heard Aesop's single voice
Contending that, depite long wrangling and much striving,
The court had just succeeded in arriving
At the exact contrary of the last wish of the dead.
"If the deceased could stand here living," Aesop said,
"We would be hearing most emphatic
Reproaches to our tribe, the Attic.
Imagine! Today's most subtle, philosophic nation
Can't give a right interpretation
Of one man's dying will!" And Aesop then and there,
On his own authority, calmly reassigned
Each sister what she least preferred –
The lot of things that each would find
Unthinkable to choose, impossible to bear.
The society darling was consigned
The drinking sister's vinous share;
The drinker got the livestock herd,
And the stingy one the maids to do her dirty hair.
The Phrygian said that of the ways
To carry out the will this had to be the best,
For if it made the girls divest
Those properties they had possessed,
Then as their worth grew known, in not too many days
They all would be betrothed to well-born fiancees,
By which their mother would be amply paid and blessed,
While they, without their father's gifts, would now fulfill
The deep intentions of his will.
The public was amazed to find
That there are times when one man's mind
Displays more sense than does a pack of them combined.

II. 20

Book Three

The Miller, His Son, and the Donkey

To M. D. M.

Because our elders have a prior right to speak,
Both fable and the arts in origin are Greek.
Yet those fields, surely, haven't yet been picked so clean
That we, arriving later, have nothing left to glean.
Fiction is a land of blank, unsettled spaces
Where every day our authors find undreamed-of places.
But let me tell a tale already ancient when
Racan was told it by the old Malherbe. These men,
Two poets who rival Horace, inheritors of his lyre,
Disciples of Apollo who teach us and inspire –
In short, our masters – happened to cross paths one day,
Both occupied with their own thoughts and cares as they
Were walking. Racan addressed Malherbe, "I ask you, sir,
Who have lived long and seen what chances may occur
In any life and, having passed through every stage
Of it by now, has all the wisdom of old age,
What path should I best follow? For it is time I chose.
My wealth, my talent and my family: all those
You know quite well. So tell me, should I settle here,
Deep in the provinces, embark on a career
In the king's army, or go to court? A soldier's life
May have its quiet pleasures; living with a wife
Its noisy battles. This world seems always an alloy
Of less-than-perfect choices, mingling grief and joy.
If I pleased just myself, I'd have no hesitation,
But I must please them all – parents, court and nation."
Malherbe replied, "Please everyone! That's very nice!
But listen to a tale, and then hear my advice.

"In some old work I read, a miller and his son –
An old man and a boy, but not a little one,

51

A lad of fifteen years – were headed for the fair,
Bringing along their donkey, planning to sell him there.
To keep him looking fresh and saleable in town
They tied his feet together, and carried him upside down
On a pole between them like a delicate chandelier,
A pair of ignorant bumpkins, idiots sans peer.
The first to see them broke into great peals of laughter.
'What farce is this?' he said. 'What can these fools be after?
The biggest ass among them is not the one they'd guess.'
The miller, overhearing, perceived their foolishness,
Untied the beast and set him walking on his own –
At which the animal, in a resentful tone,
Brayed that he'd rather ride. But, paying him no mind,
The man said, 'Son, you mount; I'll walk along behind.'
The sight of them offended three merchants whom they met.
The eldest thundered at the son, 'Young man, you get
Yourself right off! For shame! You should be mortified!
Your servant's old and weak! You walk and let him ride.'
'Good sirs,' the father answered, 'we'll do as you have said.'
The boy got off and walked; the father rode instead.
Three girls passed by. One sneered, "Now, that is very wrong!
He's putting on such airs! That young boy limps along
While that old moron, lolling on his jackass, tries
To act like some throned bishop, looking oh so wise!'
'At my age, girl,' he said, 'one doesn't put on airs,
Believe me, child, and just keep out of our affairs.'
But after more such catcalls the old man changed his mind
And had his son get on and ride along behind.
They'd barely gone another thirty steps when they
Met yet another bunch with yet more words to say.
One said, 'These folks are stupid. The beast can't take that
    load.
They'll kill that little jenny; she'll die there on the road.
Do they not pity that old helper whom they ride?
If they should reach the fair, they'll have to sell her hide!'
'Gol durn!' the miller said. 'Whoever tries to please
Everyone and his father, it's definite that he's
Out of his skull completely. Still, let us try once more!'

The two got off and walked; the donkey pranced before.
But soon another voice inquired, 'Is this the way
The world today is going? Are donkeys free to stray,
Unburdened down the road, while millers walk, frustrated?
Which of the species was especially created
To carry burdens, asses or their masters? Can it
Be doubted? Take my advice and carve that into granite.
They're wearing out their shoes to spare their ass's feet.
They've got the plot reversed. When Nicholas goes to meet
Sweet Jean he rides his ass, according to the song.
But here all three are asses! As the miller strode along,
He said, 'That's right. An ass I am; agreed; okay.
But from now on, whatever anyone may say
To do or not to do, to praise me or malign,
I'll do what my head tells me.' He did, and he did fine.

"And as for you, choose Mars or Eros or court life,
Stay in the provinces or leave. Find you a wife,
Turn monk or take a job or run for office. No matter
What you decide you'll be besieged with silly chatter."

III. 1

The Belly and the Members

These fables needed prefacing
With some remarks about that thing
Called royalty – equivalent,
Some say, to Master Belly, whose need for nourishment
Also elicits lots of corporal resentment.
Grown tired of being at the belly's beck and call,
The members of the body voted to retire
And live as he did, folk of leisure one and all.
"Without our help," they said, "he'd swallow only air.
Yet we, like beasts of burden, toil and moil and sweat.
Who for? Only for him! Nothing is what we get!
Our labor goes to waste in fetching him his swill.

53

Be idle, friends. He'll gladly teach us all that skill!"
No sooner said than done. The hands quit grasping things,
The arms kept stiff, the legs stood obstinately still.
All told the belly he could grow a set of wings
And serve himself – an error they would soon repent.
For speedily they found themselves debilitated;
Their blood used up, no nourishment now circulated.
The rebels now found all too evident
That though appearing greedy, useless, indolent,
The belly, more than any of them, served the health
And proper working of the body's commonwealth.
And this is true of monarchs and the powers they wield –
They take but also give, for as they take they yield.
All do the kingdom's work and from the kingdom draw
The daily bread that all require.
The kingdom sets the craftsman's task and pays his hire,
Makes merchants rich, seats judges in the courts of law,
Provides the soldier's pay, the laborer's livelihood,
Distributing to myriads its sovereign good
And binding all into one state.
Menenius knew this tale and told it well.
The Roman populace had come to look with hate
Upon the Senate. Malcontents were heard to yell
That it had everything, all wealth and power and glory –
It owned the empire, but for them the same old story:
Taxes and more taxes and sending sons to fight.
Huge crowds began to form outside the city gate,
Swept up by arguments that they should emigrate.
But then Menenius stopped their flight
By telling them this fable
That made them see themselves as members to the state,
Recalling each to duty, first and fundamental.

III. 2

The Wolf Who Became a Shepherd

A wolf, experiencing a drop in quantity
Of sheep input from local flocks,
Decided he would be as clever as a fox
And take a new identity.
He dressed in shepherd fashion, wore a little cloak
And found a stick to be his crook,
Nor were his shepherd's pipes left out.
And finally, to end all doubt,
He had the happy thought of writing on his hat,
"It's me that is young Jock, the shepherd of this flock."
Then, with identity made clear,
And with his forelegs posed upon his shepherd's crook,
Young Jock the False crept stealthily to where
Young Jock the True at full length snored
On his green herbal bed of sward.
His sheepdog also slept, his pipes made not one peep,
And all the flock, or nearly all, lay sound asleep.
The villain left them sleeping there.
To help persuade the flock to follow to his lair,
He thought his speaking style should fit his mode of wear.
This seemed quite logically correct –
But that was where his scheme was wrecked.
His voice could not assume the proper pastoral sound,
The howling tones he uttered made the woods resound
And gave the mystery away.
The noise awakened all from sleep,
The boy, his dog, his flock of sheep.
The wolf, in the ensuing fray,
Became too tangled in his clothes
To run and flee or fight his foes.

Clever operators always catch themselves,
For in the end, wolves act like wolves.
Of many sayings, this one's true.

III. 3

55

The Frogs Who Asked for a King

Weary of swamp democracy,
The frogs made a cacophony
So rude, so raucous, so anarchic,
That Jupiter to shush them made their state monarchic.
He dropped them down a king not in the least bit harsh,
But whose arrival caused such panic in the marsh
That all that popeyed population,
A cowardly and stupid nation,
Dived in the water, hid in the weeds,
Sank into holes, shrank among reeds,
Not daring just at first to face
This conquering king who came from some new giant race –
Though, actually, he was a toppled tree
Whose air of gravity caused awe initially,
Until at last one frog dared take a look and see.
Trembling, she emerged, then cautiously hopped near;
Another followed her, another in the rear,
And soon a mob had formed
That so forgot respect
That all together stormed
Their king and sat upon his shoulders, quite unchecked!
The king stayed calm and let the revolution run,
But Jupiter felt splitting pressure in his brain:
"Give us," yelled the frogs, "a king who gets things done!"
The monarch of the gods this time sent a crane
Who speared them, who crunched them,
Who gobbled them, who munched them
On arbitrary grounds.
And then the frogs made louder sounds.
So Jupiter spoke out, "What now? Am I to swerve
Your nation's laws to fit each new opinion poll?
The first concern you should have had was to preserve
Your government.
But having failed in that, you should have been content

56

To live in the benevolent control
Of that sweet-natured figurehead I sent.
So now fall silent and accept your curse,
For fear you'll go from bad to worse!"

III. 4

The Fox and the Ram

Old Captain Fox went on maneuvers once. He brought
A goat along, his friend the tall-horned ram,
Who never gave where he was going any thought,
Unlike the fox, past master of the art of scam.
They got so thirsty that they jumped into a well
And drank until their bellies started in to swell.
When they were full, Fox said, "Old pal of mine,
We've had our drink but I don't see an exit sign.
So just you stand up straight and tall
And slant your horns against the wall.
First, I will clamber up your spine,
Then scale your horns to get up high
And, using you as scaffold, I
In no time will be gone, bye bye –
Though not, of course, before I pull you out."
"Upon my beard," the goat replied, "that's very smart!
God, how I love to hang about
With intellectuals like yourself. If I was to start
Thinking right now and went on thinking forever,
I swear I wouldn't have figured that out, just never."
The fox emerged and left his partner in the hole,
Though not without a sermon to console
His doubts and teach him to have – patience:
"If Heaven had given you a store of common sense
Proportionate to that fine beard upon your chin,
You would not so unthinkingly have been
Persuaded into such a hole. And, now, goodbye.

Life is an upward struggle. One must always try.
Myself, I have a pressing date
And must not wait, or I'll be late!"

Before you go in, think long and hard about
How you'll get out.

III. 5

The Eagle, the Cat, and the Pig

In the top of a hollow oak an eagle made her nest;
A cat annexed the middle, a sow took up the rest.
By having boundaries all three unhindered could
Devote themselves in peace to grubby motherhood.
But, soon, the cat's deceit caused peace to disappear.
She climbed up to the eagle's nest and said, "My dear,
Our lives are imminently threatened, or at least
Our children's are, which is the same as ours,
Since we are mothers. You have seen that ugly beast
Who excavates the ground beneath us at all hours.
It's clear she means with her great snout
To root this oak's foundations out
And when our refuge comes to fall
She will rush in and eat our children, one and all.
If even one survived, I should feel less distraught."
Then, having left all in the upper level fraught
With terror, she crept down the trunk and caught
The sow just going into labor.
She said in a low voice, "My dearest friend and neighbor,
I have bad news. Should you emerge
To take your children out for air, the eagle will
Come swooping down and get them. But I urge
You not to tell a soul I said so. She would kill
Me if she heard I did." Then having sown the seeds
Of terror in this second household, she descended
To her own hole. Afraid to leave them unattended,

58

The eagle now stayed with her eaglets, and their needs
For food remained unmet. The sow was just as scared.
Great fear so paralyzed them both that neither dared
Attempt to meet their one most crucial obligation:
To keep their children from starvation.
Both stayed at home, unbudging, nervously protecting
Their offspring from the crisis each was soon expecting:
The royal bird, by underground subversion,
The sow, by sudden, overhead incursion.
Instead, both died of hunger and each family line,
The swinish and the aquiline,
Became extinct. The cat's, on the other hand, did fine.
What can't a lying tongue achieve?
What deceptions won't it weave?
When the strong locks
Were opened on Pandora's box,
Of all the mischiefs that flew out, deceit was worst
And should by all be roundly cursed.

III. 6

The Drunkard and His Wife

We all have some persistent flaw
Not cured by either fear or shame.
On this, I have in mind a tale with which to draw
A concrete illustration – for I make no claim
I don't support with an example. A drunk had parted
With all his money, addled his mind and ruined his health.
(Such types too frequently have hardly more than started
On their careers than they have thrown away their wealth.)
One day, as he lay senseless from another bout
Of pouring the wine in while pouring his brains out,
His wife conveyed him to a crypt to snore away
While he slept off his latest round of beaujolais.
When he awoke he found himself laid out in state
Upon a bier and wrapped in a long winding shroud,

59

With rows of candles flickering at his feet and head.
"What's going on?" he asked aloud.
"Is my wife widowed? Am I dead?"
And then, disguised in a demonic mask, his mate,
Dressed like Alecto, that grim Fury, stood at his side
And in an awful voice extended him a plate
Of bubbling, smoking broth. "Have some!" she said.
By now convinced he was in hell, the man replied
To this fierce apparition, "Just what is your position
Officially down here?" "I supervise nutrition
In this Satanic realm," she cackled.
"I bring hot dishes to the damned whose souls are shackled
Eternally in darkness." Not taking time to think,
The husband asked, "But don't you ever bring them drink?"

III. 7

Gout and Spiders

Having created gout and spiders, old King Hades
Addressed his ugly daughters: "Ladies,
When you arrive on Earth you will be proud of seeing
How loathed you are, how feared, by every human being.
Well, let us now consider where you will reside.
You see those huts, off to one side,
So cramped, so dismal? And there, upon the other hand,
Those gilded palaces, so sumptuous, so grand?
I offer these alternatives. Here are two straws.
Each make her choice, or else abide by what she draws."
"I hate those huts," the spider said. "I want more space."
The gout, upon her part, observed
That doctors filled the palaces and was unnerved.
She knew she never would feel safe in such a place.
Deciding on the huts, she entered the big toe
Of a man she saw in one. "While I'm in here," she said,
"I can relax in peace, and never have to dread
Some Hippocratic oaf compelling me to go

On a forced holiday." Meanwhile, the spider wove
A cozy web within the cove
Of a frescoed palace ceiling, as if its splendid room
Were leased to her for life. Not being one to shirk,
She warped her threads across the space and got to work,
Ensnaring flies galore – until, armed with a broom,
A servant came and briskly swept her house away.
She wove it back. Back came the broom. Day after day,
The wee poor beastie was summarily turned out,
Till, giving up the task, she went to look for Gout.
After a long search, when finally she spied her,
She found her in the fields, worse off than she the spider.
Her host had risen early, despite his gouty toe,
And gone off splitting rails and weeding with his hoe.
Now, it's a well-known fact about
The gout that vigorous exercise will drive it out.
Gout said, "Oh, my! I'm tiring fast. I can't stay here
Much longer. Sister Spider! Let us change lodgings, dear!"
One word was all it took. The spider softly crept
Into the gloomy hut, where no broom ever swept.
The gout, for its part, promptly went to live instead
With a bishop – whom she permanently kept in bed,
A poultice on his foot. My god! With what straight faces
These doctors give us cures that only leave us worse.
The spider and the gout saw that they could reverse
Their fortunes simply by exchanging places.

III. 8

The Wolf and the Stork

Wolves wolf things down, the taste
Means nothing. Gulp! No chewing,
Down it goes. Such greedy haste
Once nearly caused one wolf's undoing.
Gorging fraternally with his pack,
He got a bone stuck down his windpipe like a cork

And everything was going black
When, luckily, a passing stork,
Seeing him signal frantically that he was choking,
Snatched the bone out – but then presented him a bill
For her good deed. "You must be joking!"
Howled the wolf. "Your head is still
Upon your neck after you stuck it in my jaws.
And you want payment? Lady, I'm a patient dude,
But I can't stand ingratitude!
You've had your pay, so scram! Get out of here – because
You might get caught in my big paws!"

III. 9

The Lion Beaten by the Man

An artist painted a picture –
It was shown at an exhibition –
Of a lion, immense in stature,
Thrown to the ground by a man.
The public found it brave.
But then a lion silenced all the prattle.
"It's clear," he said, "the artist gave
Your side the victory in the battle,
But he was just deceiving you,
Lying without the least restraint.
The lion would be on top if art were only true,
And if my fellow lions could paint."

III. 10

The Fox and the Grapes

A hungry fox from Gascony, or Normandy perhaps,
While nosing through a vineyard spotted overhead
A luscious-looking bunch of grapes,

Their skins like velvet, coral-red,
A dish for the discriminating, rare and fine.
But when they proved to be beyond his reach he said,
"They are too green, still sour, and only fit for swine."

Would it have helped to moan and whine?

III. 11

The Swan and the Cook

Beneath a farmyard sky
With fowl of every feather
A cygnet and a gosling lived together.
Each was predestined: one to please their master's eye
And one his sense of taste. The swan would soon begin
Proudly to sail a pond, the goose would be – sent in.
They played among the ditches near the great chateau.
There often one might see them, swimming side by side,
There often racing, often diving deep below,
In rivalry forever, never satisfied.
One day the cook, one drink too many in him, took
The swan to be the goose. He caught it by the neck,
Prepared to cut its throat and fling it in the soup.
The swan, about to die, began a sweet sad song.
The cook, astounded, sobered up.
He saw that he had got things wrong.
"Might I," he asked, "have put this singer in a pot?
No, no! The gods would not have let me lift my knife
To any throat so made to sing!"

With all the many dangers dogging us through life,
A gentle tone is no bad thing.

III. 12

The Wolves and the Sheep

After a thousand years and more of open war,
The wolves approached the sheep, proposing peace.
Both sides, they said, would come out better off by far.
For if the wolves had gorged on creatures bearing fleece,
Wolf fur had often ended up in shepherds' cloaks.
One group had lacked its natural liberty to graze,
The other one to butcher folks.
Fear had kept both from following their rightful ways.
A treaty was drawn up and hostages exchanged:
The wolves gave up their cubs, the sheep their watchful
      hounds.
Commissioners confirmed that all was well–arranged,
By protocol, in proper bounds.
Time passed. The wolf cubs grew, as wolf cubs will,
To wolves, assassins of exquisite skill.
They waited till the shepherds had gone out one day
Then strangled all the fattest lambs and dragged them stark
Into the woods, from whence they sent their pack a dark
Intelligence. And suddenly the hounds, who lay
Off guard and trusting, were attacked
And murdered as they slept, the deed so quickly done
They scarcely felt a thing as they were hacked
To bits – and none of them escaped, not one.

The moral here: one must
War constantly against the cruel and unjust.
Peace in itself is good, its value is immense,
But what can be the sense
Of peace with an enemy whom one can never trust?

III. 13

The Lion Grown Old

Once the terror of the forest, now just old,
Heavy with years and grieving at his vanished prowess,
The lion was attacked by subjects he once ruled,
All strengthened by his growing weakness.
Approaching him in turn, the wolf first bit his paw,
The ox gored his side, the horse kicked his jaw.
In his last moments, low in spirit, aged and ill,
The lion had scarcely strength to roar, and he lay still.
And then he saw the ass come rushing in his cave.
"This is too much," he told him, laboring for breath.
"To die and be released is all that I now crave,
But blows from one like you will be a double death."

III. 14

Philomel and Procne

Procne the swallow, one fine day,
Shot from her nest and off she flew,
Far from cities and towns, away
Where Philomel, deep in a wood, sang *rue! terue!*
"Oh, sister," Procne twittered, "what have you to say?
It seems a thousand years ago that you withdrew
Yourself from view. Since Thrace, who's seen you, who?
You've never lived among us since – oh, no, not you!
But why remain alone and brood?
Return, sweet nightingale, and end your solitude."
Cooed Philomel, "Suppose I do?
You see my life improving?" "True!"
Said Procne. "Must your music go to waste
Upon dumb animals, or rustics lacking taste?
Was such rare talent made to grace the wilderness?
Come back and dazzle crowds in the metropolis!
Besides, the very sight of this dark forest must

Eternally remind you of the place
Where Tereus with brutal lust
Profaned your beauty's god-sent grace."
"It is the very memory of that abuse,"
Her sister said, "that keeps me here, a dim recluse.
When I see any man, alas!
I think of that and nothing else."

III. 15

The Woman Who Was Drowned

I'd never say, like some, "It's just a woman drowned –
There is no cause to be upset."
Abundant cause, I'd say, for who could not regret
The loss of any of that sex with which our joys are crowned?
That thought is hardly pointless, for it well relates
To this next fable, which narrates
The story of a woman who lacked skill to swim
And in a river met her sentence from the fates.
Her husband, as grief asked of him,
Set out to organize a search
For her remains, which he would eulogize in church.
Along the river bank where the offending current
Had recently carried her away,
He asked the people strolling there
If any were perhaps aware
Of where she'd ended up that day.
But though all said that they were sorry but they weren't,
All had advice to give. "Search downstream," one man said.
Another, "No, search up instead,
Because whatever force the river may possess
To drag her corpse down toward the bay,
The spirit of contradictoriness
Will make it float the opposite way."
The fellow's flippancy disclosed
Great lack of taste. And if that woman was disposed

To be contrary, I can't say.
But whether as a sex all women are inclined –
Or not – to have this cast of mind,
One thing is certain: all those born so will display
This trait until their dying day
And – even after – from below,
Would if they could keep saying no.

III. 16

The Weasel in the Pantry

Miss Weasel, with her model's wasted figure, stole
Into a pantry through a very narrow hole
And there she lost all self-control.
She lived it up, she ate and ate,
The lady needed no persuasion.
She crammed, she gorged – lord knows the weight
Of groceries she massacred on that occasion!
Or course, the end result was that
Her face grew round, her body fat.
Then after days of overeating, she
Was startled by some noise and tried at once to flee.
The hole was far too small. "What can be wrong?" she cried.
"This hole is not the hole. I'll try the other side."
And twice around the room she went.
"It is the hole," she said. "I'm trapped, it's evident.
Yet, several days ago, I wriggled through with ease."
A rat, observing her misdoubt,
Said, "Lady, when you entered you were not obese.
Thin, you weaseled in and thin you must weasel out.
And though the point applies to many others, too,
I see no point just now in your demanding who.
The one you'd better think about is only you."

III. 17

The Cat and the Old Mouse

A fable in a book I read
Told how a warlike cat called Rodilard the Grim
Hated all mice and wished them dead.
Keen-eyed as Cerberus he was, a shrewd commander
As cruel as Attila, as swift as Alexander,
And mice for leagues around were terrified of him.
This tale I said I read related
How in his house the mice were near exterminated
Through his rapacity, voracity, and horrible ferocity –
No propped-up board, no ratbane, could have operated
With half his efficacity or his extreme velocity.
But he had more to do, for very soon he guessed
That the surviving few, poor souls,
Were now so scared to leave their holes
That it required some ploy to winkle out the rest.
Pretending to be dead himself,
He hung head downwards from a shelf,
Suspended by one paw with which he clutched a string.
The mice thought he'd been executed
For pulling off some heist – perhaps a roast, a wing
Of chicken or a cheese he'd looted,
Or else he'd scratched somebody or had perpetrated
Such other deviltries he had been terminated.
The mice unanimously squeaked, "Hurrah! Hurrah!
The beast is dead, so Hah, Hah, Hah!"
Some now dared stick their noses out; a braver few
Poked out their heads an instant then instantly withdrew.
Then some came fully out, then more, until on tiny feet
All rushed to get outdoors in search of food to eat.
When suddenly the party stopped!
The cat returned to life and, flipping over, dropped
And crouched among them, seizing those too slow to run.
He told the rest, "There are a lot more ways than one
To win – that trick was old as war. I'm warning you,
It won't help you one bit to hide

In nests outdoors, for you'll try sneaking back inside –
And when you do, you're dead!" His prophecy proved true.
The master of deceit would once again surprise,
Bewilder and deceive them. He dusted his fur with flour
And, costumed in this bland disguise,
Crouched in a pan like a ball of dough set out to rise –
He'd warned the mice, and now their hour
Of doom was just about to strike. Of all that crew
Just one abstained from sniffing the seductive dough,
A veteran of the wars who also knew
A thing or two: evading capture, long ago,
He'd lost his tail. "Something is very fishy here!"
He yelled at the white–powdered generalissimo –
While keeping a safe distance. "You could have a sack
Of flour poured over you, and still I'd see the black
Death trap beneath. So you'll not catch me coming near!"

He said the right thing to that cat. I like his prudence –
He learned it through experience.
Which taught that lesson of maturity:
Mistrust is the mother of security.

III. 18

Book Four

The Lion in Love

Sévigné, who might serve the Graces
As model for their forms and faces,
And who, despite your being born
With every beauty, seems to scorn
Possessing it, would you consent
To listen to an innocent
And playful fable? Or will you
Grow frightened watching Love subdue
A lion? Love's a strange tyrant. Those
Are the lucky ones who know his rule
Only from tales they hear in school
And never have to feel his blows.
But though to speak before your face
Of love's plain truths may be forbidden,
A fable, being lightly hidden,
May be allowed to make its case.
Thus, warmly and with good intention,
This one petitions your attention.

In earth's first age, when beasts still spoke,
The lions decided they should yoke
Themselves to humans as allies.
And why on earth not? It seemed quite wise –
Their breed was much the same as ours
In courage and in mental powers;
Their heads were of a larger size.
So here's what came of their decision.
While hunting one day a haughty lion,
His noble family's noble scion,
Was left so weak and airy-headed
By a shepherdess he cast his eye on

That he proposed they should be wedded.
And though he would have much preferred
A son-in-law not fanged and furred
Her father thought he should agree.
For even assuming he said no,
He feared the two might some night go
And tie the knot clandestinely.
Because it was as plain as plain
This girl had males upon the brain,
Especially wild ones whose hair
Stuck out in a great flowing mane.
And so although he did not dare
Outwardly oppose the match
He warned the lion that because
The lass was delicate his claws
When he caressed could badly scratch
Her. "Might we, sir," he asked, "just whittle
Those nails off on your paws a little
And file your teeth down in your jaws,
Thus making your kisses more exciting –
Since if she need not fear your biting
Bits of her off in times of passion
My daughter can of course respond
To you in much more carefree fashion."
The lion let himself be conned,
For love had left him blinded, senseless,
With neither teeth nor claws, defenseless
As a castle deprived of its wall and moat.
When her father's dogs soon seized his throat
He scarcely fought. Let all take note:

Even the strongest, stuck by Cupid,
Becomes imprudent, mindless, stupid.

IV. 1

74

The Shepherd and the Sea

By Amphitrite's realm the sea
A man lived well, supported by his flocks, secure,
And though his income was not vast
Still it was regular and sure.
But watching all the wealthy vessels sailing past
At last so tempted him he sold his flocks,
Changed sheep to gold, gold into goods within a hold
That soon was shipwrecked on the rocks.
Now he who'd owned the sheep of old
Became the guard who watched their fold,
No longer master of the flocks that grazed the shore.
This man who'd played the part of Corydon before,
Or Thyrsis, in a masque, was now a poor Pierrot
And not the star of his own show.
With years of effort he reclaimed his flocks at last,
But then one day when winds offshore blew soft,
Puffing white sails along below, white clouds aloft,
He shouted at the waves, "You goddesses, avast!
You wish new offerings sent out to sea?
Well, tempt another man, not me!"

Do not imagine that the fable just related
Is one I've merely fabricated –
No, not at all; I've drawn the story
Straight from the harshest category
Of lived experience, hard knocks, real sweat,
To show that one red cent within your hands is worth
Five of them you may someday get.
Also, that contentment with your place on earth
Is surest wisdom. Also, that one should never listen
To siren voices touting wealth beyond belief:
For one that wins, ten thousand come to grief.
The sea will promise marvels, precious stones that glisten.
"Trust me," it sings. Then trust the wind or trust a thief.

IV. 2

The Fly and the Ant

The Fly and the Ant were bickering for a crumb.
"Dear God," complained the first.
"To think that self-conceit makes some
So blind that an accursed
Ground-dweller, pushy and insufferable,
Dares set herself equal to a child of the air!
The palace receives me, I take my place at table.
When a bull is sacrificed, mine is the earliest share –
While this poor, crawling thing
Must live three days off a straw she drags to her hole.
Well, let me quiz you, darling,
Do you ever perch on the head of a king?
Of an emperor? Of a famous beauty?
Well, I do. And, if I like, I kiss her lovely breast
And play among her curls as she gets dressed.
I enhance pale cheeks with my speck of color –
The final touch a lady of society
Will make when primping to enflame her suitor
Is placement of those beauty spots she calls her 'flies.'
So, do me a favor – go break
Your head on your stupid grain-bin!" "Are you done with
        lies?"
The thrifty one shoots back.
"The palace receives you – yes, but with a curse.
And when you take your little taste
Of what is dedicated for the gods to use,
Do you imagine that its taste improves?
If you go everywhere, it is to bring your dirt.
Upon the heads of kings, but those of asses, too,
You go and squat yourself – none will deny you do.
But where you come to light I also know
The liberty you take is answered with a blow.
You talk of 'placement' of those spots for beauty's sake;
So ugly things are used for contrast that they make.
What if they are called 'flies'? Is that a thing

In which you somehow take delight?
Did you also know that 'fly' means parasite?
Perhaps you should moderate your way of speaking:
Your fantasies are too high–flown.
They banish foreign agents, those flies of the court,
And spies, the flies of war, are hung. And in your own
Case, hunger, weakness, cold and want
Will finish you when Phoebus quits this hemisphere.
And then I'll taste the fruits of my hard effort,
I'll not be buzzing everywhere,
Exposed to every wind that blows,
But I'll be snug, living in perfect cheer.
The care I've taken frees me from future care.
I trust this lesson shows whose pride
Is foolish, whose is justified.
Goodbye, I'm wasting time. Allow me to labor.
Neither my granary nor my larder
Will ever get filled with all this jabber."

IV. 3

The Gardener and His Lord

A prosperous market gardener –
Between bourgeois and laborer –
Leased from the lord of a certain village
A fertile field and cottage, both stoutly ringed around
With a thick hedge to keep this tidy realm from pillage.
Green lettuces and sorrel flourished in its ground,
Which village Mariannes transformed into bouquets
With sprigs of Spanish jasmine and of thyme they bought
To trim themselves on festal days.
And then a hare, intruding in this Eden, brought
Such upset and annoyance that the owner sought
Assistance from the local squire.
"This animal just laughs at traps. He can't be caught.
I'm sure he is a sorcerer, sire.

Both sticks and stones are useless. Whether night or day
He stuffs his gullet full; he won't be chased away."
"A sorcerer, is he? Well, good man, he's met his match,"
Replied the lord. "My hound Old Blue will promptly catch
Him though he be the devil himself!" "But when, sire, when?"
"First thing tomorrow!" At dawn he came, with all his men.
"It's breakfast time!" he said. "Are your pullets tender?
And this sweet little thing just has to be your daughter!
Come here, my pretty! When do we get married? When
Will we give dad a son–in–law? Good man, it's then,
You'll dig into your purse, if you know what I mean!"
And, making her sit beside him, gave her arm a squeeze,
Plucked at her modest kerchief, took various liberties
She coyly fended off with such demure respect
Her father feared he might have something to suspect.
Then as the cook set pots and pans upon the fire
The lord strode in the kitchen. "Those fine hams! Have they
Been hanging there a while?" "Please have them, gracious sire,
They're yours." "They are? That's awfully good of you, I say."
He breakfasted famously, his nephews, sons and cousins,
His dogs, his horses and retainers by the dozens.
He insulted his host, drank up his wine, fondled his
        daughter –
And after breakfast's brawling followed hunting's slaughter.
As all began their preparations
The horns and trumpets pealed such rantintantarations
The good man was made deaf for hours.
But worst were all the devastations
Visited on his garden: goodbye his beds of flowers
Framed up in perfect squares, goodbye his long straight rows
Of leeks and chicory, goodbye to all that goes
In soup. The hare was crouched beneath a giant head
Of cabbage. From there, with many yoicks and tally–hos,
They started him, all galloping after as he fled.
He soon escaped them through a hole – but no small hole:
A broad highway, a horrible and gaping hole
They'd slashed in the poor hedge because his lordship
        counted

It very bad if, leaving, his men could not stay mounted.
The good man said, "So nobles play. It goes with power."
Of course, he had to say this, but all the men and hounds
Wreaked more destruction in one hour
Than all the hares within the bounds
Of that whole province could in centuries have done.

Small countries, in your confrontations,
You would be foolish not to shun
The help of kings of greater nations.
Settle your quarrels with your own hands –
Don't let them past the borders of your precious lands.

IV. 4

The Jackass and the Lapdog

He who attempts to force his talent
Beyond its scope will lack the grace
To keep from falling on his face:
Born clumsy oafs cannot turn gallant.

Of all the beings under heaven's gracious care,
Few have the gift of charm by inborn nature –
Nor is that gift one they would share
With the ass in this fable, a rough creature
Who, wanting to secure the affection of his master,
To please him greatly and impress him,
Decided that he would caress him.
"Just look at that!" he grumbled. "He,
That bitsy dog! He gets to be
On terms of full equality
With both the master and the missis,
While I get beaten till I'm raw.
And what does he do? Just gives his paw,
For which they shower him with kisses!
Well, if I have to act like that to get some praise,

It does not look that hard to do."
And having thought the problem through,
He goes galumphing joyfully to his master, brays
Fortissimo the sweetest of his roundelays
While sticking his ugly hoof impertinently in
The general direction of the master's chin.
"Oh, oh! What an endearing trick!
And what a lovesong! Quick, somebody bring a stick!"
The stick came out and soon
The comedy ended on a different tune.

IV. 5

The Combat of the Weasels and the Rats

The weasels' ancient warrior nation
Has through history, like the cats',
Shown small tolerance for rats.
And that furtive population,
I imagine, would have been
Much reduced, but for the fact
That their gloomy hideouts lacked
Wide doors that those sinuous-backed
Raiders could come bursting in.
Then one year – it was the spring,
With their numbers burgeoning –
Led by Strongtail their brave king,
For a change the rats attacked.
And the weasels, soon replying,
Under battle standards flying,
Joined their foes in mortal fray.
Back and forth the battle surged,
Victory in the scales, they say,
As the rival chieftains urged
Their battalions on that day.
Countless wounds were given, gore

Drenched the fields where heroes died.
Both lost grievously, but more
Perished on the rodent side.
Their debacle was complete.
Every stratagem they tried
Ended always in defeat.
And when mighty Pilfersnax,
Gnawabox and Eatthrusax
Bit the dust, by fate undone,
All the others fled as one.
Armored knights, marquises, earls
Scrambled to outrun the churls
In their ragged masses flying.
But it was these lowly souls,
Nameless rabble, who found holes
And survived, while *they* were dying.
Why? Because their foreheads bore
Great bronze helmets, horned or plumed,
By their richness signifying
To the weasels they were more
To be feared, so they were doomed:
What they wore made them too tall
For some hole or creviced wall
That the common folk, the small,
Easily could creep in – all.
And by far the greater losses
Were incurred by the big bosses.

Proud heads with fine plumage on them
Draw no small attacks upon them;
Carriages too grandly wide
Often meet untoward delays
Scraping through dark passageways.
And when worlds turn upside down
Though small men may safely hide,
Not so the one who wears a crown.

IV. 6

The Ape and the Dolphin

To occupy the boring weeks
On sailing voyages, the Greeks
Transported with them on the seas
Performing dogs and chimpanzees.
A ship with such a crew, they say,
Once sank on entering Athens bay,
And men and beasts within the briny
Would all have met unpleasant ends
But for the dolphins, man's wet friends –
'Tis true, they are – 'twas said by Pliny.
They rescued all with human shape;
Even the ugly, hairy ape
By anthropomorphicity
Received salvation from the sea.
A dolphin who had trouble seeing,
Mistaking an ape for a human being,
Bore him upon his back in style
Like Arion, once long before.
And then, as they drew near the shore,
The dolphin, with his charming smile,
Asked, "Sir, are you Athenian?"
"You bet," said Ape, "a famous son.
If you're in town and need things done
Just use my name. My family line
Sits high in governmental ranks;
The mayor is a cousin of mine."
The dolphin said, "A thousand thanks!
And I suppose you know Piraeus?
You're well-acquainted, I would guess?"
The ape replied, "My goodness, yes!
When we get kidding, you should see us!"
Our gross buffoon by this retort
Confused a person with a port.
How often types like this don't know

Paris, France, from Kokomo.
They rattle on at rapid pace:
Of words, a lot; of thought, no trace.
The dolphin laughed, then turned his head
To better see his passenger.
He'd saved no human but, instead,
A poor dumb beast decked out in fur.
He shook him off and went to find
Someone worth saving – with a mind.

IV. 7

The Man and the Wooden Idol

A pagan kept a wooden idol on an altar –
One of those gods with ears but just as deaf as posts.
And yet he worshipped it with ardor,
Prayed to it loudly, brought it hosts
Of costly offerings, and slaughtered sacred cows
Before it, garlanded with flowers on their brows.
He piled its altar high, expecting to arouse
Immense rewards. But never an idol of any cult,
Fed on so fat a diet, gave such a lean result.
For all his offerings and prayers
The pagan grew no richer, he begat no heirs,
He drew bad cards. Much worse, he had no better luck
Avoiding loss than others did when tempests struck,
And he grew poorer – though his god fared well as ever –
Till, tired of getting nothing, he grabbed an iron lever
And smashed the figure into bits. Lo and behold,
Out of its hollow center spilled a hoard of gold!
"When I fed you, did you help me one speck? No, never!
Get off my altar. Find somewhere else to be a god!
You act like some gross, stupid lout
Who lies lethargically about
Unless you beat him soundly with a rod.

83

The more I gave, the less your show of gratitude.
Good thing I changed my attitude."

IV. 8

The Magpie Decked Out in Peacock Plumes

A peacock shed its plumes, a magpie made a swoop
And seized them, stuck them in a fan behind,
Then started grandly strutting with the peacock group,
A bird of substance, proud, refined.
Soon someone recognized him – now he met with sneers,
Loud jeers and fleers and rude Bronx cheers.
The peacocks plucked his plumage till he had no more,
Becoming so grotesque that even his magpie peers,
When he pled for refuge, drove him from their door.

There is a magpie species ornithologists
Have not recorded, though they are not rare.
They are the well-known, common plagiarists,
Wingless bipeds who instead of feathers, wear
Their betters' castoff fashionable dress.
But I will say no more – why give poor birds distress?
Besides, what magpies do is not my business.

IV. 9

The Camel and the Floating Sticks

The first man ever to see a camel
Fled from this new-fangled mammal,
The second crept closer, still quite wary,
The third threw a rope on the dromedary.
So things at first glance frightening and strange,

As we become accustomed to them, change
And grow familiar in our eyes,
Losing their power to terrorise,
Much as when on the waves a lookout sees afar
Some unknown object and sings out, "A man of war!"
And then, as they sail closer, now sees clearly
It's no great warship but a fireship merely.
But no – correction – not a fireship, just a barge.
No, whaleboat. No, a raft – not large.
And down and down, the vision dwindling
At last to flotsam sticks of kindling.

I know of many in this world who fall
In this same category: ten feet tall
From far away, close up no size at all.

IV. 10

The Frog and the Rat

Said Merlin,
"Oft doth the entoyler get
Entoyled himself in his own net."

Although his words, to my regret,
By now have grown archaic, still, to me they seem
To put in a most forceful way
A truth as pertinent today
As in King Arthur's time. Which leads me to my theme.

A rat, well-fed in the extreme
And very well-upholstered, not to say corpulent,
As ignorant of Advent as he was of Lent,
Lived by a marshy pond, enjoying his existence.
One day a frog swam near and called to him, "Come visit!
I'll serve you up a feast!" Rat did not ask, "what is it?"
He just said yes, not putting up the least resistance.

Besides, all that she offered sounded so alluring:
The pleasures of immersion, the wonders and delights
One often meets when one goes touring.
His grandchildren one day would marvel at the sights
That he might see, the distant prospects, the exotic
Customs and new forms of government and laws
Within that world of the aquatic.
Just one small problem gave our brave adventurer pause:
He could not swim – but there his hostess would assist.
The frog produced a bit of cord she had contrived
To tow him in her wake, a twist
Of reed with which she tied his two front paws
To her hind flippers. But when they dived
Into the pond she quickly showed her true intention
Was to submerge and drown him, in utter contravention
Of every being's rights and that good faith presumed
Between two partners. For when she looked at him she saw
A morsel she would relish raw,
Like a gobbet thrown to be consumed
By a pack of barking hounds. He called the gods to aid him;
She mocked at him who had betrayed him;
He resisted; she tugged harder; their frantic fight
Caught the attention of a circling kite
Who dived and seized the rat and with the rat the cord
And with the cord the frog. Oh, happy kite! It soared
Into the sky with a two–part entrée to eat
Combining fish and fresh–killed meat.

However artful its construction,
The hidden trap, the bomb, the sting,
Often in due time will bring
Its inventor's own destruction,
As treachery and deceit may later
Return to enmesh their instigator.

IV. 11

The Tribute Sent by the Animals to Alexander

Why this next fable had such popularity
In ancient times I never have quite understood.
But here it is, reader, unadorned. And if you see
Some moral in it, well and good.

Fame having spread the word throughout creation
That a certain Alexander, said to be Jupiter's son,
Unwilling to let anyone
Exist outside his subjugation,
Had ordered all the beasts on no uncertain terms
To gather at his feet and humbly bow their heads,
All without exception: men and quadrupeds,
The birds in their republics, elephants and worms;
The goddess of a hundred mouths – as I was saying –
Having spread terror through the lands
By publishing the new-crowned emperor's commands,
Had left the creatures, once obeying
Only their own free appetites, convinced they must
Now bend to other laws. They gathered; they discussed
Possible actions and at last agreed they were
Compelled to offer homage to their conqueror
And send him costly tribute. To do the homage right
They wrote a speech the ape was chosen to recite
In his best manner – humbly, but with lots of ardor.
But the tribute – that was harder.
For what could they give? Just nothing, since
They had no money. Then a prince,
An altruist in whose domain much gold was mined,
Donated all that they might need plus some to spare,
Which meant they only had to find
Sufficient volunteers to bear
The tribute. The ass and mule both offered
Immediate help, the horse and camel proffered

Aid also. So with the ape in his new role as envoy
The four began their journey. Presently,
As they came to an arduous stretch, the little convoy
Met with a sight that struck them none too pleasantly:
Monseigneur Lion himself. "Good timing, friends!" he said.
"I was proceeding separately with my gift,
Yet, light though it be, I find it bothersome to lift
Burdens of any sort. So I suggest instead
We go along together, and if you each will haul
One fourth my lot you'll find you won't be taxed at all –
And, even better, I'll be free
To fight in some emergency,
Like thieves attacking our small troop."
Since lions seldom are said no to,
They took his pack and welcomed him into their group.
And though the tribute was to go to
The famous hero of Olympian descent,
The lion spent freely from it as they went.
After some days without event
They found themselves within a glade
Such as one reads of in old books,
Dotted with flowers, bordered by brooks,
Where sheep grazed peacefully and zephyrs played –
Truly, the native land of spring.
The group had scarcely reached the spot
Before the lion complained that he was ill. "I've got
A churning in my stomach and my head feels hot!
The four of you must now continue on our mission
While I stay here and find some herbs for my condition.
Go quickly, waste no time in tarrying –
But first give me my money you were carrying.
I'll need it." The tribute was unpacked. In joyful tone,
The lion cried, "Ye gods, see how my money's grown!
The coins have propagated, given birth to others,
Which look no smaller than their mothers –
And, naturally, their offspring all belong to me!"
He took the lot – or if not all, then all but two or three.

88

The tribute bearers and the ape, abashed,
Not daring to reply, resumed their trip. We're told
That when they said the lion had robbed them of the gold
The blame was laid on them and they were soundly thrashed.

What else could they expect? If Jupiter's scion
Had tried to punish the other one it would
Have been a case of lion against lion.
As the proverb says, thief fighting thief does neither good.

IV. 12

The Horse Who Wished to Avenge Himself upon the Deer

Horses were not our servants in the ancient past.
When man lived in the forest, munching acorn mast,
Asses, mules and horses roamed those leafy ways
And then one never saw, as one does nowadays,
Horses with saddles, horses with packs,
Horses with armor borne on their backs,
Nor heavy freight wagons or lightly sprung shays,
Nor for that matter elegant carriages
Bound for receptions, trotting to marriages.
But then one day a horse was cut off by a deer,
A beast whose speed was legendary,
And who now fled so quickly his angered adversary,
Unable to catch him, begged a human standing near
To come to his assistance. The man obligingly
Fashioned a halter, jumped on his back, began to ride
And drove him on relentlessly
Until the deer, exhausted, died.
The deed being done, the horse politely thanked
His benefactor. "Sir," he said, "I'm in your debt,
But now it's back to the woods I go." The human yanked

On his rope and said, "It's better here with us. You'll get
Nice treatment, dry litter, comfortable housing, for I see
How useful you will be to me."
But what use living comfortably
If life is lacking liberty?
Athough the horse soon saw the folly of his action,
It was by then beyond retraction,
Because the man had built the stall
Where he would live his life out, tethered to its wall.
Had he been wiser he would have seen the sense
Of calmly tolerating such a slight offense.
Because revenge, though sweet, is bought at an expense
Too dear, if for the price one must
Give up that good without which all the rest are dust.

IV. 13

The Fox and the Bust

The great are, for the most part, merely theatre masks
That by their looks deceive the idolising flocks.
The ass believes whatever he sees, but not the fox.
He studies them and stares, and when he realises
Their gorgeous faces are disguises,
He lets fly with a quip that he had once applied
To a bronze bust unveiled in honor of some hero,
Twice as big as life but echoingly hollow.
Praising the sculptor for how hard he'd tried,
Nice head," he said, "but there's no brain inside."

How many a current idol comes to mind
Who is a bust of this same kind.

IV. 14

The Wolf, the Nanny Goat, and the Kid

One spring, before the nanny goat went up the hill
To nibble the new leaves and fill
Her dragging dugs with milk once more,
She told her kid to lock the door
And if a stranger chanced to knock,
Upon her life, not to unlock
Unless he sang out, word for word,
"A fig for wolves and all their race!"
Now, as she said this, it occurred
That the wolf was passing by their place
And, having very clearly heard
Her secret phrase and realized it
Could come in handy, memorized it.
Not having glimpsed the lurking glutton,
The nanny goat departed, at which, on the button,
The wolf knocked at the door, repeating
In hypocritically bleating
Accents, "A fig for wolves!" expecting quick admission.
Cracking the door, the kid peered out in deep suspicion.
"First show me your white paw, and then I'll let you in,"
She cried. White paws, as is well known, have never been
A wolfish characteristic. So, taken aback, defeated,
This one, as rapidly as he had come, retreated.
What would have happened to the kid if she had treated
As gospel what the wolf had heard and then repeated?

Two guarantees are worth a great deal more than one.
Assurance can't be overdone.

This wolf reminds me of another one, his friend,
Who met still worse misfortune in the end.
In fact, he died. The scene was gory.
Here's the story:

IV. 15

91

The Wolf, the Mother, and the Child

A villager had a farmstead in a lonely place.
Sir Wolf was happy lurking just outside the fence,
For there inside was all the game he loved to chase:
Ewes and young lambs and new–born calves and regiments
Of turkeys – all the makings for a feast.
Then, as the thief was getting tired of waiting,
He heard a child begin to cry and, then, berating,
The mother's voice. Unless it ceased
This awful squalling she would chuck
It to the wolf, she threatened. The beast,
With thanks to the gods for his good luck,
Made ready to receive his prize.
But now the mother started cooing, "Dry your eyes,
My child. If he should ever come
We'll kill that ugly rascal dead!"
"What kind of trick is this?" the sheep–devourer said.
"To talk first one way then the other! They think I'm dumb?
Do they expect to get away
With treating a guy like me like this? I hope someday
That little creep comes to the wood to gather nuts!"
But as he said these words, the door
Of the house flung open, one of those mastiff mutts
Flew out to grab him and before
He'd run two steps his way was blocked
By pitchforks and pikes for sticking boar.
"What was the gentleman seeking here?" one mocked.
He quickly explained his innocent mistake.
"Mercy!" cried the mother. "Did my words really make
A creature such as you beguiled
Into imagining that my child
Might one day serve to glut your appetite?" Which said,
They cudgeled the poor beast until he was no more.
A farmhand chopped his right paw off and his big head.
The mayor of the village nailed them to his door
With a verse he wrote, in Picard dialect, that read:

"*Biaux chires leups, n'ecoutez mie*
Mere tenchent chen fieux qui crie."
(Good Sir Wolves, don't believe your ears
When mothers threaten their crying dears.)

IV. 16

The Wisdom of Socrates

In Athens once, tongues started clacking
When Socrates built a house. "In candor,"
One critic said, "I find the interior greatly lacking –
For one so eminent it needs to be much grander."
Another questioned the façade, and one and all
Agreed its rooms were far too small.
This house for him? Why, one could hardly turn around!
"Whatever its size, I would thank heaven," said Socrates,
"If my real friends could fill even such rooms as these."
His observation was profound.
The good man rightly realised
That, for true friends, the smallest house is over-sized.
Though everyone will lightly claim
To be your dearest friend, the words have a dubious ring,
For nothing is commoner than the name
And nothing rarer than the thing.

IV. 17

The Old Man and His Children

Unless it holds together, any force is weak.
Upon that subject hear the slave from Phrygia speak.
And if in telling it I've somewhat changed his story,
It's not to rival him but to depict our times –
I'm not about to try to best him with my rhymes.

Though Phaedrus often tried to rival him in glory,
To me such motives are at best unseemly ones.
But let us have the fable, no mere allegory,
Of one who struggled vainly to unite his sons.

An old man, knowing death would soon call him away,
Spoke to his children, gathered at his side one day:
"Dear sons" (for sons they were), "let each of you see whether
He has the strength to break these arrows bound together.
I'll show you later why the bundle has been tied."
The eldest grasped it first, then having vainly tried,
Relinquished it. He said, "I will attempt no longer
To do what I cannot. I yield to someone stronger."
A second son stepped up, assumed a muscled stance
And, when he failed, the third, still younger, took his chance.
But not one arrow broke; they found themselves frustrated
So long as the thin shafts remained unseparated.
"Weak fellows!" cried the father. "It seems I must show you
What, given the same task, my little strength can do."
Believing he was joking, they smiled – mistakenly.
He pulled the shafts apart and broke them easily.
"My sons, you see," he said, "concord is your protection.
Let all of you stay bound by mutual affection."
And then he said no more, until one day he sensed
The end was very near. "My children," he commenced,
"You must now promise me that when I'm gone you will
Stay loyal to each other and live as brothers still.
If as I go I know this promise will be kept
I'll die in peace." All three vowed solemnly, and wept.
He took their hands; he died; and they soon realised
The great estate he left was tangled, compromised.
A creditor foreclosed, a neighbor brought a suit.
At first the three together staved off all pursuit.
But the story's ending differed from its start:
Blood joined them all; self–interest drove them all apart.
Rivalry, greed and lawyers, spurring the brothers on,
Began to do their work, and soon hard lines were drawn.
They turned against each other, lied, played legal games

Until the sitting judge denied their separate claims.
The creditors' and neighbors' suits were reinstated.
What should be done? The brothers angrily debated.
One said to settle quickly, another said to stall.
Unable to agree, they were defeated, all,
And, losing everything, belatedly remembered
The bundle's strength united, its weakness once
      dismembered.

IV. 18

The Oracle and the Skeptic

Earth's hopes of fooling heaven always are in vain,
For the most secret places in the heart's dark maze
Eventually are lighted by the searching rays
The gods shine on men's deeds: their eyes see all things plain,
Including acts men think that not a soul has seen.
An impious man, the sort broiled by the Inquisition,
And who believed in God – for all that word can mean –
To the extent it proved a paying proposition,
Once entered the temple of Apollo.
He asked the oracle at the altar,
"This thing I'm holding in the hollow
Of my hand – is it alive, or dead?"
(In fact it was a sparrow, and he meant to fault her,
Whatever she answered. If she said,
"Alive!" he'd crush it; if, "Dead!" he'd let it fly, instead.)
Apollo knew at once just what the trickster planned.
The oracle intoned, "Be it alive or dead,
Show me that sparrow in your hand!
If ever there are more such clever stunts from you
You will regret it. I see far. I shoot far, too."

IV. 19

The Miser Who Lost His Treasure

Use is the one true measure of possession.
I ask those men whose reigning passion
Is simply to pile up more, to add to what they've got,
What pleasures do they have that other men have not?
Diogenes the pauper was as rich as they
And misers equal him in poverty today.
Now hear a tale from Aesop of a man whose scheme
To hide his treasure serves to illustrate our theme.

Unable to enjoy his wealth, this sad soul waited
To do so when reincarnated.
Gold wasn't his possession – he was by gold possessed.
He had a sum of money buried in a field
And his heart buried with it. He could never rest,
For night and day his head was filled
With images of it, untouchably enshrined.
And whether he came or went or drank or dined
He thought himself neglectful if ever he forgot
To fix his mind religiously upon the spot
Where all his fortune lay secreted in a hole.
But then a poor well-digger, seeing him there a lot
And guessing something hidden, got
A spade one night and found the treasure, which he stole.
Next morning, finding it was gone, the miser bawled,
He cursed, he writhed, he wept until his eyes were swollen.
"What is the matter?" someone passing by him called.
"It is my money. It's been stolen."
"Stolen? From where?" "Under that rock." "Are we at war?
We must be – or why bother bringing it so far?
Would it have not been better simply to deposit
It in your desk drawer or the recesses of a closet,
Rather than hiding it far away?
For if it were at home, then either night or day
It would be there to spend whenever you desired."
"Desired? By all the gods! You think that money grows

On trees? Or that it comes as easily as it goes?
I'd never touch that money. Never, never never!"
"Then tell me," said the other, "what you are so all-fired
Upset about, old fellow, if you would not ever
Touch it? Put that rock back, friend, and it will do
The same great lot of good for you!"

IV. 20

The Owner's Eye

Fleeing, panting, wild with fear,
A stag leaped in a livestock pen
Among a herd of oxen. "You're in danger here!"
They warned. "Find other refuge. You must leave again!"
"Brothers," he pleaded, "don't betray me. Let me remain
And, in return, someday I'll show
You where the sweetest grasses grow.
Your kindness won't have been in vain!"
After some talk they said he did not have to go.
He hid in a corner, caught his breath, regained his courage.
At dusk the farmhands came, distributing fresh forage
The same as every other night,
The stable boys and foreman, too, with hay and corn.
But as they came and went not one of them caught sight
Of foreign hide or stranger horn –
They saw no stag. The forest creature, from his heart,
Thanked his kind hosts and waited for the coming dawn
When hitched to plows they would depart
To labor in the fields, and he could then be gone.
One of the oxen, ruminating, said, "So far,
So good, but till the man who has a hundred eyes
Has had his look, poor deer, I fear it won't be wise
For you to celebrate how fortunate you are."
Just then the owner entered on his nightly round.
"What's going on?" he asked his crew.
"Those feed racks are half empty. Get a move on! Strew

Fresh bedding straw upon the ground.
I want to see these beasts from now on better kept.
And, spider webs! What would it take to have them swept?
And yokes and harness should be hung, not piled around!"
Inspecting each detail, he quickly realized
That there was an intruder. The stag was recognized;
The men brought out pitchforks and spears
And thrust him through and through, each one,
Mercilessly, despite his tears.
They cured the meat in brine. It had been many years,
Some people said, since they'd enjoyed such venison.

Phaedrus summed it up succinctly:
There's no eye like an owner's for seeing things distinctly.
And though perhaps his statement covers
Most cases, I would add to that the lover's.

IV. 21

The Lark and Her Brood and the Owner of a Field

The saying is old and widely known:
Rely upon yourself alone.
Now let Aesop convince us with his art
To take his good advice to heart.

Larks nest in fields among the wheat
When its green stalks begin to rise,
Around that time when new lambs bleat
And love rules all and every species multiplies:
Sea monsters in their depths below,
Tigers in forests, larks in fields the farmers sow.
But one of these last had once for her own reason
Let half the spring slip by her, wasted,
Its amorous pleasures still untasted,

Before at last resolving that she would,
Like nature herself in that sweet season,
Devote herself to motherhood.
In haste she built a nest, tight-thatched and well concealed,
Laid eggs in it and sat until her chicks hatched out.
Meanwhile, the grain had ripened all across the field,
Before her young had feathers yet to fly about.
And so, in great anxiety each time she went
Flying far off to find them nourishment,
She warned them in her absence they must stay
Always on guard, with watchful eyes and ears.
"If he who owns this field should come – as come he will, my
          dears –
Then listen close, for something you may hear him say
Could tell me it is time for us to flee away."
Next day, the very moment she was out of sight,
The owner of the fields arrived with his young son.
"This grain is ready, boy," he said. "So you just run
Ask all our friends to come tomorrow at first light,
Bringing their sickles, sharpened bright,
And help us get this harvest done."
The lark returning found her nestlings terrified.
At last one peeped, "They came while you were gone.
The man said they would ask their friends on every side
To come and help tomorrow, starting in at dawn."
"If that is all he said," the mother lark replied,
"We need not panic finding a new home, sweet things.
But in the morning you must listen closer yet.
For now, be happy, eat in peace and never fret."
Well fed, all slept, the chicks beneath their mother's wings.
Next morning came the sun, but of their friends not one.
The lark flew off, the owner came, found nothing done.
"This grain should not be standing now," he said. "Our friends
Are very much at fault, but any who depends
On slackers slow as these to meet their obligations
Is much at fault as well. Well, son, try our relations
And make them all the same request."
The lark came back to greater terror in her nest.

"Oh, mother, he's told his relatives to meet him here
Tomorrow just as it grows light!"
"Hush, children. Sleep. No need for fear.
Tomorrow we can still sit tight."
The lark was right, for not a soul came near.
For the third time the owner came inspecting.
He said, "I see we made a great mistake expecting
That we might possibly depend
On any but each other. There is no better friend,
And no relation closer than oneself. My son,
Never forget this. So what must now be done?
Tomorrow, grasping our sickles tightly, we –
Just us, this one small family –
Will bring the harvest in as best we can."
As soon as the mother bird got word of this last plan:
"The time has come, my darlings, we must no longer stay."
And the larks, on full–fledged wings, instantly soared away.

IV. 22

Book Five

Dedication

To M. L. C. D. B.

Your taste has served me always as a trusted guide,
And I have taken pains to merit your regard.
You've wished me to avoid a style too rarefied,
Too ornamented – one, in short, that tries too hard.
And I agree: such straining lacks the slightest charm.
Excessive fuss does any author's work real harm.
Yet one needs hardly banish everything refined –
Refinements please you, I don't hold them in disdain.
And as to that great purpose Aesop once defined,
Perhaps my efforts there have not been all in vain –
If I have failed "to teach as well as entertain,"
It's not for lack of trying but some other cause.
For, having no illusion I might seek applause
For forcefulness, with which to seize
Vice in my brawny arms and overpower it
With pure brute strength, like Hercules,
I've tried to do it in by ridiculing it,
Since this is my one talent – but up to that, who knows?
Sometimes I'll tell a tale that shows
Within one tiny foolish mind
Envy and vanity combined –
For these are the poles our lives revolve around today.
(Recall that little dunce who planned
To grow his corporate self, expand,
Till he outdid an ox.) Or else I might portray
Such pairs opposed in quality
As virtue and vice, good sense and light frivolity:
The lamb and the wolf, the ant and the fly
And many more, who in a hundred acts rehearse
A comedy of manners endlessly passing by
Upon this stage, the universe.

Men, gods, beasts: each has a part assigned,
Great Jupiter as well. And here we introduce,
In his first appearance, Mercury, his servant,
Whom he employs to carry fervent
Love notes to lovely women he wishes to seduce.
But now his task is very different – as we'll find.

The Woodsman and Mercury

A woodsman lost his means of livelihood,
His tool for earning bread by chopping wood –
That is, his axe. Ah, pitifully he moaned:
It was the one, the only axe he owned
And it had disappeared without a trace,
So he was ruined. The tears ran down his face.
"Oh, axe! Dear axe! Axe, oh! Oh, axy, dear!
Great Jupiter, cause it to reappear!
I'd have a life again if you would hear!"
His cries were heard on Mount Olympus' peak.
Mercury was dispatched. "This axe you seek
Has not been lost," the sly god said, "but just
Misplaced." Before the woodsman's eyes he thrust
An axe of purest gold. "By chance I found
This nice one near here, lying on the ground."
"Not mine," the man said. Next, the god displayed
An axe that had a polished silver blade.
It was refused. Then one of iron and wood.
"At last, you've got it! This one's mine. It's good –
And what I want, for it belongs to me."
"In that case," said the god, "you get all three.
Your honesty deserves no less than such."
"In that case," said the woodsman, "thank you much."
The story spread. Soon many a woodsman went
And lost, somehow, his treasured implement,
So many that Jupiter could not have told
The truthful speakers from the smooth-faced liars

And he sent Mercury to test the cryers.
He offered each in turn an axe of gold
And each, not wanting to seem asinine,
Made sure to answer promptly, "Yes, that's mine,"
Expecting a payoff – but Mercury instead
Paid each a lusty wallop on the head.

Just tell the truth, be happy with what you've got –
That's the best course to take, for otherwise
You'll try to grab good things by telling lies.
But will heaven be fooled? No, it will not.

V. 1

Clay Pot and Iron Pot

Iron Pot proposed
To Clay Pot that they take a walk,
But Clay Pot excused
Himself, saying it struck
Him wiser to stay there by the fire,
For, since his health was brittle,
All it would require
Would be some little, oh, so little,
Thwock! – and he'd be scattered wide.
"But as for you," he said, "whose hide
Is so much tougher than my own,
Don't wait for me, go on alone."
"Let's go in convoy then,"
Answered the pot of iron.
"If anything that's hard
Should threaten you with harm
I'll stand beside you, arm in arm,
And ward off any blow." So kind
An offer made him change his mind.
He went, with his stout iron friend
Clumping along beside. They wobbled,

Clippeting, cloppeting, over cobbled
Ways, and slamming, banging against each other
At every hiccup in the road.
Clay Pot was the one to suffer.
He had not gone a hundred yards
Before his helpful friend had battered him to shards,
And nobody but himself to blame.

In partnerships, when strengths are not the same
The weaker should anticipate
The clay pot's fate.

V. 2

The Little Fish and the Fisherman

Little fish get big someday –
"God willing," is the proviso –
But tossing small ones back to grow
Is rank stupidity, I say:
You may not catch again the fish let go today.

A tiny carp, hardly a fingerling,
Was landed by a fisherman.
"They all add up," he said. "At least it will serve
To start the meal as a small but nice hors d'oeuvre.
Let's pop it in the creel."
Then the carpling, poor thing, commenced a spiel:
"Why bother with me? I'm hardly equal
To half a good mouthful.
Just let me grow to be a carp, full–size,
And when you catch me next time, you can realize
A tidy profit selling me to some gourmet.
As I am now, I think it's fair to say
You'd need a hundred of my size to fill one plate.
One plate! Believe me, I'm not worth it. Wait!"
"Not worth it?" answered the man. "Nice try.

But, Fish, my little friend, however well you preach
You'll end up in the pan. Your speech
Was touching, but later tonight you'll fry."

A yes–right–now is better than two you'll–get–it–laters:
The first, you've got; the second, maybe not.

V. 3

The Ears of the Hare

Enraged that some horned beast had struck him twice at least
And drawn his blood, the lion condemned
All creatures on whose heads were worn
The least suspicion of a horn
To instant exile – or to anger much increased.
Goats, rams and bulls took off for foreign capitals,
Roebucks and stags sought climates more hospitable.
None stopped to argue, each one ran.
A hare who saw the shadow of his ears
Feared some inquisitor might rule that on the strength
Of being so like horns in reference to length
They would be classified as horns in all details.
"Goodbye, my cricket pal," he said. "I'm getting out.
My ears are horns, beyond all doubt.
And even if I clipped them short as ostrich ears
I still would have the self–same fears."
The cricket answered, "Those are horns?
Perhaps I'm being stupid, but it seems to me
The ears that God provided you are all I see."
"Officially, they would be horns,"
Replied the hare, "real horns like those on unicorns.
Protests won't help. The only place they would be heard
Is in the state–run psychiatric ward."

V. 4

107

The Fox Whose Tail Got Cut Off

An ancient fox – the sliest kind –
Champion chicken–snatcher, matchless rabbit thief,
Trailing fox smell a league behind,
Stepped in a snare at last and came to grief.
For, in his struggle to be liberated,
His tail, unfortunately, got amputated.
So, in this fix, sprung free but maimed, and much ashamed,
And wanting, guileful creature, companions in distress,
Upon the next fox–meeting day he claimed
The group's attention: "Friends! What should we do about
These useless weights we drag through every nastiness?
What good are tails? We would be handsomer without.
I move we cut them off. All ready for the vote?"
"It sounds like good advice," one of the troop replied,
"But, first, please turn around, and then we can decide."
At which he set in hooting on so loud a note
That no one heard poor stump-tail, however hard he tried.

Scorning to have a tail – back then it sounded lame,
And nowadays – well, just the same.

V. 5

The Crone and the Two Servants

There was an old woman who – so that's how we begin.
In her employ were two young maidens who could spin.
Such skill the pair possessed! They both were so adept
That, next to them, the Fates seemed clumsily inept.
The crone's one passion was to supervise the girls,
So every morning, just as Phoebus Goldencurls
Was rousted out by Tethys from his ocean bed,
The two were set to spinning, spinning, spinning thread.
From light in east to dark in west

They spun and spun with never a rest,
Spindles whirling, bobbins clacking,
Never for one instant slacking.
That is, each day as Dawn commenced her fiery ride,
Just as the mean old cock woke up the countryside,
Our even meaner crone, in filthy tatters clad,
Lifted up her lamp beside the lumpy cot
Where, hanging onto sleep with all the strength they had,
The two poor girls awoke, resenting it a lot!
One squinted through a half-shut eye,
One raised an arm to fend off light
As, both together, teeth clenched tight,
Said, "Wretched bird, you're going to die!
Yes, in a trice they seized that irritating cock:
The herald of the morn went on the chopping block.
But murder didn't pay, they found, not even slightly,
For since when dawn arrived the crone could not now hear it,
Forever after, like some unhinged household spirit,
She hardly let them get to bed when, tripping lightly,
She wakened them again, not once but often, nightly.
How frequently it works that way – in trying hard to get
Out of some nasty hole we plunge in deeper yet.
The girls, avoiding the Charybdis of the cock,
Discovered that the crone, to their immense regret,
Loomed in their path like Scylla's rock.

V. 6

The Satyr and the Wayfarer

A satyr and his wild brood
In their cave by a lonely heath
With bare hands tore at their food
And stuffed it between their teeth.

No tablecloth covered the rock,
No carpet cushioned their feet,

But the satyr, his mate and their flock
Of young ones were eager to eat.

A wayfarer stumbled in
Out of the rainy night,
Bone–chilled and drenched to the skin.
Said the satyr, "Come, sit. Have a bite."

The man said, "Don't mind if I do.
I'm half starved and near frozen to death."
And he cupped his cold hands and blew
To warm them up with his breath.

From a caldron they ladled some stew,
Scalding hot, so to cool it down
He held his dish close and he blew.
Said the satyr, amazed, with a frown,

"Man, none of us understands
What this blowing is meant to do."
"Well, the first breath warmed my hands
And the second one cooled my stew."

"Hit the road," said the satyr. "Just go.
I like to be kindly, but still
There's no trusting a man who can blow
Hot air or cold air at will."

V. 7

The Horse and the Wolf

Once, in that season when the west wind's warm arrival,
Undoing winter's chill, restores
Fresh youth to plants, and animals emerge outdoors
To find fresh means for their survival,

A certain wolf, abroad on one of those soft days,
Was thrilled to spy a horse someone had put to graze.
Imagine, please, his sharp–fanged smile!
"Hunting is good!" he said. "Still, what a shame
You're not a sheep, and easy game,
For hooking you will take not only strength but guile.
Well, here goes guileful." And with measured tread
He sidled toward his prey. He was, he said,
A scholar of the teachings of Hippocrates,
And, knowing the subtle powers and vital properties
Of every herb in those green pastures, he could cure
Ills of all kinds. If Don Caballo would be sure
To tell him – hiding nothing – all his symptoms, he
Would fix whatever ailed him, free.
For, seeing him grazing thus at random, unconfined,
And swallowing what there was no telling
Suggested illness to his trained physician's mind.
"I've got," said the equine beast, "this swelling,
Here on my hoof." "My son," the doctor said, "I find
This part of our anatomy
To be a spot where, often, grave conditions burgeon.
I have the honor, I must add, to be
Physician by Appointment to the Society
Of Snobbish Hobbledehorses. Also, I'm a surgeon."
Our hero thinking he would pounce upon his victim,
Befuddled by the diagnosis he had made,
Leaned closer – but the horse, who wasn't stupid, kicked him,
Reducing his jaws to marmalade.
"My just dessert," the wolf said sadly. "I'll know in future,
That *'He who sticks to what he's good at is the smartest!'*
You hoped to be a blooming herbal artist
But you were always just a blooming clumsy butcher."

V. 8

The Farmer and His Sons

Two forms of wealth all may possess:
Hard work; painstaking thoroughness.

A wealthy farmer, dying, called his sons. He said,
"I have a secret. Gather close around my bed.
This land, our ancient heritage, must not be sold,
For under it lies buried gold.
I do not know just where the treasure will be found,
But with a bit of patience and determination
You will discover its location.
The moment Fall arrives, you must spade up the ground.
Delve down, probe deeply, excavate beneath the soil,
Leave not an inch unturned where wealth might be
        concealed."
The father died; the sons at once began to toil,
Dug here, dug there, dug everywhere, until each field
Next spring produced a crop abundant beyond measure,
Though, money, none. And yet the dying man was wise
To make his children realize
That hard work is itself a treasure.

                                                        V. 9

The Mountain Who Labored

A mountain, seized with labor pain,
Began to heave and groan and strain
So noisily that none could doubt
That very soon it would thrust out
A city more immense than Paris, but
It bore a mouse – of which, so what?

As I contemplate this fable,
Which, though fiction, all a lie,

Still holds truth as its essential,
There appears in my mind's eye
An author who says, "I'm doing an epic
Of war among the gods. It's going to be titanic!"
Sounds promising. But what too often comes to pass?
Just gas.

V. 10

Fortune and the Young Boy

On the ground by an unfenced well
A schoolboy laid his head,
Stretched out at full length, then fell
Asleep – to a drowsy scholar all the world's a bed.
In a similar circumstance
Any man with a smidgeon of sense
Would have leaped twenty yards from the rim,
But now, by the happiest chance,
The goddess Fortune came and gently awakened him.
She said, "My little one, I have saved your life today,
But, next time, please behave in a more careful way.
If you had fallen in, I would have borne the blame,
Though you were guilty all the same.
For, truthfully, could one assign
The end of such bad judgment to some caprice of mine?"
That said, she vanished in thin air.

I have to say that I concur.
Nothing happens anywhere
Fortune's not held to answer for.
All outcomes are chalked up to her,
We pray she favors us in every risky game;
However ill-prepared, wrong-headed or obtuse,
If we should fail we take bad luck as our excuse.
In short, it's always Fortune that's to blame.

V. 11

Doctors

Dr. Much–Better, the well-known physician,
Called on a patient. Along to consult came Dr. Much–Worse.
The first had a treatment to cure his condition,
The second advised him to send for a hearse.
But, as the two debated measures to be tried,
Nature took its course and, naturally, he died –
Proving Much-Worse much better as a diagnostician.
Yet neither one felt less than fully justified.
One said, "You see? He's dead. I told him he would be."
The other, "He'd be living if he'd heeded me!"

V. 12

The Hen Who Laid Golden Eggs

Wanting all is greed's downfall. A demonstration
That this is true requires no other illustration
Than the fable of the man whose hen
Laid every day an egg of gold.
Believing she must surely hold
A hoard, he killed her, cut her open. But when
He searched inside her, all he found was very
Much like what's in hens whose eggs are ordinary –
And he had thrown away an asset unsurpassed.

Good lesson, this, for all the spate
Of greedy types we've seen of late
In one day losing every cent they had amassed –
Made poor by trying to get rich too fast.

V. 13

The Ass Bearing Relics

An ass bearing holy relics felt
That it was he to whom all knelt
And, thinking so, began to prance,
Imputing to himself the incense and the chants.
One who saw his error said,
"Master Jackass, rid your head
Of such vain and foolish notions.
It's what you carry and not you
To which all offer their devotions
And to which reverence is due."

So, although a judge be stupid,
The robe he wears should be respected.

V. 14

The Stag and the Vine

A stag was given shelter by a vine that crawled
So densely over trees and bushes that he stood
Within it, safe from hounds and huntsmen in the wood –
For which the pack was blamed and, for the time, recalled.
Thinking all danger past, the stag now calmly chewed
And ate his benefactor – rash ingratitude!
For now he was in view, the pack resumed the chase
And brought him rapidly to bay in that same place.
He said, "My punishment is just, I must admit.
Let ingrates learn!" The hounds encircled him, they bit,
They pulled him swiftly down – no use for him to cry
For mercy now. Those were hard men, his death was nigh.

A perfect illustration
Of those whose acts profane their temple of salvation.

V. 15

The Serpent and the File

A snake lived next to a man who made clocks –
For an horologist, not a good neighborhood.
The reptile entered his workshop looking for snacks,
But found nothing in its cupboards that looked good
Except a hard steel file, which it began to gnaw.
Entirely undisturbed, the file said, "Pshaw!
Poor simpleton, what are you trying to do?
You've met someone who is more durable than you.
Petty, deluded, crawling beast,
Before your serpent's teeth dislodge from me the least
Discernible metallic crumbs
They'll all be broken off and worn down to the gums.
The only teeth I fear are those of time itself."

This speaks to you, mean spirits of these latter days,
Who, finding nothing worth your praise,
Vainly torment yourselves in search of things to bite.
Can your teeth make a mark, however slight,
On works of beauty? No, they can't.
To you they are bronze, proof steel, eternal adamant.

V. 16

The Hare and the Partridge

One must not mock another's trials, for, who knows
He will be lucky always, never touched by woes?
Wise Aesop in his fables shows
Several examples of such reverses.
And I propose in these next verses
To tell a story just like those.

A hare and partridge lived as neighbors in a clearing,
On friendly terms, it seemed, until one morning, hearing

A pack of hounds in full cry nearing,
The hare fled to the thicket, swiftly disappearing
Where none of the dogs, not even Bro,
The sharpest-eyed, could tell at first which way he went.
But he was self-betrayed: Big Mo,
Whose nose was keenest, caught the scent
The hare's warm body was exuding
And, after thoughtful sniffing, ended by concluding
This was his hare and flushed him out. Close at his side,
Equally eager, Little Joe, who never lied,
Barked that the hunt was on once more.
When the poor creature later crawled,
Expiring, to his hole, before
He died the partridge called
In mocking tones, "You boasted that you were so fleet –
What can have happened to your feet?"
But even as she laughed, it was her turn to die.
She had believed her wings would let her safely fly
Above all danger but had not been wary of
The cruel-taloned hawk that took her from above.

V. 17

The Eagle and the Owl

"Peace!" said Eagle. Screech owl countered, "War no more!"
And then they hugged, pecked cheeks and swore,
One on king's honor, one on the honor of an owl,
Never to take a bite, or taste, however slight,
Of one another's children. "You know my chicks by sight?"
Asked Goddess Athena's fowl.
"No," the eagle said. "Bad!" said the bird of night.
"That makes the odds for their survival very small,
For as a king you never ask which one or who.
Kings see as gods, and from their point of view
One category does for all –
So, should you meet my darlings, it will be goodbye!"

"Describe them," said the eagle. "Paint me a picture, I
Will promise not to touch the little dears."
The owl replied, "Well, all are beautiful to see,
Sprightly and well–behaved, far nicer than all their peers.
Such fetching little things! You'll know them instantly –
They are unique. Just bear in mind this simple fact
And you will not commit some act
That brings cursed Fate into my house."
Then one fine evening, Owl was off to hunt a mouse,
When, soaring overhead, the eagle saw with shock,
Half–hidden by a beetling rock
Or holed–up in a crumbling wall
(Which one it was, I don't recall),
A nest of little monsters, uglier than mud,
Squawking in hellish voices fit to freeze the blood.
"These infants can't be Owl's – and they look good to eat!"
The eagle said. Not one to take half–measures, he
Gobbled them all, voraciously.
The owl on his return found just their little feet!
And then came curses, wailing, cries of rage and grief
As he implored the gods for vengeance on the thief
Who'd left him with an empty nest.
But then a voice said, "Know yourself to blame,
Or else that law that makes us see as best,
In beauty, manners and (this, more than anything)
In being fit to love, those creatures most the same
As we ourselves in looks. You gave the eagle king
Just such a portrait of your children. But did they
Resemble it in any slightest way?"

V. 18

The Lion Prepares for War

His head full of great plans for new hostilities,
The lion sent for his staff. He told his generals
To notify the animals

118

The realm had need of all their capabilities.
The elephant, as an example,
Would haul equipment, also trample
Their foes in combat, while, to prepare
For sudden counterattacks, the bear
Would stand on guard. The fox, meanwhile,
Would handle things requiring secrecy and guile;
The ape's distracting antics would keep the foe off balance.
"Let's send the ass away," said one, "he's too obtuse;
The hare will cut and run, he'll never be of use."
"Not so," replied the king. "We greatly need their talents.
The ass's frightful trumpet will make our foe retreat;
The hare will be our courier. None is more fleet.
Without them both our battle plan is not complete."

A king who is wise and prudent
Will see that even his humblest subjects are essential
And make himself a knowing student
Of all their many talents. To the intelligent,
Nobody is inconsequential.

V. 19

The Bear and the Two Guys

Well, these two guys were broke. So then they tried
Selling this furrier the hide
Of this bear – with the bear alive inside.
But they would kill it quick, they said, and then the buyer
Could peddle it to someone at a price much higher,
For this was not some common bear, it was *le Roi*.
The fiercest winds would never pierce such high class fur.
And what a size! He would make two coats at least.
These salesmen could not say enough about their beast –
Their beast, they said, not asking if the bear agreed.
So, having set their price and even guaranteed
Next day delivery, they started on the chase –

Until they saw him charging, coming at a pace
That left the two friends flabbergasted, just destroyed.
Now nothing more was said about who owned the bear;
Their contract had become invalid, null and void.
One scampered up a tree, the other was employed
In mimicking a marble statue. There,
Face down he lay, holding his breath and acting dead,
Having heard somewhere, or possibly even read,
That bears will very seldom gnaw on bodies which
Do not show any sign of life, like breathe or twitch.
King Bruin, none too quick himself, falls for the trick.
He sees this body lying prone. "Methinks
It liveth not," he growls, "but, just to check, I'll flick
It over. Ugh! I'll flick it back! And now to try
A tiny sniff." He sticks his muzzle up quite near
And he inhales. "He really stinks,"
He said, "He's definitely dead! Now let's get out of here!"
And off he lumbered to the piney woods nearby.
The climber climbed back down and went to find his friend.
It seemed miraculous to him that in the end
The only injury he suffered was his fear.
He asked, "When he stood over you he seemed to grin
And then to whisper something in your ear.
Did he say anything about his skin?"
"Why, yes. He said, 'My boy, you should have been aware –
Don't ever sell the bearskin till you've skinned the bear.'"

V. 20

The Ass in a Lionskin

Dressed in a lionskin, a silly jackass made
An awe–inspiring masquerade.
Though there was just an ass inside,
Everyone was terrified.
But then an ear, the tiniest tip, somehow protruded
And many saw they'd been deluded,

While those not on to him as yet were much amazed
To see a kingly lion hazed
By little Master Birchrod, forcefully applied,
Down to the mill by the river side.

In France we have a noisy crowd
Whose foolishness this fable shows.
Though they are only asses their designer clothes
Give them the look of lions, dangerous and loud.

V. 21

Book Six

The Shepherd and the Lion

Fables are much more than they appear to be.
In them we get instruction from the simplest creature.
For though a naked moral may beget ennui,
When clothed in narrative its precept is our teacher.
And although tales as tales strike me as trivial,
If they hold hidden truths they both instruct and please,
Which is the reason souls of great capacities
Have found the form so lastingly convivial.
These authors all in all have strikingly preferred
A style that's unadorned, without one wasted word.
Phaedrus was concise – some even said too "close,"
And yet, compared to Aesop, Phaedrus seems verbose.
But still another Greek is, more than any, linked
To true Laconic elegance, pared–down, succinct.
He kept his fables to a few quatrains in length –
Let experts say if that's his weakness or his strength.
But let's compare two fables he and Aesop made
Employing similar themes: in one there is portrayed
A silly, boastful hunter, while the other shows
Much the same character costumed in shepherd's clothes.

Here, then, is more or less the story Aesop told.
A shepherd, counting sheep returning to the fold,
Found several missing. Determined to catch the thief,
He put wolf traps around a cave in that locality –
He knew a wolf had done it: that race had criminality
Bred in its bones. The traps once set, he prayed: "Oh, chief
Of all the gods, if you will make this foolish beast
Stand here before my eyes so I can have a laugh
Before I go, at seeing him trapped, I'll kill a calf,
A very fat one, on your altar." As he ceased,
A lion came stalking from the cave. Half–dead with shock,
The shepherd fell upon his knees and said, "Alas!

No man can know what his desires may bring to pass!
If I could see the thief who preyed upon my flock
Come out and be entrapped before I'd gone from here,
I promised I would sacrifice a calf. But now,
Great god, instead of that I'll vow
To kill an ox if you will make him disappear."

So that was how the master did it. Now,
Let the disciple take his bow.

VI. 1

The Lion and the Hunter

A hunter, decked with gear from several catalogues,
Lost the most expensive of his hunting dogs –
One morsel in a lion's dinner.
He told a local shepherd, "My man, here's tuppence.
Point out the lair of this thieving sinner
So I can give him his comeuppance."
The shepherd said, "He lives upon that mountain yonder.
I pay him a protection fee,
One sheep per month, which leaves me free
To safely lead my flocks wherever they may wander."
But as the pair discussed his plan,
The lion charged, the hunter ran.
He wanted a confrontation, he'd forcefully repeated,
But when confronted he retreated.
"Oh, Jupiter, show me a place to hide!" he bleated.

The test of courage is to stand
And grasp the mortal danger with your mortal hand.
The hunter was looking for trouble, he said,
But soon as he found it he upped and fled.

VI. 2

The Sun and the North Wind

The northwind and the sun once saw a rider faring
Along a road somewhere, a cautious fellow wearing
Clothing for inclement weather: fall had begun,
When the wise traveler finds it best
To use due care in how he's dressed –
First there is rain, then brilliant sun,
Then Iris's scarf, the rainbow, warning everyone
They'll need their warmest cloaks before the season's done,
Which is undoubtedly the reason
The Latin poets called it the unsettled season.
And thus our man was ready for some rain to fall
With a stout cloak of doubled fabric, woven tight.
"This fellow," said the wind, "may think that he is all
Prepared for anything, but he lacks even slight
Awareness of the fact that I
Can blow so hard that all his buttons come undone
And, if I want to, I can make that cloak he's wearing fly
To hell and gone – to see that would be loads of fun!
You want to see?" "Hold on a moment," said the sun.
"Let's make a bet as to which one of us can first
Get that cloak taken off his shoulders. You begin.
I'll turn my rays down while you try." The northwind pursed
Its lips at once and started sucking in
Great gobs of cloud, inflating itself like a balloon,
Then shrieking like a pack of angry demons whaling
Away upon each other, spewed out a typhoon
That as it blew tore roofs off many buildings, broke
Ships' masts and sank whole fleets of vessels sailing,
All to remove a single cloak.
The traveler had taken care to check
The storm from swirling in and down around his neck,
Which saved his skin. The wind was finding that the more
It beat upon the man the stubborner he grew,
And it was wasting time without a chance to score.
At last, all that the puffing wagerer could do

Was muss the rider's hair and get his collar wet
Before its turn was done. And now the sun appeared,
Burned off the clouds and, with the skies all cleared,
Played softly on the rider's back until the sweat
Poured down beneath his heavy cloak, which he of course
Gladly removed, thus showing that violence has less force
Than gentle speaking to persuade:
Soft words do more than loud tirade.

VI. 3

Jupiter and His Tenant Farmer

Jupiter, long since, had a farm he wished to rent
And he sent Mercury to publicize and tout it.
Prospective tenants came, all bent
On getting it for less by what they said about it.
The place would cost a lot to run
And would be hard to plow, claimed one.
The rest agreed. Then, as they dickered all together,
The boldest but by no means wisest of the crowd
Said he would pay full price if Jupiter allowed
Him both to farm the land and to control its weather,
To suit the seasons to his whim,
To make it hot or cold, now stormy or now fair.
In short, all rights involving air,
Both wet and dry, would by the lease, devolve to him.
Jupiter agreed. Contract in hand, our guy
Lorded it as ruler of his local sky,
Wept rain, caused winds to blow and generally made
A climate for himself alone,
No more felt by his nearest neighbors than if they'd
Lived in America. Which proved much to their own
Advantage, since for them the harvest year was fine,
With bumper crops of grain and wine,
While Mister Man–in–charge saw little for his pains.
The next year, seeking better yields,

He redistributed his rains
But did no better in his fields,
While neighbors' granaries were filled to overflowing.
What could he do? Before the monarch of the skies
He went once more, admitting he had been unwise.
And Jupiter responded with forbearance, showing
A gentle master's leniency.

One must conclude that Providence is more knowing
As to our truest needs than we.

VI. 4

The Mouse, the Cockerel, and the Cat

A totally naive young mouse, on earth just weeks,
Once had the narrowest of squeaks.
Here is the tale its mother heard it tell.
"Mama, today I crossed the range of peaks
Around Mouseland. I scuttled just as well
As big rat children off upon adventures bound.
Well, when I got outside and looked around
I right away saw two strange creatures.
One seemed quiet and kind, with gentle features.
The other acted rowdy and ill-bred.
It squawked a lot and had this red skin on its head
And little stubby arms like that it flapped as if
It was attempting to take off,
And on its rear a scraggly bunch of feathers grew."
Of course, the picture that our small mouse drew
For its small mother's stupefaction,
As of some new American wild-beast attraction,
Was only a little rooster — *cock-a-doodle-do*!
Said he, "He slapped his sides and was so wild and loud
That though God made me brave he made me cowed
So I got scared and ran away,
Calling him all the worst things I know how to say.

129

If not for him I might have had the chance to meet
That other animal that looked to be so sweet.
It had soft fur, like ours, with pretty stripes; its tail
Was long, its face genteel, and it was so polite
The way it gazed at me – but yet its eyes shone bright!
And when I saw its ears I knew
That it would love all mice, for they were shaped
The same way ours are, and I was just
About to greet it when a hullabaloo
The other made so startled me that I escaped."
"My child," the mother answered, "that
Sweet innocent that you encountered was a cat,
Whose mask of mild benevolence
Conceals a grim malevolence
Toward all our kith and kind.
The other one, no threat to us, you well may find
Someday delicious. But as for cats, if they were cooks,
You'd find mouse recipes in all their books.
Child, if you'd live long, you'd better bear in mind –
Do not judge others by their looks."

VI. 5

The Fox, the Monkey, and the Animals

A tale is told that when a lion died
Who all his life had ruled his countryside
The animals assembled to decide
On a new king. The crown was brought from where
A dragon guarded it, deep in his lair.
Then one by one the beasts lined up and tried
It on. There was not one head it would fit.
Most were quite small, none large enough for it,
Not even those on which great antlers grew.
The monkey, smirking, clowning, tried it on too
And, holding it above him, mugged and pranced,
Did silly, apish japeries and danced

With it around his middle like a hoop,
Which so beguiled and entertained the group
That he was voted king in their election.
All came to do him homage. The fox alone
Was less than satisfied with their selection,
Though not prepared as yet to make this known.
When he had done his ritual bow, he rose
And said, "Great Sire, I have a map that shows
Where treasure has been buried. No one knows
Just where it lies, I think, but just myself.
Well, royalty by right owns all such pelf,
So it belongs to you, your Majesty."
The new-crowned king, unwilling to take chances
On losing any prop for his finances,
Rushed to the spot – and was trapped instantly.
Pretending to be coming to his rescue,
The fox showed up and said, "Oh, King, I ask you
How you could claim to govern us, not knowing
In any way where you yourself were going?"
He was dethroned, his downfall clearly due
To one small fact: a crown fits very few.

VI. 6

The Mule Who Prided Himself on His Genealogy

A bishop's mule bragged of his noble pedigree
And spoke incessantly of his mamá the mare,
To whom he owed his well-bred air
Of horsy aristocracy.
She had done everything, she had been everywhere,
And as her son he should like her
Be in the Social Register
And never in that lower class
Of mules who carry doctors – the mere idea would kill!

131

But, getting old, he was sent off to turn a mill
And it came back to him his father was an ass.

If in the end misfortune could
At least force fools to end pretence
There is no question but this would
Prove the old saw: in all events,
However bad, there lurks some good.

VI. 7

The Old Man and the Ass

An old man on an ass saw as they ambled
A flourishing meadow, ripe and green,
So he turned the old gray loose and off he rambled,
Galloping, browsing, joyfully straying,
Rolling, rubbing his back and braying
And stripping the meadow clean.
But then they saw the old man's foe
Approaching. "Hey, old gray, let's go!"
Said the man. Said the lazybones, "Why so?
What will your enemy do? What will he, haw?
Will he double my load? Will he beat me raw?"
Eager to get away, the oldster just said, "Naw!"
"Then what do I care," said the ass,
"Whose ass I am? Save yourself, let me eat grass.
My enemy is my master – that's what we asses say,
In good plain French, of course. Do you parlay?"

VI. 8

The Stag and His Reflection

Once, mirrored in a brimming spring,
A stag admired the beauty of

His branching antlers up above,
But felt it was a cruel thing
That he should have to bear the blow
Of seeing legs like spindles, vanishing below.
Examining his imaged self he sadly said,
"What proportion have such feet to such a head?
My antlers soar above all bushes in this wood,
My legs do me no speck of good!"
Then, as he babbled on this way,
He heard, close by, a bloodhound bay
And off he bolted, in a race
To reach some wooded hiding place.
Now his great horns, his fatal pride,
Entangled him at every stride
And slowed his legs, with which he tried
To lengthen out his days on earth.
At last he cursed those gifts that heaven each year applied
Upon his brow to mark his birth.

Beauty is fondly treasured, utility held cheap,
But beauty's price is often all too deadly steep.
The stag despised his legs, which gave him speed,
Adored the horns that made him bleed.

VI. 9

The Tortoise and the Hare

To hurry isn't enough: one must depart on time.
The tortoise and the hare will serve to make this plain.
"Let's bet," the tortoise says. "I'll lay you odds that I'm
The first to yonder spot!" "The first? Are you insane?"
Replies the more athletic one.
"You need a purgative, old son.
Take hellebore, four grains or so."
"If I'm so crazy, bet some dough!"
And so he does. Their stakes they stash

Beyond the goal for which they dash,
Though what they bet we do not know
Nor does their judge's name appear.
Our hare has only four of his best leaps to go,
Like those he makes that leave the dogs behind from here
To kingdom come each time they flush him out – and then
They're off across the fields again.
But having, I mean to say, some time to spare – to browse,
Or sniff the shifting winds, or close his eyes and drowse,
The hare sits back and lets the tortoise go.
Slowpoke is off and running hard!
First inch by inch, then yard by yard,
Like an old senator – full–speed–ahead–dead–slow!
Meanwhile, despising such an easy race to win,
The hare does every sort of thing – except begin.
He stretches, scratches, takes some time to ruminate,
Planning to show how fast he can accelerate.
Thus when he sees the tortoise, finally, about
To hit the tape, though like a rocket he shoots out,
He finds himself, alas, a hare a hair too late!
The tortoise gets there first and wins the day.

"Well, then," the tortoise pants, "I guess we'd have to say
That I was right and you were wrong.
What use to you was all your speed?
I've beaten you! And how, indeed,
Would you have run if you'd carried your house along?"

VI. 10

The Donkey and His Masters

A gardener's donkey constantly complained that fate
Had put him where he had to rise before the dawn.
"Compared to me," brayed he, "even the cocks sleep late.
Before they crow, 'Day's come!' I've gone.
And why? To lug some vegetables to market. That's

134

A fine excuse to spoil my sleep!" Fate finally was moved
To give the pack–beast a new master. This one proved
To be a leather–dyer, who steeped hides in vats.
The weight of the wet hides, their stench beyond belief,
Left the ass reeling, shocked, unstuck.
He said, "I miss my nice old chief,
Who sometimes turned his head away, which let me pluck,
Unpenalized, a cabbage leaf.
But now I never have such luck,
Or if sometimes I snatch a bite then I get struck."
Fate spun the wheel again, now giving
Him to a peasant who made charcoal for a living,
For whom he slaved, his servitor.
Again, loud braying lamentation.
"What now?" cried Fate, in absolute exasperation,
"This stupid donkey's life is occupying more
Of my attention than a hundred querulous kings.
Does he imagine no one's discontent but he?
May I not deal with other things?"
Fate – Dame Fortune, Chance, blind Luck or Destiny –
Was rightfully annoyed. And we,
The human lot, are all identically perverse.
We never are contented with today's conditions;
However bad the past, the present we find worse.
We tire the gods with our innumerable petitions.

If Jupiter granted all our wishes, even then,
Next day his head would ache with our complaints again.

VI. 11

The Sun and the Frogs

A tyrant's subjects celebrated when he married,
Drowning their discontents in wine.
Aesop alone perceived that they were being stupid
In thinking his wedding a hopeful sign.

"In olden days, when things were otherwise," he said,
"The sun announced it had desires
Like any other body and it planned to wed
A star it was attracted to and merge their fires.
You should have heard the uproar then
As every frog on earth began to chunk and shrill
Protestingly from bog and fen.
'What will we do,' they cried, 'if he becomes a parent?
One sun is harsh enough, but having six more still
Would boil the oceans dry and make the world a desert.
Goodbye, dear marshes! Soon our only swimming hole
Will be the river Styx!' For beasts with brains so small,"
Said Aesop, "Frogs to me seem very rational."

VI. 12

The Peasant and the Serpent

Somewhere in Aesop you will find
A peasant portrayed, a man as kind
As he was over-trustful, blind.
One winter's day, out for a stroll
On his small property, he found,
Stretched out upon the snowy ground,
A serpent, numbed and harmless, rigid as a pole,
And with mere minutes left until it would expire.
Without expecting any least
Display of thanks from the dumb beast,
He took it in and warmed it at his cottage fire.
At first it scarcely felt the heat but, gathering strength,
It gradually grew conscious, flexing its slow length,
And was itself again, a being filled with ire.
It wound its body in a coil, reared its sharp head
And, hissing at its savior, venomously tried
To strike the one whose act had raised it from the dead.
"Ungrateful beast, if this is my reward," he said.
"Then die!" And with a fury fully justified

The peasant took his axe and with two whacks created
Three snakes from one, now separated
Into the trunk, the head, the tail,
Which writhed about, attempting to be reunited
As in the old legend sometimes cited,
Though in this instance doomed to fail.

Charity is a splendid virtue.
But one must ask the question, charity for whom?
For charity to ungrateful souls may hurt you.
Such types deserve a miserable doom.

VI. 13

The Ailing Lion and the Fox

By these presents let all beasts know
That as King Lion now lies ill
And weakened in his forces so
He cannot leave his den, he will
Be pleased to have each species send
Emissaries to his presence
Where by his bed as they attend
They will assist his convalescence.
All have a Lion's solemn word
That none need fear his royal teeth.
Also, his claws will stay in sheath.
Safe passage hereby guaranteed
To both the feathered and the furred.

All the animals took heed
Of the official proclamation,
Each species sent a delegation.
The foxes, though, stayed in their houses,
For which one gave the explanation:
"We have to say that it arouses
Our strong suspicion that many a track

Leads up to the lion's gate
But not a single one leads back.
And so, your Majesty, with great
Regrets we must beg off your invitation.
Though we believe your guarantee
That we would safely pass into your lion's den,
We feel less confident that we
Would pass as safely out again."

VI. 14

The Bird Catcher, the Hawk, and the Lark

From others' cruel acts we claim
We are excused to do the same.
This universal rule applies to you:
You wish to be shown mercy? Then, show mercy, too!

A man trapped songbirds with a mirror. Taken in,
A lark alighted by its shining spectral twin –
At which a goshawk, cruising high
Above the furrows, swooped without a pause
And seized her, singing though about to die.
Having escaped the man's duplicitous construction
She found herself within the goshawk's cruel claws,
Bound for swift destruction.
But as the hawk was busied plucking out her plumage
He felt the nets close in on every side.
"Bird catcher, let me go," he said in hawkish language,
"I've never harmed thee in the least!" The man replied,
"And this small creature here – did she
Ever in the least hurt thee?"

VI. 15

The Horse and the Ass

In this world each must help the other,
For if death takes away your brother
His burden may descend on you.

An ass accompanied an unobliging horse
Who carried just a wisp of harness, nothing else,
While he, poor beast, was nearly dead beneath his load.
He begged the horse's help in carrying his pack
If he were not to die, exhausted, on the road.
"I trust my plea," he said, "will not appear ill-bred,
For half this weight would seem a feather on your back."
The horse refused with an emphatic fart,
But when he saw his comrade dead beneath the weight
He saw how foolish he had been,
For now he had to labor on
Carrying the ass's freight
And made to wear the ass's skin.

VI. 16

The Hound Who Dropped His Bone to Get Its Image

This far from heaven, everyone
Is self-deceived. Eternity's
Too brief to count the fools who run
Chasing unrealities.

All need to hear the story – Aesop's – of the hound
Who crossed a bridge. Below, he saw a hound whose bone
Looked bigger. Grrr! He leaped for it, let go his own.
He found no hound, no bone, just waves, and nearly
        drowned

While struggling to get back to shore,
Still hungrier than he was before.

VI. 17

The Bemired Cart Driver

Like Phaeton – only hauling hay –
A farmer got his cart mired deep in mud one day
In a place where human help was nowhere to be had:
One of those crease–in–the–map, provincial situations
To which blind Fate in her ministrations
Consigns poor mortals whom she wishes to drive mad.
God keep us all from such locations!
But to resume my mud–bound carter's tale.
He raged and roared, he swore until the air was blue,
Using the best swear words he knew;
He cursed all mudholes, cursed his cart, his team, his luck,
And cursed himself for getting stuck.
Then, finding cursing no avail,
At last he sank upon his knees
And loudly prayed to that immortal, famed world–wide
For his twelve labors. "Hercules,"
He said, "if you once held this whole revolving sphere
Upon your back, your arm could pull me out of here
Without half trying." From above, a voice replied,
"Great Hercules prefers to give
Assistance to those people who
First demonstrate initiative.
So, understand what's stopping you
And scrape away that mud, that mortar, like thick glue,
That clings to all the wheels as they sink deep within it,
Then grab your pickaxe, break that rock that blocks your
        travel
And fill that rut up with the gravel.
So, have you done that yet?" "I finished, just this minute,"
The man replied. "Well, then I'll help you," said the voice.

"Now, take your whip." "I've got it and – Great Scot! Rejoice!
My cart is freed! Thanks, Hercules! I'm just elated!"
"You see how easily your team was extricated?"
The voice replied. "But don't attribute it to elves."

Heaven helps those who help themselves.

VI. 18

The Charlatan

There's never a dearth of charlatans, for every age
Gives birth to more to crowd on stage.
Just recently, as one was flacking
To eager crowds a diet to hold death at bay,
Another charlatan was tacking
His notices up on many a fence,
Claiming his grasp of rhetoric was so immense
That he could teach the dullest booby to display
A more than Ciceronian gift of eloquence –
Even some dunce, some brainless clod of lowly class.
"Yes, gentlemen, a dunce, or, better yet, an ass:
If you'll give me an ass, an actual ass, a beast,
I'll give you back a speaker able to surpass
A robed professor or a priest."
On hearing this, the king sent for the rhetorician.
"Within my stable I possess a steed," he said,
A donkey of Arcadian breed, full thoroughbred,
That I command you and commission
To make into an orator." "All you desire,"
The charlatan replied, "Will be accomplished, Sire."
Then, given some money for tuition,
He guaranteed that ten years later
The ass would speak in a theater.
If not, then he himself would hang for all to see,
A noose around his neck, upon the gallows tree,
His head capped with the ass's ears

And, on his back, 'Dead Rhetorician.'
One courtier told him, "As I expect to see you raised
Upon a gibbet's crossarm, I am much amazed
That one condemned can act so cheerful and unfazed.
For when you stand upon the scaffold and petition
The king for mercy, all you'll have to aid your cause
Is a tear-jerking and long-winded repetition
Of threadbare oratorical devices, saws
And empty jargon that your sort have up their sleeves –
That sort we commonly call thieves."
"Long before then," the charlatan replied,
"The king, the ass or I most likely will have died."
He was quite right. It's foolishness to think
That we can count on being here a decade on,
So let's eat happily and and let our glasses clink –
In ten years time, it's one in three we'll be long gone.

VI. 19

Discord

The goddess Discord once caused such upheaval
Up on Olympus – over just one little apple –
That the gods expelled her from that upper level.
Below, the animal named Man
Welcomed her with a receiving line,
Her and her brother, You-cant-I-can,
Also her father, Thats-all-mine.
She did us signal honor by coming to earth here
In our superior hemisphere,
Not that below, whose peoples, opposites to us,
Are scarcely civilized, gross-mannered, barbarous –
And coupling as they do, not yoked by priest or clerk,
Are not involved in Discord's work.
To find locations ripe for Discord's talents, Fame
Rumored she was coming – and she always came.
Where people argued she ran, arriving long before Peace,

And fanned small sparks of anger into conflagrations
None could put out for generations.
At last Fame started grumbling that with no set place,
No fixed address where she resided,
Discord's true origin could never be decided.
Thus what was needed was a residence provided
Where Discord could be sent away
By every family till a day
Whose coming should be long resisted.
But since back then no boarding schools existed,
There was no place on earth designed
To keep her properly confined,
And Discord chose the Inn of Marital Relations
As permanent headquarters for her operations.

VI. 20

The Young Widow

Wives weep when they lose husbands. "Oh, alas, alack!"
They loudly cry – but finally the tears will cease;
Somehow consolement comes, and peace –
Time flies away with sorrow, brings our pleasures back.
Between the widow of the first day's grief
And the widow of a year now past
The difference to be seen is vast;
That both are the same woman seems beyond belief.
One fends men off, one has a thousand charming ways;
Sighs, real or false, escape her, uncontrolled,
While there's one note, unvarying, she always plays:
She says she'll never be consoled.
She says so, but her words lack weight,
As this next tale will demonstrate –
Or, rather, as we see in life.

A beautiful young woman's husband left
For realms above. There at his side, his wife

Cried, "Darling, wait! I'll follow you! My soul, bereft,
Wants to depart with yours and travel through the skies."
The husband made the trip alone.
The beauty had a father, sensitive and wise,
Who waited patiently until the storm had blown.
At last, to help her to recover,
"My daughter, you've shed tears enough," he said.
"This drowning of your charms cannot restore your lover.
Since there are men yet living, let the dead be dead.
I am not saying that so brief
An interval should end your grief
And let you change your mourning for a wedding gown,
Yet in a decent time, perhaps you might not frown
On a new husband, handsome, young and qualified
With all the gifts of the deceased." "Ah, me!" she sighed,
"A cloister is the only husband I will need."
The father let time's work proceed,
And for a solid month she cried.
But then a month arrived when she could not endure
This frumpy dress, that blouse and skirt, her old coiffure.
Now mourning black turned morning chic,
Worn just to show her pale, smooth cheek,
And all the exiled band of loves
Came flocking back like turtle doves,
While quips, quadrilles, flirtatious games and laughter
Each in turn came following after,
And night and day she seemed in truth
Like one fresh-dipped within the fountain of youth.
The father feared the dear deceased no more.
But when he failed to bring the subject up again,
"Where is the man," she begged, "you promised me before?
When will you bring me a husband, daddy? Tell me, when!"

VI. 21

144

Epilogue

Here let us stop, no further jaunting,
As I find lengthy volumes daunting
That too well illustrate a theme,
When all that's wanted is the cream.
I need to pant, recoup my forces,
So I may run on other courses,
For love, which rules my life, commands
That I seek new things to inspire me,
And one must do as love demands.
I'll turn again to Psyche: Damon, you'd require me
To paint her blisses and her woes.
And I consent: perhaps this task that you impose
Will meet with Psyche's favor and my verse
Blaze with new inspiration. How fortunate if of
The travails I encounter I never meet one worse
Than this, caused by her husband, Love.

Book Seven

Dedication

To Madame de Montespan

Fable is a gift to man from the divine –
Or, if to man from man, still we should raise a shrine
To that wise soul who first invented this fine art
Or, better said, this charm that first attracts the mind
And then entirely captures it
With tales of such engaging wit
That hearing them enchants the spirit and the heart.
Olympia, who casts a spell of the same kind,
If when the gods are gathered at their feasts my muse
Has sometimes been among them, deign now to peruse
These tributes that she brings
And, with a favoring glance, reward these trifling things
That are my spirit's recreation.
For then destroying time, in deference to your praise,
Will let me through this work be granted dispensation
To leap the boundary of my days.
All authors having hopes of future incarnation
Must seek to gain your approbation.
Your pleasure in my verses is my only prize:
For what we write lacks beauty till
You have explored it with your eyes
Down to the tiniest detail.
Who better knows than you of beauty and of grace?
You are all charm, as fair in words as fair of face.
My muse, expounding such a lovely theme, might ask
To treat it at far greater length,
But that must be another's task.
A master of a greater strength
Must have the privilege of your praise.
Olympia, it is sufficient if in future days
Your name gives my last work its refuge and protection.

My book so favored, I'll dare hope for resurrection.
These verses, given only your support, will rise,
Despite all envy, to full worth in this world's eyes.
It is not for myself I claim
So great a favor, but that fable in its name
Would ask it, for, as you well recognise,
We mortals have a taste for its delicious lies.
And if that means my verses give you pleasure, too,
To build Aesop a temple is what I should do –
But I would build no temple other than to you.

The Animals Stricken with the Plague

A sickness that sows frightful seeds,
Sickness that heaven's anger framed
To be fit punishment for earth's immense misdeeds:
The plague (for evils must at last be named),
With power in one day to flood deep Acheron,
Now struck the animals full force.
And though not all would die, all will to live was gone –
When death is nigh, why struggle to delay its course?
The usual snarling over morsels ceased,
The foxes and the wolves no longer chased
The innocent and curly-fleeced,
The turtle doves flew off in mutual distaste:
If love is gone, joy is erased.

At last the lion called a meeting. "My dear friends,"
He said, "I think these trials show that heaven intends
To tell us that our sins have made us all accursed.
So let us find the one of us whose crimes are worst
To draw the lightning on his head alone
And, hopefully, at one stroke atone
For all. For history teaches that in times of crisis
One often makes these sacrifices.
So search your consciences, look deep inside,

Reveal the ugly thing you always thought to hide.
Hold nothing back, wipe clean the slate:
A public confession is good for the state!
My awful appetite, for example, has made me prey
To gluttony. I've eaten flocks of sheep. Had they
Harmed me at all? No, not in any way.
So that was wrong, of course. But wait —
There is more. I must admit that sometimes it occurred
That, inadvertently, besides the sheep, I also ate
The shepherd.
So I will be your victim — if that proves necessary.
But each must first confess as honestly as I,
For in the name of justice, the guiltiest must die."
"Oh, Sire," said the fox, "We have the best of kings,
Whose scruples show his noble soul. But, I ask, why
Is eating mutton a sin? Those low, retarded things
Were honored when you ate them. And, I observe,
Those shepherds got what such imperialists deserve,
The human race, exploiters all." To huge applause,
The fox sat down. Nor did one soul dare criticize
The tiger or the bear or such high-ranking jaws
As having broken even the tiniest, little laws.
And the ferocious mastiffs were just friendly guys
Who'd never bitten a soul, without good cause.
It came the ass's turn. "I recollect," he said,
"That once in spring I crossed a field
Of grass so sweet and tender I commenced to yield
To devilish desires that popped into my head
And took a bite broad as my tongue of that good hay.
I had no right. My conscience warned me to say nay!"
At that, the assembly shouted, "Shame upon the ass!"
And then a wolf, a preacher of the saintly class,
Declaimed that nothing less sufficed
Than that this curséd beast posthaste be sacrificed,
This scabby, scurvy object, source of these bad events.
His minor tort became a capital offense.
How gross a crime it was to eat another's grass!
No penalty short of death could pay

151

For such a sin – and that is just what came to pass
Without appreciable delay.

Depending on your social height,
The law will see your crime as black – or else as white.

VII. 1

The Unhappily Married Man

If goodness always went with beauty, why, of course,
I would be off tomorrow, searching for a wife,
But as reports of a divorce
Between these two have long been rife,
And as many beautiful bodies that should rightly give
Good souls fine homes in which to live
Do no such thing, forgive me but not on your life
Will I be off tomorrow, searching for a wife!
I've gone to many weddings but have never yet
Desired my own, for though a near totality
Of humans takes this riskiest of steps, regret
Proves every bit as often the reality.
For instance, here is the case–history of a man
Who, having grown regretful, had no better plan
Than sending his tart–tongued, stingy, jealous bride
To languish in the countryside.
Nothing suited her, nothing was done right.
The household rose too late, retired too soon at night.
She changed her mind capriciously – now black, now white,
Now some new whim entirely – until at last she had
Driven the servants frantic and her husband mad.
"Master says too dear! Master says too cheap!
Master is too busy. No, Master is still asleep."
Master grew so weary of all she said about him
He sent her back to her parental place, without him,
Where Phillidas and Corydons in rustic togs
Traipsed after turkey flocks or minded droves of hogs.

Eventually, expecting she might perhaps have grown
More docile, he sent for her again. "My dearest own,
How have things gone?" he asked. "Has the time raced?
Has country innocence proved to your taste?"
"Quite minimally," she said. "What bothered me, my dear,
Was finding the people there more shiftless than those here.
The welfare of their flocks concerned them not the least.
I let them know their failings and in return I got
Cursed and derided by that ill–bred, unwashed lot."
"Madame," her husband answered, "If you are such a shrew
That even those who only need encounter you
Briefly in the morning, then not again till night,
So quickly come to be offended by the sight,
What can one expect of servants who must bear
The burden of your fury all the day and year?
And what can a poor husband do
Whom night or day you do not trust apart from you?
Goodbye. Go home to your village. If ever the time arrives
When in this life I'm seized with wanting you again,
Let me in death be forced as penance for my sin
To be forever chained to two such darling wives."

VII. 2

The Rat Who Retired from the World

The Levantines among their legends tell
The story of a rat whose midlife *crise*
Led him to take refuge in a Holland cheese,
And live there like a hermit in his cell,
Where, since his ball of wax went all around,
His global isolation grew profound.
With his feet he dug, with his teeth he chewed,
And in no time at all he'd hollowed a space:
His hermitage, serving as lodging and food.
What more could any rodent need?
He grew obese, for heaven's grace

153

Enlarges those who take true heed
Of vows of godly consecration.
But then one day a shabby deputation
Came begging at his door– his fellow rats,
They said they were, petitioning his aid.
It seemed their little state was threatened by the cats,
Who'd ringed Ratopolis with a blockade.
And since their nation's treasury was broke
Not one of them had one red cent left in his poke.
Now, all they asked of him
Was some financing for the interim,
A little cash until the aid that they'd applied
For recently became effective.
"Good friends," the solitary sighed,
"Such worldly matters now are not in my perspective.
How can a humble, poor recluse
Do anything of use
Other than lift his voice in prayer
That heaven will see your plight and care?"
And then the saintly rodent slammed the door.

Who is portrayed, do you suppose,
In this tale of a selfish rat you've heard me tell?
A Christian brother? No, a dervish, an infidel.
For Christians are always charitable, God knows.

VII. 3

The Heron

Slow–motioned, spare, on long legs faring who knows where,
Came Heron once, his long neck helving his long beak.
He edged his way along a creek
Whose ripples were transparent as the cloudless air.
And there old Mistress Carp led round and round, below,
Old Pike, like her attentive beau.
The heron then might easily have caught his fill;

154

The fish swam leisurely, for him to take at will.
But he decided it behooved
Him wait till appetite improved –
He had his hours for eating, lived by rigid rule.
A due time later, when his appetite had stirred,
Proceeding now to search, the bird
Saw drifting from their weedy hideaway a school
Of tench: not to his taste, he wanted better, sweeter,
For he was finicky, an eater
Like City Rat, from Horace's old fable.
"I? Eat tench?" he said, "I, Heron? On my table,
So thin a dinner? Just who do they suppose I am?"
The tench were sent away. And then a gudgeon swam
In reach. "Echh, gudgeon! What a banquet for a heron!
For gudgeon, God forbid, my beak should open?"
He opened it for much, much less. As it would happen,
The fish all vanished in their fishy fashion.
Now hunger gnawed. At last he counted it a treat
To find a tiny snail to eat.

Don't be too difficult –
The least demanding often get the best result.
Who stays to bet the pot quite well may lose his purse,
Who sneers at minor gains may gain both less and worse,
As many men have found – it isn't to herons
That I preach. Just listen, humans:
And you will know it is for you I've drawn these lessons.

The tale that follows I've assigned
To one much of the heron's mind.

VII. 4

The Girl

A girl of an affected kind
Pictured the man she planned to marry:

155

Young; well-built and handsome; charmingly refined;
Not without passion, yet – a bit to the contrary –
Not jealous in the least. And also, she decided,
Witty, very well bred and very well provided.
In short, he'd have it all. (Yet who can have it all?)
Still, fate was kind; distinguished suitors came to call.
The whole contingent she derided
As not half good enough. "To me?
Propose to me? These pitiful clods? The idiocy!
Men are so stupid, and it shows!"
One lacked finesse, one had a silly-looking nose;
One had these faults, one had those.
Not one would do; all were rejected –
The most disdainful females are the most affected.
The best men gone, the mediocre took their place.
She scoffed at their pretensions. "They're lucky I don't chase
Such dullards from my door. Do they suppose I moan
For their companionship? By the grace of God I sleep
Without regret each night, although I sleep alone."
The beauty seemed content to keep
Believing her own words, but as the time went on
Age brought its ravages. Where had her lovers gone?
An anxious year went by, then two. From some recess
Regret emerged. The amorous games she used to play
Had other players; she heard laughter less and less;
Men looked at her then looked away.
Now she tried mud-packs, face-creams, every kind of lotion,
But found that though applied with feverish devotion
None helped her to escape from Time,
That famous thief, that prince of crime.
An aging house may be restored without a trace
Of disrepair, why not a face?
She changed her tune. Her mirror told her, "Do not tarry!
It's time you found a husband. Marry!"
I can't say if desire preached to the same effect,
Though it may lurk, we know, in even the most correct.
But in the end she counted herself supremely blessed

156

To find a foul-mouthed boor to marry none had guessed
Attracted her more than the rest.

VII. 5

Wishes

Far to the west of Xanadu
There once were spirits – genies! – who
Kept houses tidy, mended, polished, swept floors clean
And gardened, sometimes, in between,
Yet if you touched what they had done
It turned to moondust. By the river Ganges, one
Of these kind spirits kept the garden for a pair
Who lived in modest comfort there.
He worked with quiet devotion, loving both his host
And hostess but, undoubtedly, their garden most.
Who knows what aid the zephyrs, creatures of the spring,
May have provided him, but he took pains to pour
Before his human hosts a store
Of pleasures, richly burgeoning.
Yet the best proof of his affection
Was his desire to stay there evermore, despite
The urge all genies share for flight,
Untethered, in some new direction.
But then his fellow spirits, in pure caprice perhaps,
Or in the wars of politics,
Convinced their president by underhanded tricks
To transfer him to Norway where, among the Lapps,
He would be lodged where rivers froze,
In a hut whose roof lay deep in everlasting snows.
Before his time was up he came before his hosts.
He said, "I'm forced to leave you, though
The sin I'm guilty of I don't presume to know.
Still, there is nothing I can do. These foreign posts
Can't be refused. One has to go.

My time is short – a month at most, perhaps a week,
But let us use it. Make three wishes. That will do
For me to give you what you seek –
Just three, not more." To humans there is nothing new
Or difficult in making wishes. With one voice
The two gave wealth as their first choice.
And wealth in an immense amount
Was showered on them, more than they knew how to count.
Their granary was full, their wine casks overflowing;
The glut of all they had kept growing.
But how to cope with it? The time it took, the care,
The reams of record–keeping all of it required!
If ever two had been perplexed it was this pair.
Great nobles asked to borrow money; thieves conspired
To swindle them; the sultan taxed them for his share.
Enslaved by all they had acquired,
They told each other, "Poverty
Is better than this kind of wealth. Now let us be
Set free of these false goods that only bring us grief.
Riches, begone! Sweet goddess of contented rest,
Companion of good cheer, allow us the relief
Of moderate fortune, having again what we possessed!"
And at these words the goddess men call Moderation
Materialised, and with their second wish returned
Them gracefully to their original situation,
As lucky as before, like all the population
Who waste their time on wishes, but who should be
          concerned
To put that time to use with industry and craft.
The genie and the couple laughed.
Then at the last, before he rose
And headed northward through the skies
They wished for that great gift whose value always grows:
They asked for him to make them wise.

                                                    VII. 6

158

The Lion's Court

Wanting to know more about the many nations
The gods had given him to rule by right of birth,
King Lion sent out deputations
To all the corners of the earth
To read aloud his royal writ
With his great seal affixed. To wit:
His various subject populations
Must send their delegates to court
For plenary deliberations.
But first, grand opening celebrations
With circus acts of every sort
Would showcase the stupendous power of the king.
His Louvre received their delegations.
But what a Louvre! The stench was overpowering
Of rotting corpses. The bear was seen to hold his nose –
To his regret. The monarch, hugely irritated,
Had him despatched to Hades where, he said, such shows
Of squeamishness might possibly be tolerated.
The ape at once, with sycophant sincerity,
Applauded their glorious leader's just severity,
He praised his rage, his claws, his den, but most of all
That fragrance wafting through the hall:
There was no sweet perfume, no flower beneath the sun
That would not stink like garlic by comparison.
His obvious flattery won him instant strangulation:
This Lion Majestic was Caligula's close relation.
And now he asked the fox, "So, what is it you smell?
Be frank about it. Mince no words. I bid you, tell."
The fox immediately told
The lion he was sorry but he had this cold
And with no sense of smell he really couldn't say,
Which saved his hide another day.

Take my advice, don't get yourself in a position
Where you must try to please a king,

But if you do, be neither weakly flattering
Nor forthright – try to say nothing, like a politician.

VII. 7

The Vultures and the Pigeons

Mars once stirred all the air with shrieks and cries
Born of a struggle for a certain prize
Among the birds – of course not those the Spring
Calls to her court beneath the greening boughs,
Where by their ways and amorous songs they sing
They waken Venus in our midst and rouse
Our hearts once more to passion; nor were they
The ones that draw her chariot on its way
Across the sky: no, these were razor–clawed
And hook–beaked vultures, warring to the death
Over a dead dog's body. It rained blood –
I don't exaggerate – but I lack breath
For all the grim details that I might tell.
Suffice it, then, that many a hero fell
And many a chief was slain in either flock,
So many that Prometheus on his rock
Hoped his deliverance might be done that day.
It was a stirring thing to watch their fray;
It was great pity to see myriads fall.
Daring, bold strength, surprise, deception: all
Came into play, for so imbued were both
With murderous rage that neither side was loath
To using means of any sort that hurled
Their enemies into the nether world:
From earth and sky new citizenry sped
Into the vast, walled kingdoms of the dead.
Moved by this carnage, a tender–hearted nation
That lived nearby – that race whose lustrous collars
Shine with a soft sheen of shifting colors –
These faithful birds, roocooing with compassion,

160

Endeavored to bring peace by mediation.
They sent their most ambassadorial pigeon
To expedite the process, and he wooed
Both sides so soothingly they soon agreed
To cease their fracas, whence peace again ensued.
Alas! the peace was of small benefit
To those deserving praise and thanks for it.
The brutes of both camps instantly turned on
The pigeon flock and thousands soon were gone,
Their towns left desolate, their fields untilled
And grown to weeds, their many voices stilled.
Poor souls, they had unwisely offered aid
To savagery – and found themselves betrayed.

A rule by which all statesmen should be guided:
Seed war among ill-doers, keep them divided.
Failure to do so means you won't have peace.
That's just a thought I had – which said, I'll cease.

VII. 8

The Fly and the Omnibus

Up a long hill, slipping in sand, a brutal grade,
In sun without one spot of shade,
Six horses pull an omnibus.
The team is sweating, panting, near to drop,
So all get down, old men, stout wives, the priest up top.
A fly comes buzzing by, decides a stimulus
Is what these slowpokes need, and down at once it dives,
Stings here, stings there and, thinking its attention drives
The whole machinery around,
It perches on the harness shaft, the coachman's nose,
And finds its theory is sound:
The wheels revolve, away the whole procession goes.
Reserving all the glory to itself alone,
It zips officiously about

Like a staff officer who roams a staging zone
Assigned to motivate the troops as they move out.
"Let's win this fast," he bellows. "Make them feel our will!"
In this shared enterprise, the fly complains,
It knows the leader's loneliness, takes all the strains.
Not one is helping push these horses up the hill –
The priest goes on reciting prayers:
("Don't waste a moment, Father!") And hear the way
One woman sings: ("That's just what we all need today!")
The fly keeps up a constant buzzing in their ears,
A hundred such inanities that no one hears,
Until at last, exhausted, they are at the crest.
The fly says, "Halt. All stop and take a breather. Rest!
I've brought the expedition up the mountainside,
So now, my dear good horses, time to pay the guide!"

Thus some people meddle,
Smack in the middle
Of other people's business, acting as though
It is they who run the show.
Someone should tell them, "Just buzz off! Go!"

VII. 9

The Dairymaid and the Pail of Milk

(I've taken this tale of comic ilk
From an old farce, *The Pail of Milk*.)

Perrette, a country wife, went confidently striding
Toward town, a well-filled milk pail riding
Upon a cushion lightly balanced on her head.
Hurrying to get there, eager, dressed for speed
In flat-soled shoes and a brief petticoat, she sped
Absorbed in dreams of money she'd
Soon get for all that milk and then
She'd buy a hundred eggs and when

The chicks from these were grown each hen
From this new flock would raise another brood again
And her hard work would be rewarded.
She told herself, "I can raise chickens easily
Around my cottage, keeping them so safely guarded
That any fox would have to be
A very clever one indeed
To leave me not enough to barter for a pig,
Which I will fatten up on bran – that's cheap to feed.
Of course I'll get a little one and when it's big
I will resell it. What a profit that will yield!
And what's to stop me, with my gains so multiplied,
From buying a fine cow with her small calf beside?
I see it in our herd, cavorting in the field!"
Imagining the jumping calf, Perrette jumped too –
And spilled the milk. Her vision of quick profits shattered.
The calf, the cow, the pig, the chicks – away all flew.
In tears, the mistress of this wealth so rudely scattered
Went home to mollify her sweeting,
From whom she greatly risked a beating.

Whose thoughts don't run in the same vein?
Who doesn't build castles, off in Spain?
The wise, the simple and the silly,
Milk–maids or conquerors, willy nilly
Get lost in daydreams – such a pleasant occupation!
Our minds are captured by alluring fantasies:
Much honored by a grateful nation,
We are rich past counting; beautiful celebrities
Wait for our call. When I'm alone
I dare the greatest champion to face me in the ring.
I'm off in space! I wrest the throne
From a harsh tyrant and cheering crowds elect me king.
My people love me. When I place the gorgeous crown,
Dripping with diamonds, on my head the people roar!
But then it always happens: something brings me down –
To find I am John Bumpkin, as I was before.

VII. 10

The Parson and the Corpse

A corpse went slowly, solemnly, riding
To its last home, to start residing.
A priest stepped cheerfully past,
Impatient to bury it, fast.
Well-wrapped for travel our departed,
Lying in state upon a bed
In a great carriage, soon got started,
His garment, alas, a coffin, duly lined with lead –
The fashion for winter, spring, summer and fall:
The dead never take it off at all.
Beside the high-wheeled hearse, the priest
Droned psalms and prayers for the deceased,
Sang *requiem, sanctus, miserere,*
In short, did all the ordinary.
"Dead Sir, no need to fret, I'll see you get a very
Fine send-off," he said. "So, how much will you pay?"
Jack Parson gazed with glinting eyes,
As if he meant to rob the body of some prize,
And with his glances seemed to say,
"Dead Sir, you owe me a service tax,
Payable partly in cash and partly in candle wax,
And partly in other little clerical supplies."
He counted on a generous fee, with which he'd get
A vintage cask of wine. Also, his niece – sweet girl! –
And her chambermaid, Paquette,
Needed new petticoats. His mind was in a swirl
Of happy fantasising, when – catastrophe!
The vehicle violently struck
Some obstacle and with the shock
Tipped over – goodbye, carriage, goodbye, fee –
For, out flew the cadaver, catapulting
Straight at the parson's head
And breaking it – thus resulting
In murder of the living by the dead!
Now parson and parishioner,

Both dressed in lead, rode on together.
The story of our lives is neatly told
By Jack Parson and his ilk
Who expect the dead to give them gold,
Or by the milkmaid and her jug of milk.

VII. 11

The Man Who Ran After Fortune
and
The Man Who Waited for Her in Bed

Who is not running in the race
For Fortune's favors? I only wish that I could stand
And watch the crowds rush past, all eager to embrace
This apparition they pursue from land to land,
Chance's skittish daughter, leading them on and on.
At times she waits, they reach to have her – but she's gone!
Poor souls, I sympathize, for, surely, any born
To be such fools deserve our pity not our scorn.
"You know that man," they'll say, "who had so little hope,
That simple cabbage farmer who became a pope?
Aren't we just as deserving?" Of course you are, and ten
Times moreso. You are all of you deserving men,
But what good is deserving? Has Fortune eyes? And then,
The papacy, is all its power
Worth one's tranquility – tranquility, that flower
So precious those who have it share
The bounty of the gods? Yet it is rare
That those possessing Fortune find
The treasure of a peaceful mind.
Ignore this goddess, then she well may come to you,
For, goddess though she be, she is a woman, too.

Two friends were both of them the heirs
To ample wealth and well-established place

In their provincial town. But one still yearned for more:
He wanted Fortune for his mistress. "Since no man,"
He said, "can ever be a prophet, as you know,
In his own country, what about our leaving here
And trying our luck elsewhere?" "You will have to go
Without me," his good friend replied. "I have no wish
To better my surroundings or my lot in life.
But suit yourself, obey your restlessness. In time,
You'll surely be returning and, until you do,
I promise faithfully to get a lot of sleep."
Ambition – or plain avarice, if one prefers –
Drew our adventurer down narrow paths and wide
Until in time he found his way
To that strange place which that strange goddess finds
More to her taste than any other –
That is, the court. And there he settled for a season,
Attending the royal person's wakings and goodnights,
Those hours all said were best – in short,
Attending everywhere and getting nowhere fast.
"So what's the use?" he asked at last. "I must move on.
Yet this is Fortune's habitat, no doubt of that.
I see her daily, entering first this one's place,
Then that one's. What is going on that I can't also
Convince that easy wench to come and stay with me?
I was well warned when I was told the people here
Would never tolerate a man who wants to rise.
Farewell, dear friends at court, dear friends at court, farewell!
Until the end, you'll dance to any flatterer's tune.
I hear that Fortune has built temples in Surat,
So I'll go there." No sooner said, but he embarked.
Stout hearts of bronze they had and diamond–clad, to boot,
Those humans who first dared to set a course past charts
And sail on unknown seas where the abyss plunged down.
Yet as he voyaged outwards, ever and again
The vision of his village lingered in his mind,
As he endured those endless months of storms and calms,
Of piracy and rocks, those ministers of death.
At what harsh cost he journeyed to the distant coasts

For what he might as well have found by staying home!
At last he reached Mogul, and there they said Japan
Was now the place where Fortune yielded her rewards
And he set off in haste. The very seas grew worn
With bearing him. And all the fruit
That these hard voyages had brought him
Was wisdom simpler folk had taught him:
"Keep to your country ever, let nature be your teacher."
Japan held nothing more to satisfy this man
Than had Mogul. At last he understood
That leaving his village did no good.
He quit the race he could not win,
Changed course for home. And when, far off, at last he saw
His hearth fire's smoke ascending skyward, weeping with joy
He said these words: "Happiest he who keeps to his home,
Who seeks at most to govern himself,
Who does not know but by distant hearsay
The affairs of court, the tossing seas –
Thine empire, Fortune, which hovers before us,
Of honors sought and goods acquired,
All chased to the ends of the earth and all at last empty.
Now I have stopped. I'll stay here. This is better."
But then as he went on, deploring Fortune's ways,
He found her, sitting in the doorway of the house
Where his old friend lay sleeping, undisturbed by dreams.

VII. 12

The Two Cocks

Two cocks co-existed. Then a hen chanced by
And warfare flared, all peace was gone.
Eros, why must you start these things? You toppled Troy,
You brought the nasty quarrel on
That dyed the River Xanthus with the gods' own blood!
Then this. Our feathered warriors battled stubbornly,
The squawk of combat echoed through the neighborhood

And every male who wore a comb flocked round to see.
More than one Helen of fair plumage
Became the victor's prize; the loser in the scrimmage
Retreated deep within his coop to sulk and mourn
His glory lost, his true loves lorn,
The loves his rival now, fired up by his defeat,
Possessed before his eyes! And every day the sight
Rekindled his burning hatred and his will to fight.
He honed his beak and, very fiercely, flapped his wings
While sparring bravely with the winds,
Until he'd worked himself into a jealous fury –
Which proved unnecessary. The proudly strutting victor
Flew up to the henhouse roof to crow his epic story
And was carried off by a swooping vulture:
Adieu sweet loves, farewell to glory.
All that male pride was snuffed in the vulture's horny claw.
In short, by a fatal turnaround
The loser in the battle had
Once more become the cocky lad.
You should have heard the cackling sound
From eager hens as they flocked round.

Fortune loves nothing better than a rude surprise –
As boastful victors all need someone to remind them.
For though they've beaten fate and won the prize,
They shouldn't relax – she's sneaking up behind them.

VII. 13

On Man's Ingratitude Toward Fortune

A merchant became rich through lucky circumstances.
In voyage after voyage all his vessels found
Fair winds, calm seas; none met with rocks or ran aground;
Kind Fate exempted him from punishing mischances.
While Atropos and Neptune took their toll of others,
The goddess Fortune brought his cargoes safe to port.

His lenders and investors were his loving brothers;
His merchandise, of every sort –
Tobacco, sugar, Canton porcelain, rare spices –
Was snapped up at the highest prices.
Extravagance and folly vied for all he sold;
One only talked to him with gold.
And as his swelling wealth increased
He had his pack of hounds, his gilded coach, his stud
Of stallions bred from champion blood.
His notion of a fast was like a wedding feast.
A friend, amazed at all this glittering excess,
Asked him to tell the secret of his great success.
"The secret? I'm the secret! It's my know-how, see?
I have a talent for investment. I know when
It's safe to risk my money. My wealth is due to me."
Since profit was so easy, he risked it once again –
And found that his investments were no longer charmed:
Poor judgment caused his plans to fail.
One over-loaded vessel sank in the first gale.
Another one, too lightly armed,
Was set upon by pirates, boarded and soon lost.
A third one reached a port of call
But found no one to buy his wares, at any cost –
Extravagance and folly now helped not at all.
And then he found he had been slyly double-crossed
By his dear partners while he looked the other way,
Leading his life of pleasure, building new chateaus,
And he'd grown poor within one day.
His friend, astonished seeing him in tattered clothes,
Asked, "What has done this?" "Fickle Fortune turned on me!"
He sighed. "Why then, console yourself. Though she denies
Herself to you, still you should be
Contented, for she's made you wise."
Did he believe this? I can't guess.
But this I know: we all attribute our success
To our hard work and mental powers,
Yet if, due to some fault quite obviously ours,
We fail, it's Fortune we berate.

It is that old familiar song:
We won? So credit us! We lost? Blame that on fate.
For we are always right; it's destiny that's wrong.

VII. 14

The Fortune Tellers

Opinion often turns upon some chance occurrence
And as opinion shifts the next new vogue arrives.
We are all swept in the same currents
And, whether rich or poor, each strives
To best his neighbors, plots, excludes, connives,
Few worrying if their behavior is unjust.
It is a flood. What can one do? Why, simply wait
And let things run their course – such crazes always must,
As they have always done, eventually abate.

A woman dealing in palm reading and clairvoyance
Became the rage in Paris. If one wished to recover
A missing glove or kerchief or a wandering lover,
Or found an ancient husband a terrible annoyance,
Or had a nagging mother or a jealous wife
Or any other problem complicating life,
One rushed to cross her palm with gold
To have her tell one only what one wanted told.
She put on an impressive show,
Half mystic hoohah, half the brashest impudence,
And as she often guessed, by pure coincidence,
Some secret none were thought to know,
The public was amazed. It was incredible!
Though ignorant as a post, she was an oracle.
The oracle lived up a stair,
Lodged within a garret where
Without more assets than pure gall
She rapidly acquired sufficient wherewithal
To buy a government appointment for her spouse

And leave the garret for a house.
Next day a new soothsayer took the place once more
And wives and daughters, rich men, poor men, as before –
All Paris – came, expecting to be well advised
About their fates. The garret had become the shrine
Of a new sybil, through having been well–publicised
By its first tenant. This second woman had a fine
Way with her words and spun an artful, teasing line:
"Me? Read your future? Sirs, oh, do not mock me, please!
I scarce can read my abc's."
And yet, despite her protestations,
She always could be made to mutter divinations
If primed with cash enough to pay two lawyers' fees.
It made her much more credible that in the room
Were just four listing chairs and a long–handled broom
That reeked of witches' sabbaths and weird sorceries,
While had she spoken truths amidst fine tapestries
All would have scoffed at her. The garret was the reason
She was in vogue and she who'd left it past her season.

The sign brings people in the door.
I've seen, up at the court house, a badly rumpled suit
Earn heavy legal fees. A crowd, all looking for
A big attorney to defend their cases,
Mistook the man inside it for a councillor
Of fully national repute.
But, ask me, on what rational basis?

VII. 15

The Cat, the Weasel, and the Young Rabbit

One fine morning, sly Dame Weasel
Seized a young rabbit's ancient castle
And summarily occupied it –
Without resistance, since nobody was inside it,
Its master having left and not as yet come back.

171

As she was settling in, the absent owner, Jack,
Was in attendance at the court of goddess Dawn,
Carousing gaily, frisking, browsing
Amid the broom and thyme before the dew was gone.
But then, returning to his subterranean housing,
He found the weasel at the window, nose stuck out.
"Oh, gods of hospitality, how has this come about?"
Asked the poor creature thrust from his ancestral hall.
"Ms. Weasel, leave my house and shut the door behind you.
If not, I'll tell our local rats to pay a call."
The sharp-nosed lady sneered, "Allow me to remind you,
I found this place abandoned when I came.
I occupied it first, so I have legal claim."
Besides, did he not think it rather droll
To speak of war about this dismal little hole
There was no way for him to enter but to crawl.
"And even if it were a kingdom, I can't see,"
She said, "what law puts it eternally in thrall
To Jack, the son of Peter, rather than of Paul,
Or Tom or Dick or Harry, or, for that matter, me?"
Jack said, "I am the lord and master here because
Of ancient customs and traditions, by whose laws
The ownership runs through a long unbroken line
That starts with Peter, goes to Simon, ends on John,
Which is myself, my father's son. So it is mine.
You think mere occupancy makes your claim the stronger?"
The weasel said, "We should not bicker any longer!
Let us consult Judge Velvetpaws, a wise old cat
Who leads a saintly life of quiet contemplation
Not far from here, fur-robed, fine-fettled, fitly fat,
And famous for his skill at arbitration.
Jack Rabbit readily concurred,
And soon the pair arrived before
The judge, splendiferously furred.
"My children," said the judge, "draw near,
Draw near. Old age has made me deaf. Speak in my ear."
Suspecting nothing, both approached until they stood
In reach of kindly Velvetpaws,

Who, suddenly catching both with his sharp claws,
Hungrily ate them, ending their argument for good.

This very much resembles what happens in debates
Between the kings of little nations
When they request the helpful arbitrations
Of kings of greater states.

VII. 16

The Head and the Tail of the Serpent

The snake is a creature with two ends
That are not either one man's friends.
The head, the tail: both ends have earned,
As far as humans are concerned,
An ill repute much like the Fates'.
In fact, the two once had debates
As to which end was more accursed
And should accordingly be deeded
The privilege of going first.
The head had always been the one that had preceded
Until the tail cried out to heaven: "God!" it pleaded,
"I'm always being forced to slither
Wherever *she* wants, hither, thither.
Is she so meanly unobservant
As to suppose I wish to be her humble servant?
I thank you, God, I was created
Her sister, not her slavey, fated
To follow meekly where she goes.
Inside us both the same blood flows,
So you should treat us equally.
Besides, as everybody knows,
I am as poisonous as she.
So this is all I ask – indeed,
It's very little – Lord, you need
But say the word – just let me lead!

173

I will be perfect as a guide;
Trust me, she'll be satisfied!"
Heaven responds to us at times with cruel kindness
And often grants our prayers to our real detriment:
It should be deaf to pleas we utter in our blindness –
But this time it was not. The tail end, bent
On leading, saw no better in broad daylight than
If it was shut inside an oven and it ran
At random into people, statues, trees and rocks,
Which after one too many of such sudden shocks
Killed both, the leader and the led. Unhappy the nation
That falls to just such blind, wrong–headed navigation.

VII. 17

An Animal in the Moon

When some philosopher commences
To claim that we are always lied to by our senses,
Another says, "Not so! Forsooth,
I swear that our five senses always tell the truth!"
And both are right. Philosophy is quite correct
In saying that if we depend uncritically
Upon our senses they mislead us; yet, if we
Allow with care for the effect
Of distance from the object, its environment,
And both the eye observing and the instrument,
Why, then our senses lie to us in no respect.
For Nature's way of ordering these things is wise –
But that's another subject, not for treatment here.
As I observe the sun, how shall I gauge its size?
From here on earth this giant body looks a mere
Three feet around, but if I flew into the sky
And saw it from the vantage point of its own sphere
How else could I conceive it than as creation's eye?
Its distance makes my eye misjudge its majesty
Until my hand by sides and angles geometrically

174

Takes its true magnitude. The ignorant confound it
With a flat disc; I give its roundness depth; I fix
Its globe in space and make the earth revolve around it,
And contradict my eyes, those harmless tricks
They play on me. My mind, which guides my eyes, reveals
The truth that bland appearance by its mask conceals.
I do not trust my vision when, with glance too quick,
It shows the world's apparent scenes,
Nor what my hearing tells me by its slower means;
My mind corrects my eye when water bends a stick.
For reason has the final say; my eyes,
With reason's aid, don't fool me though they tell me lies.
If I believed appearances – the failing's common –
I'd think the full moon's rising face portrayed a woman.
It really doesn't? No. Then what's the explanation?
The moon is nowhere flat; its differences in elevation,
Invisible from so far off, cause the effect.
Above the sunlit plains are mountains that project
Dark shadows that by contrast with the brightness trace
Perchance an ox, an elephant, a human face.
In England recently there was a famous case
Of similar misjudgment. Astronomers, moongazing,
Were thrilled when in their focus suddenly appeared
A strange new animal. They cheered
At finding a marvel so amazing.
This sudden alteration in the firmament
Most surely spoke of some terrestrial event,
Perhaps a war in prospect, with its alliances
And enmities. The king, informed, came hurrying
To see this monster for himself – the sciences,
He strongly felt, were worth a king's encouraging.
Staring through the eyepiece, reverently rapt,
The monarch saw the monster was a mouse entrapped
Between the lenses – the cause of all that talk of war.
The nation laughed. What lucky folk you English are!
When might we French, like you, have leisure to enjoy
Such peaceful occupations? Now we must employ
Our time in harvesting the fruits of bravery

Upon the field of Mars: it is our enemy
Who runs from combat, we who seek it out, for Victory,
Whose darling Louis is, will surely follow him, and we,
Made famous by his deeds, will live in history.
Yet Memory's daughters, the nine muses, have not fled.
They yield their pleasures still, delighting all our hearts;
We want the joys of peace, not requiems for the dead.
Charles understands these joys; his bravery imparts
The promise that through war his England will be led
Back to the tranquil pleasures of these present days.
But if he fends off war and damps these quarrels down
He will be deified – who would deserve more praise?
For was that time when great Augustus wore the crown
In peace less glorious than that first era when
The conquering Julius reigned? And if peace comes, why then,
May we not practice peaceful arts, like Englishmen?

VII. 18

Book Eight

Death and the Dying

The wise stand ready, baggage packed;
Death cannot take them by surprise,
For they are warned within themselves
About that time whose coming we must all expect.
That time, alas! embraces all our times,
So that however time is split, in days or hours
Or seconds, no least time exists when Death might not
Demand its tribute paid: all time is its domain.
And even that first instant when a monarch's son
Opens his eyes and sees the light
May prove as well to be the one
When he forever shuts them tight.
Let greatness serve as your defense,
Allege your beauty, virtue, youthful innocence –
Death has no shame, it rapes them all.
This world some day will lie in its dark treasure hall.

No fact of life is dwelt on more,
Yet there seems nothing, I must say,
That we could be less ready for.
A dying man, beyond a hundred years of age,
Complained to Death that she was too precipitate
In forcing him to leave in such a hurried way,
Without the time to make a will,
Without a proper warning. "Can one rightly die
When one has social plans? Give me a brief delay!
My wife will not be happy if I leave without her;
I have a new grandchild not yet provided for.
Let me have time to put a new wing on my house.
Oh, cruel goddess, you are so abrupt!"
"Old man," Death said, "my coming should be no surprise,
Nor could you ever claim that I have been impatient.
You've lived a century. Find me in Paris two

Such ancient mortals, find me ten in all of France!
You say you should have been much sooner notified
To give you time to wind things up.
And then I should have found your will was signed,
Your grandchild made secure, your house at last complete.
But can you say I did not warn you when the source
Of strength by which you walked and moved,
When your vitality, your grasp,
When all of you has failed? You neither taste nor hear,
And everything you peer at seems to disappear.
For you, the daystar need not take the pains to shine.
You grieve the loss of pleasures you no longer feel,
And you have watched me take your friends,
All dead or dying or infirm.
Now what was all of that, if not a warning sign?
Come on old man, stop arguing.
Although you fail to make a will,
The nation will continue still."

And Death was right. I would desire at such an age
To take my leave of life as from a splendid feast,
Thanking my host, then going promptly on my way –
For how much longer could the journey be postponed?
Still whimpering, old man? Well, see these young men die,
See them go marching, see them run
To deaths that, although truly glorious and brave,
They know are certain and, perhaps, in pain.
But I cannot persuade you – it is not worth trying,
For those most like the dead are most in fear of dying.

VIII. 1

The Cobbler and the Financier

A cobbler sang the livelong day –
What a marvellous sight he was to behold,
What a marvel to hear! Well, he warbled away

180

More content than all the wise sages of old.
His neighbor, by contrast, with riches to spare,
Seldom sang and slept hardly at all:
He was in high finance, a millionaire,
And if by sunrise his eyelids finally started to fall,
The shoemaker's tralalala–ing opened them wide once more.
Till at last the plutocrat started to wonder why
A caring Providence had neglected to think
Of making sleep a commodity one might buy
In the market place, like one's food or one's drink.
He summoned the singer to appear
Before him. "Now, good man," he said, "please specify
The gross amount you earn per year."
"Per year?" the jolly cobbler snorted.
"I don't count up that way. There's nothing to be reported,
No bottom line, no profit growing day by day.
I'm happy if at year end I can say
I'm hanging on. Each day brings in its bread."
"Then tell me what you make per day," the rich man said.
"Some days more, some days less, but one bad thing
          about it –
It is so bad! We'd be much better off without it –
The bad thing is the days stuck all throughout the year
We aren't allowed to work. We're ruined with holy days.
Sir Curate every week packs in more saints to praise."
Amused by his blunt speech, the financier said, "Here,
I wish to change your life, to raise you to a throne.
Within this sack you'll find a hundred gold écus.
Guard them well. They are for you to use
For anything you need." The cobbler imagined there shone
In his two hands more glittering gold
Than all the miners on the earth, all told,
Had dug in a hundred years. Clutching it, he hurried
Back to his house and there in his cellar buried
His hoard of gold and, with it, all his joy and pleasure.
He sang no more: he'd lost his voice
The moment he possessed that which destroys our leisure.
Sleep left his house – it now was residence of choice

For anxious cares, suspicions, a groundless sense of fright.
All day he kept a lookout and, at night,
If some stray cat made noises, creeping,
The cat had got his money! At last he ran, poor man,
Back to the mansion where his woes began,
Where he no longer kept the financier from sleeping.
"Give back my songs!" he cried, "also my nightly snooze!
And here! Take back your gold écus!"

VIII. 2

The Lion, the Wolf, and the Fox

Decrepit, gouty, hardly able still to hobble,
A lion wished to have a cure for old age found.
To tell a king that something is impossible
Is never wise, so orders went around
That every species had to send
A physician to attend
His Highness – and they came, doctors of all descriptions,
Prepared to dose him with prescriptions,
All but the fox, who stayed holed up though not excused.
With fox away from court, the wolf abused
His absent comrade in the monarch's ear,
And soon the offended lion made it loudly known
That Fox must be smoked out and summoned to appear
Before him. This was done. Fox came before the throne,
Certain he saw the wolf's influence here.
"Your Majesty," he said, "I fear a false report
May have been spread about my absence from the court.
The truth is, Sire, I was away
Upon a pilgrimage to pray
For your good health. And I found experts to consult
While traveling, who said there is a way to treat
This languor that, neglected, might, one fears, result
In grave effects. They said a simple loss of heat
Through age has caused the symptoms you have felt.

The cure is simple, too. You take the pelt,
All hot and reeking, from a wolf fresh-skinned alive
And wrap it close around you. The heat you thus derive
Is a most sovereign remedy for age's chill.
That nice Sir Wolf, should you so will,
Can serve your majesty as royal dressing gown."
The lion was pleased by this advice;
The wolf was seized and in a trice
Was flayed, dismembered, carved, and taken down
To bite-sized bits. The monarch dined on wolf ragout
And wore wolf fur around him, too.

Politicians, cease destroying one another;
Try to be statesmen, not assassins of each other.
Your evil deeds outweigh your good by four to one,
But to evildoers evil will be done.
The beckoning path on which you're driven
Ends in a place where none's forgiven.

VIII. 3

The Power of Fables

TO MONSIEUR DE BARILLON

Should a king's ambassador stoop to hear
Small, unheroic stories for the common ear?
What of these slight and playful verses I present?
Will you accept them? And if perhaps at times they dare
Assume a somewhat grander air,
Will you not think them just a shade impertinent?
You've more to do than disentangle
The weasel and rabbit when they wrangle,
But – read their tale or not – prevent,
I beg of you, this continent
From joining arms against us. Let
A thousand enemies, all bent

On our destruction, gather, yet
I'd have no fear, but should the English parliament
Desire our kings to tire of their old friendship – this
Would strike me as much more amiss.
May Louis never rest? What other Hercules
Would not at last grow weary fighting enemies
That, like the Hydra, sprout another head for each
His arm strikes off? If you, so eloquent, so deep
In your resourcefulness, can reach
Into their hearts and mend this rift,
In gratitude I'll sacrifice a hundred sheep
Upon your altar – no small gift
For one who lives upon the steep
Side of Parnassus. In any case,
Do me the honor and the grace
Of willingly accepting this small offering
Of incense, this narrative put into verse I bring
And, with my warmest wishes, dedicate to you.
Its subject suits your task, of which I'll speak no more,
Since I well realize that you find praise a bore –
Praise even the envious must grant that you are due.

In ancient Athens once, a nation
Of a self-regarding, shallow-minded, population,
An orator, perceiving some danger to the state,
Rushed to the agora and in stern tones, with great
Vehemence of passion, attempted to dictate
To their democracy his plan for their salvation.
He was not listened to. So he began again
With rhetoric fit to rouse the sleepiest of men,
Called on dead patriots to make their voices heard.
But though for all his worth he thundered and he dinned,
He found that not one soul was stirred,
His words were lost upon the wind.
The beast of many heads and small intelligence
Was so impervious to his shafts of eloquence
That no one deigned to hear – all looked the other way,

Intent on childish squabbles, not what he had to say.
What did the speaker do? Found a new path to follow.
"Great Ceres," he began, "went journeying one day,
With the wriggling eel and the swift-winged swallow.
They came to a river: the eel swam across, the swallow flew –
And they got over without delay."
"But Ceres," the crowd demanded, "What did Ceres do?"
"What did she do? Grew furious at the lot of you!
That childish tales could set her people so abuzz,
That you of all the Greeks should foolishly ignore
The danger that is at your door.
Why don't you ask of me what conquering Philip does?"
At this reproach the crowd was shaken,
The fable having made them waken:
They listened now with concentration:
All due to fable's fascination.

We're all Athenians in this way, all cousins kin.
And even I, having just dispensed my moral bit,
If I were told the fable of *The Ass's Skin*,
I would with greatest pleasure turn my ear to it.
It's an old world, I grant you, yet each will be beguiled
Till the end of time by stories, forever still a child.

VIII. 4

The Man and the Flea

We nag the gods with our demands on their attention –
And often in matters too trivial for human mention,
For all of us, whatever our situation,
Think deep concern for us is heaven's main obligation
And that, however insignificant we are,
Our tiniest step, our slightest whim – since it is ours –
Should mobilise the pantheon of Olympian powers
As if the Greeks and Trojans once more were at war.

A man – a fool – had his shoulder bitten by a flea
That fled into his rumpled sheets and hid.
"Oh, Hercules," he said, "your duty is to rid
The earth of this new Hydra spring has sprung on me.
And you there, Jupiter. Yes, you! Instead of waiting
Up on that cloud as if there were no tomorrow,
Why aren't you busy exterminating
All of this impudent race with great electric jolts?"
To kill a flea, the fool thought it his right to borrow
The club of Hercules and Jupiter's thunderbolts.

VIII. 5

Women and Secrets

Secrets are heavy – to carry one far
Is more than women have the strength to do.
And, looking at it that way, I would say there are
More than a few men who are women too.

To test his wife in this regard, a husband said,
One night when they were close in bed,
"Oh god, what's happening? The agony! Ooh, awk!
It's splitting me apart! I'm giving birth! Just look!
Look, look! I've laid an egg!" "An egg?" "Right here,
A nice, fresh egg. But listen, dear,
You have to promise me that you won't talk,
Or I'll be called a hen. This must not be revealed."
His wife, to whom the world was new
And full of many wonders, said her lips were sealed.
On every deity she knew
She swore a vow of silence – but this was in the night,
And her vocation vanished with the dawn's first light.
When day had barely broken, up she got,
This eager talker, going at a trot
To see her friend, the wife next door.

"My dear," she said, "what I'm about to tell must not
Go farther, or he'll beat me sore.
My husband laid an egg last night, the size of four,
But in the name of God don't let the news get out!"
"You're joking, aren't you," said her friend. "if you suggest
I'd do that kind of thing. But rest
Assured, you can relax. You have no need to doubt."
The egg producer's wife went home again with pride,
While her excited friend, fired up as she could be,
Went off to spread the tale across the countryside –
But now, for one egg she said three.
And it did not stop there: the girlfriend's friend said four,
A fact she whispered cautiously in every ear –
Though what was there by then to fear
Without a secret any more?
As to how many eggs, the power of fame was such
That, mouth by mouth, their number grew
And by the time the day was through
There were a hundred in the clutch.

VIII. 6

The Dog Who Carried His Master's Dinner on His Neck

With visions of fair women always in their eyes
And with their hands caught up in money's calculation,
Few men guard the treasures they should prize
With adequate determination.

A dog was bringing his master's dinner home from town
In a large basket, its handle hung around his neck.
It smelled so good! He would have loved to wolf it down,
But, showing restraint, he kept his appetite in check,
Unlike our tribe, who, one and all,
When sweet temptation dances near, are prone to fall.

How strange! that dogs might give us lessons in sobriety
That one can't get in man's society.
At any rate, this dog, adorned with such a necklace,
Was set on by a mastiff, eager for the food.
But his attack proved over-optimistic, reckless:
The dog set down his package, growling. There ensued
Fierce combat. Other dogs arrived
And piled into the fracas – those
Mean curs that always have survived
By preying on the public and have small fear of blows.
Our dog was perfectly aware
That if he fought them all he only faced defeat,
And he decided then and there, that since they'd eat
All that there was, he might as well enjoy his share.
And so he wisely told them, "Don't be angry, sirs.
I'll just have my small bite, then you can take the rest."
Then all in turn had at it, the mastiff, then the curs,
Snatching, grabbing, tearing, each doing his crude best,
Convivially feasting, greedy each to take
His share of the communal cake.
I see in all of this the image
Of a human village
Where goods are meted out according to one's rank.
The sheriff, the president of the bank –
Such fellows have their hands in deep. The strongest give
The others lessons in survival. And so they live,
Skimming as they go their heaps of change.
And should some upright person for some strange,
Deluded reason think of challenging their rule,
He soon will learn that he's a fool.
And having learned what is for real
Will often be the first to steal.

                                                              VIII. 7

The Joker and the Fishes

Everyone loves a joker, but not I, however.
It takes great gifts, the highest art, this being clever.
For fools alone God made these pests
Who torture humor with their jests.
I've often wished to try a fable
To illustrate the type. Perhaps someone who reads
This one may say, perhaps, if the attempt succeeds.

At an investment banker's table,
A joker, far from the head of it, was passed a platter
Of little fish – the big ones had long since been taken.
He held the dish up close and was observed to mutter
Some words at it, then put it by his ear and listen –
Now he had the group's attention.
The room fell silent with suspense –
At which the joker, speaking in tones of utter
Gravity, explained that, out of his intense
Concern that a dear friend had possibly been wrecked
In sailing to the Indies over a year ago,
He'd asked these fish if they had news to this effect.
Alas, they'd told him that they were too small to know
Of times so distant. But it was their group's suggestion
That bigger fish were likelier to know his fate.
"Has anyone," he asked, "a big one I might question?"
How amused all were I'm not prepared to state,
But in response they served a monster on his plate
So huge, so old, it must long since have learned
The name of every dreamer who had ever yearned
For unknown worlds, then sailed away and not returned –
And who, eyeless for centuries, within the steep
Abyss stared at the ancient emperors of the deep.

VIII. 8

The Rat and the Oyster

A rat of cornfield habitat, not much for brains,
One day found life so boring on the old homestead
He chucked it all – cornfield, corn shocks, the endless *grains* –
Abandoning his rathole to tour the land instead.
When he had barely stuck his nose out, "Gracious!"
He said, "The world is just so big, so huge, so spacious!
There's the Caucasus, and there the Apennines arise."
(The slightest molehill was a mountain in his eyes.)
Then several days on, the traveler reached
A sandy shore where there lay beached
Great scads of oysters that the sea had brought –
A fleet of sailing ships, was his first thought.
"Certes," quoth he, "My father was a paltry sire.
He dared not go abroad – a thorough coward he.
But I, I have beheld the maritime empire,
I have crossed deserts where no drop to drink had we."
He'd heard some country pedagogue once spout
Such bits that made him keen to tour about –
Not being the sort of scholar rat who merely gnaws
On books, and so knows nothing deeper than his jaws.
Among a host of oysters lying closed was one
That lay completely open, yawning at the sun,
Brushed by the gentle breeze, happily beaming,
Breathing in tiny sips of air, its countenance gleaming,
So plump, so white, and succulent beyond compare.
Now when the rat perceived the oyster yawning there,
"What's this I spy?" said he. "It looks like tasty fare.
And if the dish should prove as toothsome as it looks,
The feast I have today should be one for the books."
At which young master rat crept soft across the ground
Anticipating pleasure, waving his tail around –
When, suddenly, he felt it caught within a trap
As, once again, the oyster, with a stupendous snap,
Reclosed – pure ignorance the cause of his mishap.

This fable holds more than one lesson: first, we learn
That those who lack all worldly grounding
May find the commonest things astounding.
And, following this, we also can discern
A truth that should be widely taught:
He who would catch is often caught.

VIII. 9

The Bear and the Gardener

A certain bear, a craggy sort, unlicked and crude,
Consigned by fate to life in mountain solitude,
Was slowly going mad – not so extraordinary,
Since prisoners lose their reason, kept in solitary.
For although speech is good and silence better still,
Both have malign effects if carried to excess.
No beast or bird made sounds to fill
The silence of that wilderness
The bear inhabited until,
Bear though he was, he found himself completely bored
With such a lonely life. Meanwhile, near that same spot
An old man lived who was as bored with his own lot –
Although he did what he adored,
Which was to garden. He could well have been a priest
Of Flora and Pomona, goddesses that bring
Spring flowers to bloom and autumn fruits to ripening:
A splendid occupation, but I'd prefer at least
To share my garden with a close, considerate friend –
For gardens never speak, unless within this book –
And feeling thus, our bored old fellow one day took
Leave of his mute charges and started off to look
For company. With that same thought in mind, the bear
Upon that very day had started to descend
His mountain and the two met, coming round a bend.
The man recoiled in fear. How could he hide, and where?
What should he do? He had no way to disappear.

At times like this the tactic that works best is sheer
Bravado, like a Gascon's, so he hid his fear.
The bear, no good at greetings, growled, "Come visit me!"
The man replied, "Great Sir, you see
In the near distance there my humble habitation,
Where it would greatly honor one of my low station
Were you to share, upon the grass, a light collation.
I have milk; I have fruit: perhaps not quite the sort of diet
Your Bearnesses are used to, but please come and try it."
The bear said yes; they went. And by the time the pair
Had reached his place, the two had bonded, man and bear.
And though it's clearly better to be
Alone than with some chattering booby,
That wouldn't be a problem, since the bear might utter
Two words a day at very most,
Which meant the man would be at liberty to putter
About his garden while his partner was engrossed
With hunting game or chasing off those pesky creatures –
Which we call flies – that lit upon his dear friend's features
As he lay napping. And so one day when one of those
Annoying parasites lit smack upon the nose
Of the old man as he was taking his siesta –
It was the stinging kind, a most egregious pest, a
Vicious thing – the bear got mad. "I'll fix it good!"
The stout fly catcher said. "And this is how I'll do it!"
With that, he grabbed a boulder with his forepaws, stood
On his hind legs and, using all his strength, he threw it,
Straight downward, managing in the event to smush
The fly and, with good aim and rotten logic, crush
His poor friend's skull and lay him out in rigor mortis.

The lesson here, summed up in short, is:
An ignorant friend can often be
More dangerous than one's most hostile enemy.

VIII. 10

The Two Friends

In Monomotapa lived two true friends, so true
That nothing one possessed was not the other's, too.
For friends were every bit as dear
In that far place, they say, as here.
One night, when each was busy sleeping soundly
And putting to good use the absence of the sun,
One of them woke, alarmed, then hurried at a run
Straight to the other's gate and, shouting roundly,
Aroused the servants snoring in the castle hall
Where Morpheus had tiptoed in and touched them all.
His sleeping friend awoke, took up his purse and sword
And let him in. He said, "You seldom roam abroad
When others sleep; I've always held you of that number
Who set high value on their hours of slumber.
Have you perhaps lost all your fortune in some game?
Here's mine. Or must you duel to defend your name?
Then you must take my sword.
Or are you simply feeling bored
With sleeping all alone? I had a pretty slave
In bed beside me. I'll call her if it's she you crave."
"Dear friend," he said, "my want's not it or that or she.
I thank you though for your concern for me.
I saw you in my sleep, and you seemed sadly grave,
And so I hurried here for fear it might be true.
My silly dream has prompted all this wild to-do."

A subtle question, reader, but worth examining:
Which would you say showed more affection on his part?
A veritable friend is, oh, how fine a thing!
He looks for your true needs within your deepest heart
And spares your having to spell out
Emotions hard to speak about.
Some dream, some trifle scarcely worth the thinking of –
We fear whatever touches someone whom we love.

VIII. 11

The Goat, the Sheep, and the Pig

In a high–wheeled cart together, jaunting to the fair,
Rode a goat, a sheep and a pig – but business took
    them there,
Not pleasure: they were for sale is how this story goes –
The driver hadn't the least intent
Of treating them all to puppet shows.
Friar Pork kept squealing as they went,
As if a hundred butchers had him by the tail;
His clamor was enough to make one's hearing fail.
The other two, by nature not so apprehensive,
Were startled by his cries for help. They had no fears
Of awful things to come. "This uproar is offensive!"
The coachman told the pig, "You're deafening our ears!
Just what is your excuse? Why such ungodly noise?
These two good folks, both better–bred than you,
Might teach you etiquette. Where is your equipoise?
Look at this sheep. Has she made a to–do?
She hasn't made a peep, not even once.
She is wise to keep quiet." "She's a dunce!"
The pig replied. "If she knew what's in store
She'd scream like me, till her lungs were sore.
And this other oaf would scream in dread
At the very top of her stupid head.
They think someone will only want to pull
From the goat her milk, from the sheep her wool.
Well, I don't know – they may be right. But, as for me,
Since edibility
Is all that I am good for, it is certain
I'll soon be taking my final curtain."

The pig's conclusion was sharply logical,
But what good did that do? When evil
Must come, to weep and tremble changes nothing.
The wisest then is the least foreknowing.

VIII. 12

Thyrsis and Amaranth

FOR MADEMOISELLE DE SILLERY

I'd put Aesop aside
To rhyme Boccaccio,
But then a goddess cried,
"Aesop must stay, not go!"
(She loved my fables so.)
Well, simply to say no
With unexcused impunity
Is hardly a wise course
To take with a divinity,
Particularly one
Whose beauty tends to stun
A mortal with its force.
And that, as we might know,
Is Sillery, who wants
The Messrs. Wolf and Crow
To stay in their old haunts
And speak through me in rhyme.
Sillery! Paradigm
Of beauty's power, few
Men are so sternly steeled
They would not humbly yield,
As to a queen, to you.
For what else could they do?
But to go on. You find
My fables too obscure;
Well, since the brightest mind
May sometimes be unsure
About what things may mean,
The stories I'll tell next
Will need no notes to glean
The meaning of each text:
The first shows shepherds in a sylvan scene, and then
The wolves and sheep will speak in poetry again.

"Ah, Amaranth!" the shepherd Thyrsis sighed one day
To that young shepherdess. "If only you might catch it,
This same enchanting sickness that I've got, you'd say
That there could be no pleasure on this earth to match it.
Please let me show you with what bliss it can affect you –
I swear to you it's nothing you need be afraid of.
Would I wish to deceive you? I totally respect you
With all the sweetest sentiments true hearts are made of!"
And Amaranth at once replied,
"What does one call this sickness? Has it got a name?"
"It's love!" "A pretty word. But how is it identified?
What symptoms does one feel?" "You ache with a sweet flame
Beside which any monarch's royal pomp and treasure
Is lifeless stuff. You lose your mind! You can find pleasure
Lost in the woods alone, where if you chance to look
Into the mirror of a brook
It's not your own but someone else's face
You'll see in it and will keep seeing everyplace,
While having no eyes for the rest.
I know a certain shepherd just that way obsessed
With still another shepherd in the village here,
Whose voice or name or simply being there, close by,
Makes that first shepherd blush and sigh
Both from desire and timorous fear."
And then came Amaranth's reply,
"Oh, oh! Is that the sickness that you warned about?
It's nothing new to me. I think I've caught it too!"
And Thyrsis thought his scheme to woo
Had won, till Amaranth blurted out,
"That's just the way I feel for Clidamant!" And Thyrsis
Went on his way, frustrated and with many curses.

Many who hope that their selfish actions
Will gain them wealth through sharp transactions
Often fill other people's purses.

VIII. 13

196

The Lion Queen's Funeral

When the lion's mate died
The animals hastened to his side
To do their duty by their chief
By mouthing those polite cliché's of consolation
That only add more weight to grief.
The monarch notified his nation
That at said time, said place, all might attend the grand
Imperial rites of lamentation.
His ministers would be on hand
To usher in the congregation.
Who could refuse such a commanding invitation?
The time arrived. Within his den – for a lion the same
As his cathedral – the ruler wailed. About him, howling,
Barking, braying, hooting, each in his fashion yowling,
His court did as he did, until the noise became
Unutterably deafening.
What is a court? I see it as a polity
Whose members – happy, sad, of every quality
From eager to apathetic – seek to please their king
By feeling as he feels or, failing to, still try,
Chameleons by nature, pet apes that imitate
Their master, whose one spirit serves to animate
A thousand mindless bodies. It is at court, say I,
That men most plausibly might seem to be machines,
Automatons, mere ticking clockworks figurines.
But back to our tale. Amidst the weepers, there was one
Who stood unmoved: the stag shed not a single tear.
What else, indeed, should he have done?
This death for him was sweet revenge. In the past year
The lioness had strangled both his wife and son.
And so, no tears, not one. Some toady saw and told.
And even lied that he had laughed! As Solomon said,
The anger of a king is fearful to behold –
A lion king's, especially. But this stag seldom read.
"Ignoble backwoods thing," roared the lion, seeing red,

197

"Instead of keening with these others, you profane
Our sorrow with rude laughter. But we will not deign
To soil our sacred claws on you. Wolves, never falter!
Avenge the queen! Tear him apart upon the altar
To please her guardian spirits!" To which the stag replied,
"Great Sire, we are past those mourning hours!
All sorrow is now out of date. Your late, fair bride
Appeared to me near here upon a bed of flowers.
I knew at once that it was she. She said. 'I pray,
Dear friend, that you will see to it that when I mount
To join the gods, no one will weep on my account.
For now amongst Elysian Fields I gladly stray,
Conversing with saintly souls like me along the way.
Yet let the king still mourn my passing for a time,
For that well pleaseth me.'" The words were barely out
When everyone began to shout,
"A miracle! Her earthly form has grown sublime!"
And the stag was now rewarded, not punished for a crime.

When you've done something to offend
A king and he grows pettishly irate,
Be sure to dangle before his eyes
Amusing dreams, sweet flatteries and pleasant lies,
And after he gobbles down your bait
You'll find you have become his friend.

VIII. 14

The Rat and the Elephant

In France, men often act like big celebrities
When they are rank nonentities –
A trait so common in our nation
It should be called the French disease.
The Spanish have it too, but in a variation:
Their pride is of a different strain,

Much crazier, but not so vain.
Let us now see an image of our own.

A rat of the smallest size encountered an elephant
Of the most corpulent
And he proceeded to disparage
The ponderous gait of the beast of such majestic carriage,
Who had on his huge back bestowed
A staggering three–layered load.
As he came swaying down the street,
Upon the highest story perched
A sultaness; below her, lurched
Her cat, her dog, her parakeet,
Her jester ape, her ladies maid
And all her household staff. The rodent was dismayed
To see the awed respect that all the world displayed.
"It is as if the space one's body occupies –
However large or small – must surely signalise
One's level of importance. But that is wrong, so why
Do all you humans act so thrilled as he goes by?
Is it his massive bulk, which makes small children cry?
Whatever our size, I say, each one's significance
Is every bit as great as any elephant's."
He would have continued his eloquence
But the cat got loose and in an instant
Proved that a rat's no elephant.

VIII. 15

The Horoscope

On roads men take to flee their fates,
They frequently discover destiny awaits.

A noble had one child, a son he loved too well.
To hear what perils were in store for him he went

199

To an astrologer and asked him to foretell
The dangers in his path, which knowing might prevent.
He was advised his son must stay
Far from all lions till a certain age – in fact,
Till he turned twenty (the prediction was exact).
Believing it the only way
That would with certainty ensure
That his dear child would live protected and secure,
He ordered that the boy must never, till that day,
Set foot outside the palace, where there was ample space
To gather with his friends, to laugh, to romp, to race.
Then when he had begun to reach
That age when youthful spirits burn to join the chase,
The father told the household everyone must teach
The boy to scorn such sport. But though
They lectured, counseled, preached and pleaded
No argument they made succeeded,
For, as anyone might know,
There is no changing temperament.
The young man, restless, reckless, more obstinately bent
On doing the forbidden the more it was denied him,
With all his new emotions boiling up inside him,
Was keen to try those dangerous pleasures.
He knew what he was kept from by the fear of fate:
For in that house, among its treasures,
Were myriads of pictures, hung in every room –
Some painted upon canvas, some woven on a loom:
Bright landscapes of the peopled world beyond the gate
Or scenes where men chased beasts across the countryside.
A picture of a lion roused his indignation.
"You ugly monster! It is due to you," he cried,
"That I must live imprisoned in dark isolation!"
With every word he spoke the rage he felt increased
Till with his fist at last he struck the harmless beast.
Beneath the tapestry a hidden nail projected,
Which pierced his hand and left him mortally infected.
And that dear head, in spite of all the doctors tried,
Was lost, due to the efforts on the father's side

To keep his child from harm. And just the same mistake
Did Aeschylus in. When an oracle, so it was said,
Warned that a house someday would fall upon his head,
He moved outdoors beneath the sky, for fear a quake
Would bring his roof around his ears if he stayed home.
One day an eagle, flying with a tortoise caught
In its huge talons, saw the playwright's hairless dome
And, thinking it the rock outcropping that it sought
With which to smash the tortoise's hard house, let go
Of it and finished off poor Aeschylus below.
These two examples should make clear
That horoscopes, if true, would make
Those who believe them victims of the ills they fear.
But they're absolved of blame, for, as I'll show, they're fake.
I cannot think that Nature has in any wise
Tied her own hands, nor tied our own so fixedly
That we can read our destinies within the skies.
From persons, places and the times – from all these three
In all of their conjoinings do we realise
Our fates, not from conjunctions astrologists expound.
Although a shepherd and a king might well be bound
By birth to the same planet, one will come to hold
A shepherd's crook, and one a scepter made of gold.
And why? Great Jupiter wills it. But what is Jupiter?
A mindless body. By what means then may one infer
That it affects these men in two such different ways?
How could it influence this distant world of ours?
How permeate all things, projected here from Mars,
From the sun's orb or the deep void of endless space?
An atom's difference at the source
Would send it on a different course
Those charlatans would find impossible to trace.
With all the recent grave events
In Europe, it would seem that one
Of all that lot would have seen warning evidence
Among the planets, yet how many have? Why, none!
Can shifting points of light at that enormous distance
Provide these weak observers insight by their motions

Into our own inconstant, retrograde emotions?
They claim their orbits govern all of our existence.
But they cannot. No more than we do they maintain
A steady path. Yet these men feign
That with their compasses they can
Scribe out the fate of every man,
A claim that's no more truthful than
The dubious tales I've told – the one
About the too–well–cherished son
Or that of Aeschylus: astrology, though blind
And totally mendacious, by accident is bound
In every thousand tries to find
At least one answer that is sound.

VIII. 16

The Ass and the Dog

Each one must help the other: that's the law of nature,
And yet the ass defied it once –
Though why, I can't imagine, since
He's such an inoffensive creature.
Untouched by any thought, but gravely dignified,
The ass was once proceeding through the countryside
Companioned by the dog and followed by their master.
The master paused to nap, the ass began to pasture
Within the meadow where he slept.
Such tasty greens he saw – except
There were no thistles. Yet, why act
So finicky always? Though it lacked
That special dish, the meal would serve.
One small omission from a feast
Would not deter him in the least
And he began to graze with verve.
At which the dog, near perishing with hunger, said,
"Dear friend, stoop down a bit so I can take some bread
Out of that pannier on your back." He went unheard.

The ass grazed on determinedly, without a word,
Unwilling to give up the chance for one more bite.
But finally he answered, "Friend, I would advise you
To wait till Master wakes and he will give you quite
The usual amount he normally supplies you.
He should be waking soon enough."
But meanwhile, from the nearby wood
Emerged one more voracious beast, a wolf
Who soon approached them as they stood.
"Oh, please protect me, dog," the ass begged instantly.
The dog moved not a muscle. "Friend," he said, "I would
Advise you rapidly to flee
Till Master finishes his nap. I'm sure that he
Is going to wake up soon enough.
And, meanwhile, if somehow the wolf
Should overtake you, a good blow
Straight to the jaw with your new shoes will lay him low,
Believe you me." But as the dog's fine blather filled
His ears with nonsense, the wolf attacked him, he was killed.

Each one must help the other: I said it and it's so.

VIII. 17

The Pasha and the Merchant

In Turkish lands, a Greek with goods to trade
Had his path smoothed by a great pasha's aid –
For which it was a pasha's price he paid,
Not a mere merchant's. Feeling much dismayed,
The Greek would often shake his head and sigh,
"Protectors are expensive things to buy."
Three lesser Turks approached him. Though each lacked
The pasha's power singly, if they backed
His enterprise, they claimed, their strengths combined
Would do as much yet cost him less, he'd find.
Impressed, the Greek agreed to pay their fee.

This was reported to the pasha. He
Was told he would be wise to play these three
Some little trick that sent them soaring straight
To paradise with a nice message to
Mohammed. He must act at once, not wait,
Since otherwise, united, they would do
The same to him. For, surely, they had heard
That there were men about who at his word
Would take revenge upon them. Thus, a cup
Laced with some poison soon might send him up
Instead, to govern things in paradise.
The pasha listened to this good advice,
Then, much like Alexander who, when warned
Of treachery by his physician, laughed
And carelessly drank off the proffered draught
Of medicine, so he now coolly scorned
All show of caution and confidently strode
To supper at the merchant's, where he showed
Such self-assuredness in words and actions
One could not have believed that he felt fear.
"My friend," he told the Greek, "it would appear
That you no longer want my benefactions.
And my advisers tell me I must be
Concerned with what may follow. But to me
You seem a man of conscience who would shrink
From giving any guest a deadly drink.
I think no ill of you. As to these three
Who offer to supplant me with their joint
Protection, rather than take the risk of boring
You with such reasons as might set you snoring,
I'll tell you a tale that's short and to the point.

A shepherd had a mastiff dog to guard his sheep.
Somebody asked him whether it was wise to keep
A brute that ate a loaf of bread
At every single meal. What he should do instead
Was give it to the village squire
And then in place of it acquire

Two smaller dogs, or even three.
For it would cost him less to keep three small dogs fed
Than one that big. Besides, the three of them would be
Better than one at watching. Yet none perceived the flaw
In this advice: although he ate more than the three,
He had, for fighting wolves, a three times bigger jaw.
The shepherd gave the beast away
And got three little dogs instead
Whose size saved him a lot of bread
But who ran fast from any fray.
The flock was much diminished, as you yourself will be
Should you go with such rabble. But if you are wise
You will return to me."
The Greek believed him. The moral of this tale applies
As well to nations small in size,
Which when all's said and done might just as well submit
To some great super power's writ
As to make pacts with many other weak allies.

VIII. 18

The Usefulness of Learning

In ancient times a quarrel began
Between two townsmen. One, though poor,
Was an accomplished, literate man,
And one, though rich, an ignorant boor.
The second, hoping he might cow
His rival, haughtily professed
That all who were wise would surely bow
Before the fortune he possessed –
"All who were fools" would have been more
To the point, for who can be impressed
By wealth alone, devoid of merit at its core?
He frequently was heard to rant
At the savant,
"You think yourself a man worth heeding –

But who frequents your dining table?
What use is all your endless reading, reading, reading,
Shivering in your garret up beneath the gable,
Wearing in December what you wore in May,
And none to serve as your valet
But your thin shadow? This republic
Has all too many of you types who never spend.
What we need, I say, to benefit the public,
Is men who scatter riches with an open hand.
God knows they are useful! We give employment
To artisans, merchants, those who make skirts
And those who wear them – saucy flirts! –
By what we do for our enjoyment.
And it is we to whom your books are dedicated,
Execrably written, well remunerated."
Such words, impertinent in the extreme, soon met
The sort of fate that they richly deserved to get.
The scholar held his tongue – he had too much to say.
A war broke out that punished his detractor worse
Than any satire done in verse.
Their town was taken, the two men fled away.
Now, at whatever door he knocked,
The ignorant man found his entry blocked;
The smart one, on the other hand,
Found his talent and learning in much demand,
Which made him the victor in their quarrel.

Moral:
Ignorance may talk but learning pays its way.

VIII. 19

Jupiter and the Thunderbolts

Enraged by our constant sinning,
Jupiter one day roared,
"It's time for a new beginning!

I'll expunge this ill-behaved horde
That never leaves me in peace
And people the lands where they dwell
With a less troublesome race.
Mercury, go to Hell
And fetch me that Fury – she,
The cruelest of the three.
Oh, race I have loved too well,
This time you're going to get it!"
But then, once having exploded,
Jupiter promptly subsided.
You, kings he has sent us, by whom
Our lives and our fates are guided,
Between the onset of anger
And the storm that threatens doom
Leave one night's breathing room.
The god whose wings are agile
And whose tongue is smoothly clever
Flew off to the three dark sisters.
Among them he chose neither
Tisiphone nor Megaera
But pitiless Alecto,
Whose pride at being chosen
Led her to swear by Pluto
That the mongrel swarm called human
Would instantly be hurled
To the depths of the nether world!
But having now changed his mind
Jupiter reconsigned
Her to Hades' abyss – yet aimed
One angry bolt at a nation
Of treachers, here unnamed.
Now, since those beneath the fire
Of his stupendous ire
Were children of his creation,
He sent his lightning wide
To burn desolate countryside,
And leave them terrified

Yet safe from the conflagration –
A father strikes to one side.
Then, what resulted? Our breed,
Only made bold by the deed,
Continued its age–old tricks,
So offending the other gods
That the ruler of the clouds,
To appease them promised, by Styx,
He would raise a storm once more
And smash us this time for sure –
Which was met with Olympian laughter.
It would, said the gods, be better
If one who was not their begetter
Would do it, with other weapons.
Clearly, the task was Vulcan's.
He found, to load in his mortars,
Two kinds of boulders. The first
Are the lesser gods' missiles – once sent,
These never deflect till they burst
On the mortals for whom they were meant.
The second, however, may swerve
And, sometimes, missing their mark,
They will for an instant serve
To light the surrounding dark
As, harming none with their streaks,
They crash upon distant peaks.
Know then: these latter are thrown
By great Jupiter alone.

VIII. 20

The Falcon and the Capon

A voice will often call you, full of guile and cunning,
But if one does do not come running:
Be like Jack Neville's dog: if Jack called, "Good boy, here!"
The dog, no fool, turned a deaf ear.

A citizen of Le Mans, one of the capon guild,
Was forthwith summoned to be tried
At a tribunal held inside
His master's house (in fact, the hearthfire) and there grilled.
Although the servants sent to catch him said, "Here chick,
Nice chicky, here nice chick," attempting to disguise
Their true intentions, this Norman–and–a–half was wise
To them and let them call. "Too obvious, you guys,"
He clucked. "You'll never catch me with that stupid trick,
And for good reason." Meanwhile, on its perch nearby
A falcon sat and watched him fleeing.
Whether from instinct or from sad experience,
No capon has much faith in any human being,
And this one, averse to being caught at all events,
Would have next day been guest of honor at a feast
While resting on a plate, an honor not the least
Attractive to a chicken's mind.
The bird of prey addressed him: "I'm astonished by
Your lack of understanding. You're of that ignorant kind,
Thick–witted, cowardly. However one may try
There is no teaching such low types. Yet I, I fly
Into the sky and hunt, but then I know to land
When master calls, on his gloved hand.
There he is now, at the window, watching. Don't you hear?
Are you deaf? He calls you!" The capon said, "I understand
Too well why he is calling. Isn't it all too clear
What he intends, he and that big knife–wielding cook?
Would you come to that wheedling, *cluck, cluck, cluck*?
Just let me flee and do not jeer
At my impulse to flight the moment that I hear
Such dulcet voices calling. If falcons were one bit
As likely every day to end up on a spit
As capons are, you'd not reproach me for my fear."

VIII. 21

209

The Cat and the Rat

A queer quartet of creatures: Clipperclaw the cat,
The melancholy owl, sharp Nibbleknot the rat
And gaunt Dame Weasel of the sinuous body –
Rascals all four, whose ethics were shoddy –
Dwelt in the hollow trunk of an old, gnarled pine.
Their doings brought a human with his nets one night
To weave a trap about them, of malign design.
Next morning at the dawn's first light
The cat stole out while it was yet too dark to see
And she was snared – soon destined to be fur, no doubt.
The cat began to yowl, the rat came rushing out,
One in despair, the other in glee –
For there in the snare his worst enemy lay!
The cat began to plead, "Dear friend,
Where I come from folks all say
That you have done kind deeds no end.
So help me leave this trap where fatal circumstance
Has put me. What a lucky chance
That it is you of all your family I've had
This strange attraction to! I know I must seem mad,
But I adore you. There! I've said it and I'm glad.
I thank the gods for it, and pray
To them as holy cats all do at break of day.
I am enmeshed. My very life is yours to guard.
Prithee, undo these knots!" "Just what is the reward
You promise me?" the rat replied.
"I swear to be, upon my side,
Forever allied to you!" the cat declared.
"For your defense alone will my sharp claws be bared.
I care not who may threaten you, he'll feel my steel.
The weasel who would eat you up,
The horrid hootowl who would sup
Upon your flesh, will rue the day!" Said Rat, "Get real!
Me be your liberator? I'm not so dumb as that!"
And down he scuttled, toward his hole,

Where, just outside, the weasel sat.
Next, he fled upwards. There sat the owl.
Now, since the direst danger is the one to flee,
The rat ran back at once to help the cat get free.
He gnawed one knot and then another, round and round,
Until the net was naught, the hypocrite unbound –
When, suddenly, out sprang the man!
At which our new allies took to their paws and ran.
Time passed, the crisis faded, life returned to normal.
Out for the air one day, the cat professed surprise
At seeing the rat slip by him, acting stiff and formal.
"Dear brother-in-arms!" he cried. "Do you not recognize
Your old ally? You act as though
I were your foe. Your coldness cuts me like a knife.
Embrace me! Would I forget you saved my life?"
"And I?" the rat replied. "Could I also
Forget your nature? No treaty on this earth
Could make a cat be grateful. What are assurances worth?
Can one ever rely in any degree
On alliances formed through necessity?"

VIII. 22

The Torrent and the River

Roaring and churning in its bed,
A stream rushed off a mountainside,
A horrifying torrent: in its path all fled;
It set fields trembling, far and wide.
No traveller had yet dared try
To pass the barrier it made
Until, pursued by bandits, hoping not to die,
One rider plunged across, though mortally afraid.
He found its noisy threat mere froth and shallowness,
The danger only in his mind.
And so, encouraged by success,
He galloped on, the bandits still somewhere behind.

At last he reached a different stream,
A placid river, scarcely flowing, lost in sleep,
A crossing any child could manage, it would seem,
Its banks soft sand, not rock, and gently sloped, not steep.
He entered, and his horse soon carried him away
Beyond the reach of thieves, but not of that dark flow.
Both steed and rider drank the Styx's undertow.
Poor swimmers come to grief, now they
Fled on through shadows deep below
To cross far other rivers than the ones we know.

Be wary of the quiet kind;
The other sort – pay them no mind.

VIII. 23

Education

Lardcan and Caesar, pups of a single litter,
Descended from famous dogs, winners at many shows,
Were reared by different masters in dissimilar manners.
One roamed the wild forests, one lay by the kitchen stove.
Each at the first was called a different name,
But variance of nurture
Gave to the one a valiant nature
And softened the other – a kitchen scullion
Gave him the nickname, Lardcan.
His brother chased through many a high adventure,
Brought countless stags to bay and finished many a boar.
He was the primal Caesar of all the canine race
And proper care was taken that no illbred bitch
Would taint the pedigree with her unworthy blood –
While Lardcan, neglected, bestowed his tender attention
On any object straying past.
He spawned the numerous race
Of kitchen curs so common here in France,

A gutless bunch that runs from any hint of danger,
Creatures the antipodes of Caesars.

Great fathers may produce dim-witted sons,
Soft living and bad unions have ruined the noblest lines.
When nature and its gifts are lightly tossed away,
How many Caesars are transfomed to Lardcans.

VIII. 24

The Two Dogs and the Dead Ass

If the virtues are sisters, then no doubt
The vices are a pack of brothers:
The moment one of them invades our hearts the others
At once come crowding in; not one may be kept out –
And certainly not those most apt to live
Beneath one roof, cooperative.
Yet as regards the virtues, seldom will they stay
Together in one person at their fullest sway;
As firmly as one grasps them, they will slip away –
So courage may turn testy and wise prudence cold.
Among the animals, the dog has been extolled
For watchful loyalty but can
Be a fool and a glutton as much as a man.

Witness this pair of mastiffs on a beach. They see,
A long way off, afloat upon the waves, a dead
Jackass, whose corpse the wind is pushing out to sea.
"Pal, you have better eyes than me," the first one said.
"Just for a second, would you care to cast your glance
Way out across that vast and featureless expanse?
Is that an ox? A horse, maybe?"
"Hey, what's the difference, partner? Meat is meat!" replied
The other mastiff. "But the question to decide
Is how we get it. It is far away and we

Will have to swim upwind. Well, here is what I think.
We open our thirsty throats and drink
All of that water in until the corpse has floated
Back here upon the sand and soon, when it has dried,
We will be plentifully supplied
With rations for a week." They drank until, too bloated
Even to breathe, they burst and in an instant died.

Man is the same. Aflame with some great prospect, he
Has not a clue to its impossibility.
How endlessly we pray, what years we dedicate
To the pursuit of wealth or an exalted rank.
"Supposing I had piles of money in the bank!
Vast acres swelling my estate!
Supposing I learned Hebrew! History! What if I
Would study science!" And what if you drank the ocean dry?
Man never will be satisfied.
To realize the projects flowing from one brain
Would take four bodies' efforts, nicely unified.
Yet even then I would maintain
That, barely halfway done, their energies would wane.
Though four Methusalehs back to back assumed the role,
They'd never content one dreaming soul.

VIII. 25

Democritus and the Abderites

The common crowd's opinions are my lifelong bane!
How rashly formed they seem, how biased, how profane.
Perceiving all things dimly, having veiled their eyes,
The masses measure others by their own small size.

This was a lesson Epicurus once was taught
As a disciple of Democritus, in Thrace,
In the city state of Abdera. Its people thought
Democritus was mad. Such a small-minded place!

Why would they think so? Well, recall that old refrain:
At home, no man's a prophet. Nonetheless, it turned
Out they were all the mad ones, Democritus was sane.
Misjudging him, the Abderites became concerned
And sent off emissaries to Hippocrates
Imploring him to come and find
Some way of curing poor Democritus's disease.
"Our fellow citizen," they said, "has lost his mind.
Reading has ruined Democritus.
If he knew less he'd have more sympathy from us.
There are more worlds, he claims, in number infinite,
And each of them may have in it
Another Democritus. But not content with such
Odd fantasies he adds a more fantastic touch:
The atoms, invisible offspring of a fevered brain.
And he imagines as he sits there that he flies
Across all space, this judge whose wise
Decisions mended our disputes. Yet now, insane,
He babbles to himself. He knows the universe,
Himself he does not know. Divine physician, please
Return with us, before his madness grows yet worse!"
Though little trusting in these men, Hippocrates
Sailed with them. And – confirming yet again how great
A role chance plays – just as the traveler was landing,
The man supposed to lack all sense and understanding
Had just begun to contemplate
The seat of consciousness in animals and man.
Where can it be? The heart? The head? He sat in shade
Examining a brain's deep maze; beside him ran
A brook and at his feet were laid
A multitude of books. As usual immersed
In thought, he scarcely roused himself at first
At his old friend's approach. Their greetings,
As one would certainly expect of wise men's meetings,
Husbanded time and words. And then the two conversed
With eloquent reasoning on man and mind, which led
In turn to ethics. But all they said
Scarcely needs here to be rehearsed.

Is it the case, as I have read,
That God's voice is the people's voice? If it were so,
They'd be infallible. But this tale serves to show
That they are not. The answer is no.

VIII. 26

The Wolf and the Hunter

Foul rage to pile up wealth, blind monster lying curled
Around those precious goods the gods provide the world,
Must all my works and words against you come to naught?
How long before you learn the lessons I have taught?
Can man, as deaf to me as to the ancient sages,
Not tell himself at last, "I have well earned my wages;
Now I'll enjoy their fruits!" Friend, you must hurry then
For life is all too short. I'll say that word again,
A word that's worth a book: Enjoy! "I will!" But when?
"Starting tomorrow." Friend, remember that death may,
Be waiting on the road. You must begin today
Lest you should meet a fate as miserably gory
As that of the greedy hunter in the following story.
Aiming his crossbow he brought down a deer, a doe;
A fawn ran past; again, he shot; it fell also,
Still at its mother's side, stretched out upon the ground,
A kill that a more modest hunter would have found
Sufficient, doe and fawn. But then, from the deep wood
A boar, immense, superb, stepped into view and stood,
A prize too tempting to give up. He cocked his bow
Then sent another creature past the Styx – although
For once Fate found her shears too dull to cut the thread.
Time after time she tried but, very far from dead,
The wounded monster lay defiant as it bled.
Now he had game enough, but there's no satisfying
The appetite for conquest: as the boar lay dying
He saw a little partridge, bobbing its humble head

216

As it moved slowly down the length
Of the furrowed field beyond. But as the archer drew
The bowstring taut again, the boar with its last strength
Got up and, charging, slashing, with its great tusks slew
Its foe and fell upon him, dead. The partridge flew.
This fable treated covetousness in that first section;
This final part holds avarice up for your inspection:

A wolf who happened on this scene of carnage said,
"Oh, Fortune! For this gift, I promise in your name
To dedicate a shrine. Four bodies! And all dead!
Quite suddenly I have grown rich! But, just the same,
I'd better ration them. It isn't every day
One has this kind of luck." (The miserly often say
This sort of thing to rationalize.) "I have got more
Than enough to last a month at least,"
He told himself. "One body; two; three bodies; four,
If I have counted right. For four whole weeks I'll feast,
Starting day after tomorrow – meanwhile, I will first
Eat this small string off this bow thing – it has to be catgut;
By its smell I know it is nothing but."
And with these words he bit the bow,
Which shot an arrow through his tripes and laid him low.

Which brings me to my theme: this life must be enjoyed –
As shown by these two dunces, both of them self-destroyed:
The first by greediness undone,
While stinginess killed the other one.

VIII. 27

Book Nine

The Faithless Trustee

By the Muses' favoring
I have been inspired to sing
Of mute animals: my name
Might have gathered, had I sung
Of speaking heroes, smaller fame.
So I've taught the gods' own tongue
To the wolf, who with the dog
In my works speaks dialogue.
And still others in these pages,
Acting parts as fools or sages,
Hold debates on many stages –
Where the fools at times prove winners,
As in life they often do.
In addition, here you'll view
Smooth–tongued con–men, wicked sinners,
Tyrants, ingrates, flatterers, asses
And, of foolish dimwits, masses,
Joined by liars, legions of them.
"All men lie," King Solomon went.
If by 'all' he merely meant
Common souls, not those above them,
One might possibly assent
To that judgement, but if 'all'
Means just that, both great and small,
I would argue otherwise
And that those who tell such lies
As Aesop told or Homer, are
Not true liars when they spin
Tales of beasts or gods at war.
Though such dreams have never been,
Still, their artful vision shows
Naked truth concealed within
Beautifully mendacious clothes.

What these two have written will –
I proclaim it – live until
The end of time, or longer still,
If that could be, for there's no way
That one could lie as well as they.
But a liar of the kind
You'll meet next, a false trustee
Paid in his own currency,
Is thief and idiot combined.
But here's the tale. A Persian trader bound away
For distant parts left in his neigbor's trust one day
A bar of iron, a good hundred pounds in weight.
"My iron, please," he said when he at last got back.
"Your iron? Gone! It seems that at some recent date
A rat has eaten it, alack!
I've scolded my staff soundly, but what is one to do?
There always is some hole for rats to get in through."
Pretending he believed this wondrous story true,
The merchant calmly waited several days and then
Kidnapped the neighbor's son before he cordially
Invited the man to dinner. "I must refuse," said he.
"For this day I am the most miserable of men.
I have a son I love. He is my pride and joy.
Alas! What did I say? Till now I had a son;
Now I do not. He has been taken by someone.
Friend, weep for me! I can't accept. I've lost my boy."
The merchant answered: "In the late dusk yesterday
I saw a screechowl seize your son and fly away
In the direction of a crumbling castle tower."
The father said, "Do you expect me to believe
That any owl alive could have sufficient power
To lift my son's full weight? You think I'm so naive?
My boy would doubtlessly have massacred that bird."
"I don't know how he did it, I'm saying it occurred,"
Replied the merchant. "I saw it with my own two eyes.
I cannot think what justifies
Your doubting me in the least. What's there to wonder at
In seeing an owl – in the same country where a rat

222

Eats a hundred pounds of iron – fly
With a child who weighs just half of that?
The neighbor, seeing what the lie
He had so blandly told had done,
Returned the merchant's iron and got back his son.
A contretemps of much the same sort once arose
Between two travelers. The first was one of those
Who cannot tell a tale without hyperbole –
They always look through microscopes and all they see
Becomes gigantic. If one listened to their words
One might believe that little Europe swarms with herds
Of African–sized monsters. "I once saw," he said,
"A cabbage whose stupendous head,
Was bigger than a house!" "Well, that does not
Impress me," said the other man. "I've seen a pot
Big as a church." "I question your veracity,"
The first replied. "There's never been
A pot that big. What use is such capacity?"
"It has to be that big to cook your cabbage in,"
The other said. One man was clownish, one was clever.
When lies become absurd, it is a vain endeavor
To answer them with logic. The quickest way to stop them
Is to hear them out with humor, then cheerfully to top them.

IX. 1

The Two Pigeons

Two pigeons loved each other with true tenderness,
But then, for one, their cote grew boring:
He dreamed of distant wilderness
And made big plans to go exploring.
"Is my dear brother leaving me?"
The second cooed. "No pain could be
Worse, to my mind, than being parted,
But not to yours, you cruel-hearted!
At least, can't all the dangers and the cares you'll see

Make you less bold? Oh, wait until spring winds blow warm!
Who says you have to hurry? A crow I lately heard
Kept prophesying woe for some unwary bird.
I will have nightmares now, in which you come to harm
In nets, or falcons hunt you." And, knowing they must part,
He wept, "Will my sweet friend be cared for? Will he find
Good feed, safe roost, and comforts of that other kind?"
These questions made our brash adventurer's small heart
Beat anxiously, but the desire to see and know
And restlessness of spirit made him bound to go.
He said, "Oh, please! You must not cry.
Three days at most will satisfy
My curious soul. And then I will be back with tales
To tell my brother, filled with picturesque details.
I will divert him – for, remember, 'Those without
Experiences lack anything to talk about.'
You'll be delighted with the stories that I tell.
I'll say, 'Can you imagine? I was *there* that day,
And I did this or that, I really did,' I'll say,
Until you get the feeling you were there as well."
Now both of them were weeping as they said goodbye.
The traveler took off – but soon clouds hid the sky:
A storm was rising, he needed to find shelter fast.
He found one lonely tree that when the wind blew high
Gave scant protection. He was battered by the blast
And left near-frozen by the time the tempest passed.
Then drying his wet wings as best he could, he wheeled
Aloft again and saw, below him in a field,
Another pigeon, pecking wheat grains scattered there.
Famished, tempted, down he flew – to find, concealed
Beneath the alluring surface, a deceitful snare –
Which fortunately proved so worn with use and weak
That, with great effort, using claws and wings and beak,
He struggled free, exhausted, feeling near to dying
And minus many feathers. But now still worse occurred.
A cruel-taloned hawk spotted our hero flying,
Trailing torn net behind, which made the desperate bird

Look like a galley slave escaped and on the run.
The hawk was diving, talons set, when, from the sun,
An eagle, wings extended, plummeted and struck
The hawk in turn, at which the pigeon, still in luck,
Escaped once more, amd, as the hawk and eagle fought,
He fluttered to a farmhouse roof, a place
Where he might safely rest, he thought.
But now a rascal boy – that age without a trace
Of pity – took his slingshot, so,
And sent a stone that squarely hit and very nearly
Finished the poor fowl off, a blow
That left him staggering, lamed severely.
And so it was with spirits flagging.
Regretting his boldness, one wing dragging,
That he now made his way back to their cote
Without more incidents of note.
And then our parted souls with joy were reunited.
One need not ask what pleasures all their pains requited.

Lovers, happy lovers, do you wish to fly
To unknown lands? Then let your journeys be close by!
There may each pair of lovers find,
Each in the other's eyes, each in the other's mind,
Infinite new worlds that endlessly supply
New discoveries – and let all else go by!
I too have loved, sometime. I would not then have traded
The Louvre and all its treasures nor all the stars in space
For the least brook in which my shepherdess had waded,
Or clearing in the woods made magic by that face
Whose youth and beauty lighted every place
Her fair eyes shone upon, and for whom I knelt to swear
My first vows at Love's shrine among the myriads there.
Alas! Are those days gone? Must I now live bereft
Of all those visions that once charmed me, left
To my unquiet soul's devices? Would my heart dare
Ever again be set ablaze,
Or would the beauty that transfixed me leave me cold?

Have I turned old?
Am I beyond my loving days?

IX. 2

The Leopard and the Monkey

To raise some cash, the leopard and the monkey both
Did sideshow acts. Each from a painted booth
Worked on the crowd. The leopard purred,
"Good people, my rare glamor is the latest word
In fashionable circles. The king himself expressed
A wish to see me and, should I die, he wants a vest
Made from my skin, which is so variously spotted,
So speckled, so freckled, so diversely dappled, so gaily dotted."
The spots were a big attraction. Throngs came filing in,
Took one brief look, then promptly filed back out again.
The monkey, on his part, said "Yo! Good people! Don't stand
There gawking. For Pete's sake come and see my sleight
        of hand.
I do a hundred different tricks. Friend Leopard has
A lot to say about variety, but his
Is just what's on his body, while what mine is
Is from my spirit. Your humble servant, Giles the Clown,
From that same family tree as Amos,
That Roman ape who grew so famous
As the pope's pet jester. Yessir, Giles is fresh in town,
Just off three ships a–sailing, and primed to talk to you
In perfect French. And you will see him do his new
Ballet and loop the loop through hoops – and all you'll pay
To see him is one dollar. Dollar, did I say?
I meant one dime. And those not wholly satisfied
Will get back every penny when they step outside."

The monkey had it right. Variety I find
Appealing, yes – but of the spirit, not of dress.
The first provides abundant pleasures to the mind,

The other in an instant bores us to excess.
Oh, that the famed, those spotted leopards at our fair,
Had talents equal to the clothes they wear!

IX. 3

The Acorn and the Pumpkin

What God does he does well. But rather than search far
Across the universe for proof of this, I'll go
Into a field where pumpkins are.

A village thinker, considering how pumpkins grow,
Wondered what God was up to when he created them:
"These great humongous fruits on such a minchy stem!
The Maker got it wrong – their placement is a joke.
If it had been left up to me
I would have hung them on an oak!
Such fruit belongs on such a tree.
It seems a pity, Boyo, that you were not consulted
By him they preach about in sermons.
A better world would have resulted.
Now, for example, let's take acorns,
No bigger than my pinkie's little upper joint –
Wouldn't they be better on this vine?
God was mistaken on this point.
Boyo, the more you ponder these fruits and their design
The more it's clear that somehow they got switched around."
Such heavy thinking made his eyelids start to close.
"One needs more sleep," he said, "when one is so profound,"
Then stretched himself beneath an oak to doze.
An acorn fell from high above and struck his nose.
He woke and passed his hand across his face to find
The acorn tangled in the whiskers on his chin.
His throbbing nose brought on a sudden change of mind.
"Oh, oh, I'm bleeding! But what if it had been
Some much more massive object falling from this tree?

227

What if this acorn was a pumpkin? But I see
That God did not want that. I have no doubt at all
He chose to make this acorn fall
Just when it did and for his own good reason." Then,
Praising God's great wisdom, Boyo went home again.

IX. 4

The Schoolboy, the Pedant, and the Orchard Owner

A boy was proud: in school he'd learned to be
An ignorant piece of brash rascality –
An outcome rendered easier by his youth
And by a teacher whose pursuit of truth
Could only kill it. The boy devoted hours
To pillaging his neighbor's fruits and flowers.
This neighbor, a great favorite of Pomona,
Was granted every fall in all he'd grown a
Rich harvest of her finest fruits, beyond
What others got, of whom she was less fond.
And he would get, when spring came back once more, a
Rich blossoming of the finest flowers from Flora.
One day he saw our schoolboy swaying in the crown
Of one of his fine trees, quite heedless, his big boots
Destroying buds, those frail precursors of the fruits
Fall promises, and even bringing branches down.
Appalled, the orchard's owner made
An angry protest to the pedagogue, who duly
Appeared ahead of a parade
Of youthful scholars, each of them yet more unruly
Than that one in the tree. But hauling this untaught
Crew of young savages into the orchard brought
Untoward results. Despite his selfless dedication
To furthering their education
By an instructive lesson none would soon forget,

228

He found that as he lectured, with many an apt quotation
From Cicero and Virgil, the boys began to get
So restless as they stood there having their eardrums tortured
That finally they went rampaging through the orchard
And in a hundred places wreaked worse devastation.

I hate these eloquent speeches given
In the wrong places, droning on till one is driven
Out of one's mind. Which one is worse,
The schoolboy or the pedant? Curse
Them both equally, is how I look at it.
And as to having them as neighbors, I'm averse
To either one. No, I'd not like it, not one bit.

IX. 5

The Sculptor and the Statue of Jupiter

"What shape to chisel from the rock?"
A sculptor asked himself one day
As he considered a new block
Of marble in his atelier.

"A simple lustral basin? Waste
Of good marble. Table? No. Too odd.
It must be something in good taste –
Of course! That's it! I'll do a god,

A very great one, whose commands
Make mortals tremble: 'On your knees!
I hold the lightning in my hands,
I rule all earthly deities!'"

The sculptor then began attacking
The block of marble with his steel
Till Jupiter stood naked, lacking
Only the voice to make him real.

And the next instant, it is said,
Before the idol he had made
The artist knelt in quaking dread,
The first of all to be afraid.

Much like that artist, in all ages
Poets, too, have demonstrated
A readiness to fear the rages
Of gods they have themselves created.

They show a close resemblance here
To little children, always trying
To soothe their speechless dolls for fear
They will grow fussy and start crying.

Belief goes where emotion leads –
Which will explain those errors found
In pagan thought, flung out like seeds
Across the world on fertile ground.

Artists in ancient times produced
Works that their fiercest passions fired:
Pygmalion was thus seduced
By the stone Venus he had sired.

To the extent one can, one tries
To have one's dream of paradise –
We're all on fire for lovely lies
But homely truth turns us to ice.

IX. 6

The Mouse Who Was Turned into a Girl

A mouse an owl had captured in its beak broke free
And tumbled headlong from the sky.

And that would have been that had it been left to me,
But a Hindu picked her up. And why?
Because one acts as taught by one's society.
The mouse, of course, was bruised and sore.
And though our sort may set small store
On what becomes of fellow creatures such as she,
The Hindus think a lot of them and, what is more,
They treat them with true brotherly regard, for when
A monarch's soul at last takes flight
They have it in their heads it may come back again
To spend its next life in a mite
Or similar low creature at the whim of fate.
(Pythagoras much later would incorporate
This notion in his doctrines.) Seeking to be kind,
The Hindu begged a wizard to cause the restoration
Of the girl's soul back to some prior incarnation.
The wizard gladly acquiesced in the transferral
And changed the mouse into a girl
Fifteen years old, a creature of such loveliness
That Paris, son of Priam, would have been no less
Smitten by her than Helen. With paternal pride,
The Hindu said, "You need but say whom you decide
Upon as husband, for great suitors far and wide
Will vie for the distinction of making you their bride."
"My choice, in that case, is the one
Who is the strongest," she replied.
Then, kneeling down, the Hindu cried,
"My son-in-law is you, oh, Sun!"
"Not I," the sun said, "that thick cloud
Can effortlessly stop my rays within his shroud.
Take him instead." The Hindu asked the thunderhead
"Are you, in terms of birth, sufficiently endowed
To be my daughter's husband?" "Alas, no. I dread
The angry wind, who drives me anywhere he blows.
I will not make the slightest effort to oppose
The claim of Boreas to have her."
Becoming vexed with this palaver,
The Hindu yelled, "Then, wind it is! Without delay,

Wind, come and take this beauty." Rushing to obey,
The wind came on – until a mountain blocked its way.
So now the mountain had the ball but, though it had,
It tossed it back. "I would be mad,"
It said, "to claim her. There's this rat I'd have to fight.
He'd put a hole in me." At the word, 'rat', a light
Shone in the damsel's eyes. At last, her Mister Right!
Quite often passionate romances
Arise from such odd circumstances.
"He's such a rat!"one hears, but she –
And she as well – would not agree.
(This is between just you and me.)
One's origins will always tell.
This fable proves that point quite well
But, viewed more critically, its details don't hold water.
For who would choose the sun as husband for a daughter?
And would a giant's strength be outdone by a flea's,
Hard as the flea might bite him? If so, it's clear the rat
In turn would have to yield the beauty to the cat,
The cat to the dog, the dog to the wolf. And after these,
By hinduistic logic, the claim to her would run
Once more around the circle till it reached the sun.
Which brings us doubling back in reconsideration
Of metempsychosis. The wizard proved by his creation
Not that the doctrine's true but that it lacks all worth.
For if it were the case all creatures on this earth
From mites to mice to men – quite literally all –
Would borrow their souls from a common store
Of animating substance, like coins all of one ore
But differing values. And whether any soul would crawl,
Or walk erect would turn upon the body fate
Had put it in, and only that. But would a beauty shun
A beauty like her own? Would she not choose the sun?
She chose the rat. And yet it seems beyond debate
That women's souls and mice are totally at odds.
The laws of nature – they are God's –
Are never broken. They decree

That every being has its single destiny.
Though we try magic spells or seek
The devil's aid to change, we stay ourselves, unique.

IX. 7

The Fool Who Sold Wisdom

Don't stand in range where fools can reach you –
Of all the things that I have said,
There's nothing wiser I have to teach you
Than to run from a man who has holes in his head.
One often sees them near a crown.
The king finds it amusing when their barbs bring down
Some self–important fop, some fraud, some courtly clown.

A fool went shouting all about the town,
That he sold wisdom. Soon, people were thickly pressed
Around him, each more credulous than the rest.
But after a bit one saw disgruntled faces,
For what their money bought
Was a swat on the ear and a thread – in length, two paces.
Most got angry – but anyone who thought
About it might have seen that this made them appear
In a worse light yet. Far better in this case
Had each one walked away, silently rubbing his ear
And clutching his thread, a rueful smile on his face.
For to think that one perceives a rational motive here
Makes little sense. Randomness better explains
The fantasies in damaged brains.
Still, one of his puzzled victims, hoping to resolve,
First, the sudden blow and then the proffered thread,
Consulted a sage, who scarcely paused before he said,
"These things are hieroglyphics, simple ones to solve.
All those who hope to prosper would do well to place
Between themselves and fools a space

Which this thread measures. If they do not,
They will receive a similar swat.
You weren't cheated. The fool sold wisdom – which you got."

IX. 8

The Oyster and the Litigants

One day, two pilgrims trudging by the ocean spied
An oyster cast up by the tide.
They eyed it hungrily, they pointed at it, they
Both bared their teeth, each ready to contest for it.
One stooped to grab it, only to be pushed away
By his cohort, who said, "It would be best for it
To go to him who first became aware of it.
The other gets no share of it
Except to watch the winner dine."
"If that's how we decide it, brother,
Thanks be to God my eyes are sharp," replied the other.
"Well, there is nothing wrong with mine,"
The first one answered. "And I saw it first, I swear."
"So, what! You saw it, but I smelled that it was there!"
Who owned the oyster? The two continued to debate it,
Till Lawyer John came by and said he'd arbitrate it.
He picked the bivalve up and, as the two looked on,
He gravely pried it open, smacked his lips and ate it.
Then in judicial tones, the oyster being gone,
He gave his verdict: "After due deliberation
The court hereby decrees that in full compensation
Each will receive one shell, free of all cost. Now cease
All further bickering and go back home in peace."

Imagine what it costs these days to bring a suit;
Count up what's left to the poor families who begin them;
You'll see it's Lawyer John who makes off with the loot
And leaves both parties holding bags with nothing in them.

IX. 9

The Wolf and the Scrawny Dog

Remember the carp, that little guy
So eloquent in his own defense,
Who still went in the pan to fry?
My point back then was that it shows great lack of sense
To drop what's in your hand because you hope that later
You'll make a catch immensely greater.
The fisherman was right – and yet the carp was, too:
All do what they must do in order to survive.
But now I'll tell a tale to drive
That earlier lesson home, lest any doubt it's true.
A wolf, as foolish as the fisherman was wise,
Once met a dog outside the town
And was about to set on him and bolt him down
When the sly mutt protested, "Sire, I am no prize
As thin as I am now – so you should wait to kill me
Until my master's daughter weds, for, as you know,
That means a feast. And then I'll get such scraps to fill me
That I will put on weight despite my best intentions."
The wolf believed him, let him go.
Some days elapsed. The wolf approached the town to find
If now the dog had grown to eatable dimensions.
But, staying in this time, the rogue called through a grating,
"I'll come right out, my friend, and surely you won't mind
My bringing along the porter. You'll get us both combined
As your reward for patient waiting."
The porter was a dog of an enormous size,
A born wolf-killer, as even he could realize.
He said, "Your servant, Porter," and ran off in a tick,
Showing himself quite nimble if a trifle thick.
To be a proper wolf it seemed that he would need
A few more lessons to succeed.

IX. 10

235

Nothing in Excess

Nowhere in the whole creation
Do I see beings that observe
Within their lives that moderation
Nature's ruler wished them always to preserve.
Have any done so? Not a one.
For better or for worse, that never will be done.

Blond Ceres' gift to humankind, the precious wheat,
Will often sprout so much too thickly in the fields
It uses up the soil and then, self-starved, it yields,
From too rich germination, little good to eat.
Nor are trees any better – all life finds excess sweet!
To discipline the wheat, God let the sheep within it
To browse upon its surplus shoots and neatly thin it.
But they came trampling in, insatiably chewing
And seeming so to threaten the complete undoing
Of all he had designed he told the wolves to come
And keep the sheep in limits by devouring some.
But they devoured them all or, if not all, they tried.
So heaven to resolve the matter
Put man in charge of punishing these latter –
And humans in their turn defied
All heaven-made laws for their restriction,
For man of all the animals is most inclined
To carry his actions to excess.
Search as you may, you will not find
One living soul not guilty of this dereliction.
"Nothing in excess," all say with great conviction –
But no cliché is oftener preached or practiced less.

IX. 11

236

The Taper

The bees, according to the ancients, were confined
At first to Mount Hymettos' slopes, where gods resided,
And in those flowering meadows dined
On delicacies the soft winds in those parts provided.
Now, when the many-chambered golden palaces
Of these industrious daughters of the sky had all
Been breached and sacked and their ambrosial chalices
Poured out – or, in plain French (to call
A hive a hive), when the hives had all been drained,
Then candles were molded and tall tapers formed
From the soft beeswax that remained.
One taper, seeing how soft clay emerged, not harmed
When put in fire but turned to brick
That triumphed over time, decided to try the trick.
And, like a new Empedocles (cremated due
To his own foolishness), it threw
Itself into the kiln – a bad idea. That taper
Just didn't have the stuff to be a philosopher.

Everyone is different: never get so muddled
As to believe that you are just like someone else.
The wax Empedocles, rather than hardening, puddled –
Though both were crazy: flesh burns, wax melts.

IX. 12

Jupiter and the Voyager

How perils would enrich the gods if only men
Kept promises to heaven made when fears beset them!
But finding themselves safe they totally forget them:
Not heavenly but earthly debts concern them then.
"Jupiter is not one to hector
People to pay up," said one of those doubting scoffers.

237

"He never sends a bill collector
To make them honor their past offers."
Oh, no? Well what then, I would wonder,
Is Jupiter telling us with his thunder?
A storm–tossed voyager promised a hundred head of cattle
To the god who crushed the Titans in celestial battle –
Though, since the man owned not one head,
He might as well have offered him elephants instead.
Once safe on shore he burned some bones upon a pyre.
The smoke rose up to Jupiter's huge nose. "Big Sire,"
The man said, "take this offering. The part you get
Is the rich smell of beef you breathe in with the smoke.
I owe you nothing more. I have made good my debt."
Jupiter laughed at this as if he'd heard a joke,
But some days afterward, the angry god undid him
By sending him a dream to bid him
Go to a certain place where treasure lay concealed
Beneath the surface of a field.
Waking, he ran with fiery haste to find the spot.
He met with thieves along the way
And, being penniless as they,
To mollify them he promised faithfully to pay
A hundred golden talents to their lawless lot
Out of a treasure buried in a place close by.
The thieves had doubts about the spot
And one of the brigands said, "Old guy,
You're making fun of us. So die
And go to Hell, where Pluto reigns supreme as king.
Give him your golden offering."

IX. 13

The Cat and the Fox

The Cat and the Fox, like saintly citizens in fur,
Went on a pilgrimage. They were
Two hypocrites, two arch con–artists, hairy pawed

Finaglers who defrayed their costs en route
With many a pilfered chicken dinner and, to boot,
Many a cheese acquired by fraud.
The road was long (read 'dull' as synonym for that),
And so to pass the time they argued, Fox versus Cat.
Now, arguments help a lot when life gets boring –
Without them we would be forever snoring.
Our pilgrims argued themselves hoarse,
Then, having argued, had recourse
To tearing everyone else apart.
At last, the Fox said, "Cat, you think you are so smart,
But can you rival me? I have a hundred slick
Deceptions in my bag." Replied the Cat, "One trick
Is all I have in mine, but I would say it's worth
A thousand such as yours." A new dispute began.
But as the words flew back and forth
A pack of hounds came toward them, running.
The Cat said, "Fox, reach in your bag for some sure plan,
Some scheme to save your skin, employing all your cunning.
Meanwhile, here is the trick I do."
And, well and swiftly, up a tree he safely flew.
His hundred tricks, the Fox soon found,
Helped not at all. He went to ground
A hundred times, but was a hundred times dislodged
By a smoking stick or a Basset hound.
Wherever he dashed, however he dodged,
The dogs left him no place to hide.
At last, two greyhounds caught him as he tried
To sneak a back way out. They got him in one bound.

Too many options: that's a recipe for losing.
They all look good, but precious time is lost in choosing.
Have just one plan, but that one sound.

IX. 14

239

The Husband, the Wife, and the Thief

A husband passionate for his wife,
Passionate in high degree,
Believed, despite his pleasures in their bed, that he
Led an unhappy married life,
Untouched by joy, for, since his bride
Gave him no smiles, nor sang his praises,
Nor looked his way with hot-eyed gazes,
The poor man felt undeified,
With never any sign by which he might surmise
That he was truly loved – which I find no surprise:
It meant he was a husband. Yet, what odds?
It's nothing against marriage if his lacked the spice
Of love to make a paradise
For which he would have thanked the gods,
For what else should he have expected?
His spouse was an old fashioned wife
And never once in her whole life
Had shown him tenderness enough to be detected.
But then one night, as he upbraided her, a thief
Broke in and, interrupting this sad tale of grief,
So scared the wife that, seeking now to be protected,
She snuggled against her husband's chest.
"Friend thief," he said, "without you, it must be confessed,
I would not have enjoyed such bliss. So you may steal
As your reward whatever in this house you feel
Would be appropriate. Take the whole house, in fact."
Now thieves are seldom ever wracked
With guilt or given to restraint, so this one sacked
The place without a qualm. My inference is clear:
The strongest passion in the human heart is fear,
Which even overcomes aversion
And, sometimes, love, though love may win upon occasion.
As evidence for that I cite a man who yearned
So ardently for his wife he set their house on fire
And passionately took her as the building burned.

I must admit that I admire
Such passion and have long savored this small tale
That typifies the Spanish soul,
Built on a grandly different scale,
Less mad than loftily beyond control.

IX. 15

The Treasure and the Two Men

A man was destitute, his wallet grown so thin it
Had just the devil lodged within it,
And so, without the slightest hope
Of altering his situation,
He thought it best to take a rope
And hang himself before he perished of starvation –
A death with small appeal for those
Not taken with so gradual a termination.
With this in mind the poor man chose
An old, abandoned house where with a heavy maul
He went to drive an iron stake into a wall
From which to hang the rope and then himself as well.
But the old wall proved weak and, after a few blows
From his sledge hammer, crumbled suddenly and fell,
And from it fell a treasure. Swiftly, our desperate man,
Leaving the rope behind, gathered the coins and ran,
Not pausing to tot them up but with his hopes revived,
Whatever their sum might be. Soon after, there arrived
The treasure's owner, to find the wealth he'd counted on
All gone.
"After such loss," he said. "What can I do but die?
Should I not hang myself? Could I? I could. I can.
There is the rope, prepared. It only lacks the man."
He strung it up and soon was swinging clean and high,
Perhaps consoled as he was dying
To think he had been spared the added cost of buying
The rope that now, in one of fate's unlooked-for switches,

Had come to him, while some new owner had his riches.
Few are the avaricious souls who have not wept
At just how little at the end of day they've kept.
The treasure they piled up was for the benefit
Of thieves or relatives or it
Was lost forever, buried somewhere in the ground.
And what of the surprising way
Dame Fortune has of swapping destinies around?
Just that it is the sort of prank she loves to play,
And that she is more pleased the more bizarrely grim
The outcome. The fickle goddess had the whim
Of seeing a man hang who never till that day
Could have imagined such a fate awaited him.

IX. 16

The Monkey and the Cat

As fine a dish of mischief as one might hope to see,
A monkey and a cat, lived in their master's dwelling
In awe of no one in it, whoever it might be.
The cat, named Mouser, wasn't one that needed belling,
For he would rather steal a cheese than catch a mouse,
While Bertrand, the sly monkey, was a snatch–and–grabber.
Indeed, if anything was missing in the house
They were the guilty ones and not some sneaky neighbor.
One day as they lolled by the hearth these rascal brothers
Decided that they should acquire
Some of the chestnuts they saw roasting in the fire,
A deed that, as it profited them and injured others,
They found twice as appealing. "Mouser, now's the time,
Old pal," said Bertrand, "to use your mastery in crime.
Get me those chestnuts. If God had
Outfitted me with claws I would of course aspire
To pull those chestnuts from the fire,
But he did not. So it is up to you, my lad."
His words were scarcely out before the monkey saw

242

The cat extend a careful paw
And whisk away some ashes, instantly withdraw,
Then reach again, repeatedly,
And pull the chestnuts out, first one, then two, then three,
Which Bertrand ate as this went on.
A housemaid with a broom arrived
And, whoosh! the two of them were gone,
Though Mouser, we are told, felt ill-used and deprived.

No different are the princes of those smaller lands
Who, hoping to please their greater neighbors,
Dabble in fires but for their labors
Get little more than well-singed hands.

IX. 17

The Kite and the Nightingale

After the kite, that aerial thief, had raised alarms
And been yelled at by children, flying past their farms,
A nightingale fell in its claws. Spring's herald pled
To be allowed to live. "What good is it," she said,
To eat someone made purely out of sound? Delight
Your ears by listening to my song instead.
I'll sing to you of Tereus, of lust and dread."
"What's Tereus? Is it a food to tempt a kite?"
"Why, no. He was a king in whom the burning fires
Of passion made me victim to his cruel desires.
That is the tale I'll tell you. Listen, while I sing
My song. You'll find it ravishing.
Everyone adores my voice."
The kite replied, "Now, this is choice!
My stomach's rumbling and you speak to me
Of music. Duh!" "I speak to kings. They are enraptured."
"Well, dearie, next time you are captured
By some great king, then maybe he
Will love the fairy tales he hears.

243

But for a kite that's all a joke. Hee, hee!
A hungry belly has no ears."

IX. 18

The Shepherd and His Flock

"What! One more gone from me? They keep
Getting dragged off, this feckless bunch.
The wolves keep eating them for lunch!
How many in this flock? More than a thousand sheep,
So many I could hardly count them all, and yet
They've let the wolves get Robin now, my gentle pet,
Poor Robin sheep, who for the merest crumb of bread
Would follow me through the village square,
Faithfully trotting where I led,
Up hill or down – to the world's end if I'd gone there.
It is so sad! He listened whenever I would play
Upon my pipes and smelled me coming a mile away.
Poor Robin sheep, alackaday!"
Then, having wept for Robin and assured his name
Would have a wide and lasting fame,
The shepherd passionately urged the flock, great rams
And lesser ewes and even the smallest of the lambs,
That if they stood together the wolves would be defeated.
"But if you don't," he said, "then one by one they'll catch you."
"Upon sheep's honor we will stand as one," they bleated,
"Unbudgeable as a stone statue."
They'd gladly throttle, they told their herder,
The wolf who'd done poor Robin's murder.
Believing them to be sincere,
The shepherd praised them, raised a cheer.
But later that day, before the night,
A wolf appeared and all the flock at once took flight.
(It was no wolf but shadows that set off their fear.)

Fire up weak troops with your best oratory,
They'll shout: "Hurrah! The battle's good as won!"
But the first whiff of danger brings a different story;
No matter what you say or do, they'll break and run.

IX. 19

Discourse to Madame de La Sablière

Iris, I would praise you – none too hard to do –
Had you not said such "incense" has no charm for you,
Unlike your mortal sisters, who would wish their days
Unfailingly would bring them novel kinds of praise.
There is not one of them who is set yawning by
Soft flatteries. Yet do I blame them? Never, I,
For not just womankind, but gods and monarchs too
Are addicts of this potion poets boast they brew.
This nectar that we offer Jupiter above,
Or proffer earthly gods for their intoxication,
Why, Iris, it is praise, for which you have small love,
Preferring in its stead a lively conversation,
In which one chance remark may start
A hundred subjects up, and the quick play of wit
As you converse must always play a special part.
Though earnest types may frown a bit
On hearing that, let us ignore their frowns, for it,
Along with serious learning and imagination
That sees what eyes cannot – all these,
From grand concerns to less–than–trivialities,
Are needed, I maintain, in a good conversation,
Which is much like a blooming garden where in spring
The bees, exploring flower after flower, bring
Pure honey from their intermingled harvesting.
This being understood, do not think ill of me
If as you read these fables you find woven through
Some thoughts on a philosophy

That has been talked about as new,
Ingenious, daring, keen. Have you
Heard tell of it? It clearly means
That animals are mere machines,
Their actions only choiceless, automatic motions,
Their bodies lacking souls, vacant of all emotions,
Like clocks, stone blind, devoid of will,
But with a steady cadence marking seconds still.
Yet open them, look in their hearts –
You'll see no trace of spirit, only moving parts:
Gear A impels gear B around,
Thus causing C to turn and so the hour to sound.
And animals are of this ilk, these thinkers say.
It seems the place where an external 'object' first
Impinges on a creature's body will relay
The force of that initial impetus away
To an adjacent part (its 'neighbor', we would say),
From where in its turn it is transmitted and dispersed
Throughout the body, point by point, in a succession
That finally becomes what they term an 'impression.'
And how is this impression made?
By strict necessity, they tell us.
Though animals, to laymen, may appear afraid,
Downcast or joyful, full of love, in pain or jealous,
Make no mistake: no will or passion is diplayed
In anything they do. – How should we see them then? –
As ticking clocks – And us? – As something else again.
So said Descartes, a man who would have seemed a god
In pagan times, who rose as far above our plane
Toward the pure spirit as others sink below, who plod
Along inert as oysters and with as little brain.
This author reasoned: of God's children only man
Can tell himself, "I think; also I know I can."
Now, Iris, it seems clear beyond the slightest doubt
That if beasts think it is without
Reflecting on the thing perceived
Or on the thought itself. But what Descartes conceived
Goes a step further. He believed

That animals don't think, in any slightest way.
Yet neither of us, I or you,
Is forced to hold his doctrine true.
Imagine a hunt, in which the fleeing prey,
Hearing hallooing voices in the woods behind him,
An echoing of horns, the dogs upon his track,
This ancient roebuck, burdened with years and a great rack
Of massive antlers, exhausted, knowing they will find him
Despite his efforts to confuse them, doubling back,
At last compels a younger buck to act as bait
And with unwearied legs to draw away the pack.
How rational his actions to avoid his fate!
His sly backtracking, unexpected turns and twists,
To leave his enemies off balance and deceived:
Such wiles seem worthy of our greatest strategists,
Whose names in death we honor on heroic lists.
Yet butchering was all the honor he received.

It's known that when
A partridge hen
Has chicks that still are featherless and cannot fly
At the approach of danger, to vanish in the sky,
If she should see a hunter coming with his hound
She will act wounded, fluttering along the ground
As if her wing is broken and she's easy prey.
She lures them onward, drawing them step by step away
From her dear brood, until at last the hunter cries,
"Quick! Grab her, dog!" But, as it leaps for her, she flies!
Leaving the man to follow, vainly, with his eyes
As she soars off in sweet elation.

Near the north pole are tribes that live
In ignorance as primitive
As in the first age of creation.
But they, as I said, are humans; the animals there build
Works of a fine sophistication.
They put up dams that curb the rivers when they flood,
Enduring structures spanning bank to bank, so skilled

They are as builders, laying in logs they pack with mud
To make strong barriers the currents cannot breach.
Their projects are communal; the elder beavers teach
The younger, giving them no respite from the work,
But with stern discipline allowing none to shirk.
Plato's ideal republic surely
Did little more than imitate
The life of this amphibious state
Whose members in winter live securely
In dwellings each small group erects,
These wise, foresighted architects
Who cleverly construct the bridges by which they
Cross frigid waters and which until this present day
Our northern cousins only stare at, at a loss
For how it's done, as they plunge in and swim across.
That beavers are mere bodies void of intellect
Is an idea that I forever will reject.

But this next tale lends my belief far greater weight:
I heard it from a king, one who has garnered fame
As the defender of the north, whose very name
Stands as a bulwark that protects his Polish state
From Ottoman attack – and kings are never liars.
He told me, then, that in his distant border shires
Live animals caught up in an unending feud.
The bad blood that the sons inherit from their sires
Keeps ancient hatreds long renewed.
He said that foxes are these creatures' nearest kin
And humans are not nearly so adept as they
At making war, not even those of our own day.
Their use of raiding parties and of spies within
Each other's ranks, of ambush and reconnaissance
And all the myriads of tricks
Employed in warfare's cursed and terrifying science –
That daughter of the river Styx
And mother of dead heroes – shows their intelligence.
To tell the epic of their combats it would need
The Acheron to give us back great Homer – oh,

If only that could be! – and if it then also
Allowed our modern rival of Epicurus freed,
What would he say as to these latter observations?
Just as I've said, that to effect such operations
In animals, nature needs only simple means;
That memory is corporeal and those last scenes
Of animals I've put in verse require no cause
For all their acts that is not found in natural laws.
If something that an animal has sensed before
Impinges on its outer body once again,
This new impression, moving inwards to its store
Of memories, will find its likeness there and then
Return in the same sequence to its outward part,
Where, with no need of thought, it now effects the start
Of suitable behavior. We, however, act
By other laws completely. That which governs us
Is our free will, not instinct or brute stimulus.
I speak, I move, I sense within me that thing lacked
By every animal: a mind, which the machine
That is my body perfectly obeys. Between
The mind and body runs a line exact.
Indeed, as we consider both of them we find
We have an even clearer notion of the mind
Than of the body. The mind commands our every act.
But there's the point: how does the body understand
The mind's instructions? A tool is guided by a hand,
But who guides that? Or – think! – whose is the force
That guides the cosmos? Does some seraph set its course?
There surely is some spirit that resides in each
Of us that sets those parts in motion that will go
To forming our "impressions." How? I do not know.
The answer lies somewhere beyond all human reach.
Nor can Descartes tell why it's so.
In this at least we are his equals here below –
But what I do know, Iris, as a certain fact,
Is that no animal of all the ones I've shown
Exhibits such a spirit in its smallest act.
Man is its temple, man alone.

And yet one must concede that animals as well
As humans have a trait plants lack, though they too live.
But when you have considered this next tale I'll tell
Say what rebuttal might one give?

IX. 20

The Two Rats, the Fox, and the Egg

Two rats went out in search of food for their next meal:
They found an egg, not big, but for their size ideal:
What benefit to them if they had found an ox?
So with good appetite and cheer
They went to share their egg, when who should now appear
At just this inconvenient juncture but Sir Fox?
How to protect their prize? They had no way to pack it,
Then carry it with their forepaws, held between the two;
To roll it or to drag it on the ground might crack it.
Yet what else was there they could do?
Ingenious necessity at once provided
A neat way out. They saw the thieving fox was yet
A quarter mile away, which left some time to get
To the snug hole in which the two of them resided.
So one now lay upon his back and, with each leg
Stuck in the air, formed a soft cradle for the egg,
Allowing his companion, pulling him by the tail,
To drag him, somewhat bumpily, upon the trail
That led them safely home. Hearing such evidence,
Who'd still say animals have no intelligence?
If I were asked to judge the case, I'd be inclined
To credit them, as much as children, with a mind.
For, do not children from their moment of arrival
Engage in thought? If this is so it's not essential
To know oneself before one thinks. I do not claim,
By the same token, that animal thought is just the same
As that of man, but that it is far more than blind
Clockworks unwinding. I picture a substance so refined

250

One strains to comprehend it. It is the stark quintessence
That is an atom, light tinctured to pure luminescence,
A something I cannot define, yet more alive,
More volatile, than fire. From solid–seeming wood
Arises the pure flame. Why won't this image serve
To represent the mind's emergence, like the gold
Extracted from the lead? An animal, I find,
Has feelings, judgement also, but of the simplest kind
And fallible in any case.
Which means an ape could never in the least degree
Engage in reasoning. But we, this human race,
I see as having minds whose measure
Is infinite compared to other creatures – we
Possess, each one of us, a two–fold treasure.
Its first part is that soul found equally in all:
Blank idiots and children, the foolish and the wise,
And every other being that we think to call
By the term 'animal', of any shape or size.
The treasure's other part, a second soul, is kin
Instead to those of angels and it wants to rise
And follow their celestial legions in the skies,
Yet could be free though prisoned in
A point's pure fixity. Whatever its origin,
This treasure, strange as it is, is real and never dies.
When we were children, this being born of heaven seemed
No more than a pale light that gleamed
From deep within us, weak and much obscured.
But as our years increased, at length
Our power of reasoning matured
And that soft radiance, gathering strength,
Pierced the dark veil of shadows that surround
The other soul, forever to the body bound.

IX. 21

Book Ten

The Man and the Snake

A man saw a snake.
"Evil one!" he said. "What I do next will make
All the universe feel better!"
And then the perverse critter
(Meaning the snake and not the man,
If you've confused the two – one can),
Resignedly letting itself be caught,
Was seized, put in a sack and – very much the worst –
Condemned to die at once, if guilty or if not.
But yet, to demonstrate his sentencing was just,
The man made a brief oration:
"You, ingrate of the first creation!
Letting criminals go free
Is nothing but stupidity:
Ergo, you die, and then
Your anger and your fangs can't threaten me again."
The snake, in its own language, managed a reply:
"If all who prove ungrateful were condemned to die,
Who could get a pardon – is there anyone?
The criminal that you describe is you, as I
Can prove by your own actions. Open your eyes and see!
My life is in your hands – so cut it short. Your justice
Is your caprice, your prejudice, your mere convenience.
By such laws you may sentence me,
But know that dying sets me free
To say the ingrate of creation
Is not my race of serpents but your human nation!"
These words produced a pause, the human stayed his hand,
But soon he answered back, "This rhetoric is futile.
I have dominion here, as heaven's wisdom planned.
Still, let us arbitrate." "So be it," said the reptile.
A cow agreed to hear the case. Each made his plea.
The cow said, "There's no doubt! What need of asking me?

The snake is right. It's true, so why pretend it isn't?
For many a year I gave this man my nourishment;
He wouldn't have survived but for the gifts I've given.
Yes, it was all for him – my milk, my children even.
He never went from me without his arms full laden.
When age made him infirm, I nursed him back to health.
My purpose was as much his pleasure as his wealth.
Well, now I'm old, how does he comfort my last days?
He puts me out where there's no grass. If I could graze,
I might get by. But see, I'm tethered to a stake.
I should have had more gratitude from any snake!
That is my judgement. Now, just go away."
The man appeared astonished. What a thing to say!
He told the snake, "We can't believe this stuff.
It's gibberish. She's lost her mind. She's high on hay!
But here's an ox. He looks believable enough."
"So call him," said the snake. The ox was slow to come.
He ruminated all their words in his huge head,
Then said at last it seemed to him that oxen led
The hardest lives. They did the heavy jobs with dumb
Acceptance, laboring endlessly on that long round
That as it comes full circle sees the ground
Replenished yet again with all that Ceres gives,
Or barters, anyhow, to everything that lives.
And when a season's work was done,
What did the oxen get? Why, every single one,
More kicks than kindness. Then, when they grew aged
          and halt,
Men seemed to think it honored them to shed their blood
To buy divine indulgences for human fault.
So spake the ox. And then the man: "My, what a flood
Of rabble–rousing elocution!
He's boring. Turn him off. All those big words he used
Can't hide the truth – he's working for the prosecution!
This witness also is recused."
A tree was next appointed to preside,
And it had worse to tell. For at its rooted feet

The man had often taken refuge, both from heat
And cold, from wind and rain. And it had beautified
His public gardens and his countryside.
But more than giving shade, it bent to yield him fruit.
And in return some foolish man would chop it down –
That was the wage for trees, despite what they produced
In every season, liberal with their flowers that crown
The spring, the autumn fruit and summer shade, the boon
Of winter warmth – without an axe, if only one will prune.
For trees, well–treated, naturally live long.
Now furious that his last appeal had lost,
The man was wild to win at any cost.
"I was a fool," he said, "to be polite to these –
Why deal with trash, dumb beasts or stupid trees?"
And suddenly he slammed the sack against the wall
And ended the discussion, once for all.

The strong don't trouble about what's right,
For everything in sight
Was made for just their sakes –
Beasts with four legs, people with two,
Even snakes.
If anyone opens his mouth to object
They slander his name. Well, if this is correct –
And, clearly, it's true –
Then what's to be done?
Well, either keep quiet, or speak out and run!

X. 1

The Turtle and the Two Ducks

A turtle grew tired of her earthbound existence
And planned on a trip, this leathery dame –
How alluring far countries look in the distance,
How hateful four walls can seem to the lame!

She told two ducks about her dream of going touring,
And they were greatly reassuring:
"You see that broad highway up there?
We'll take you on it. We will go by air
Clear to America. You'll see such places!
You'll see kingdoms and republics, you'll see races
Yet unheard-of – and you will grow wise,
Observing different customs under different skies,
Just like Ulysses." (Ulysses? Well, now, really!
To bring him into it was silly.)
The turtle liked their proposition.
And so, the fare agreed, the birds fixed up a slick
Contraption for their transport mission.
Crosswise between her jaws they passed a stick.
"Bite hard," they said. "Make sure you don't let go."
Then, each one holding one end in its bill,
They lifted off, and all below
Experienced a sudden thrill
To see the turtle, slowest of the slow,
Proceeding, house and all, across the sky.
"Miraculous!" all screamed. "Above our heads their hurtles
The very queen of turtles!"
"The queen!" she said. "Yes, truly, that is I!
Don't laugh, you boors, as royalty goes by!"
She would have done far better not to make a sound,
For, opening her mouth to talk,
She let go of the stick and plummeted to ground,
Splatting at the feet of all who stood to gawk.

Foolish vanity, vain affectation,
Share a family relation
With brainless babble and imprudent action:
All are of the same extraction.

X. 2

258

The Fishes and the Cormorant

There wasn't any pond around a cormorant's roost
That didn't pay him tribute; whatever its dimension,
If fishes swam in it, it yielded him a pension
And he ate well. But with the years, as age reduced
The ease with which he moved and blurred
His once sharp eyesight, the poor bird
Ate less and less, though there were fish aplenty yet.
For cormorants must forage for themselves and he
Not only was too old to see
Into the depths but lacked, as well, both line and net
And so he starved. What could he do? Necessity,
That doctor of ingenuity, provided him
This stratagem: within a pond, just at its rim,
He saw a crawfish. "Friend," he said, "do not delay.
Swim down and warn the fish that they
Are soon to die, because the man
Who owns this pond next week will institute a plan
To fish them out and carry all of them away."
The crawfish swam to spread the news.
A crowd assembled: great excitement; a delegation
Was sent to get the cormorant's views.
"Your Excellency, this information,
Is it reliable? You guarantee it's true?
Who can corroborate it? Tell us what to do."
"Go somewhere else," he said. "But how are we to do it?
"No problem. I will ferry you,
One at a time, to my safe haven. I'll fly you to it.
No one but just myself and God above knows where
It is, what roads to take to reach it,
This fishy refuge, the creation
Of Nature's gentle hands. Man's treachery can't breach it,
And it will save your little nation."
Deceived by this false apostle of salvation,
They were transported to a place of desolation
Beneath a cliff, where he confined them

Within a pool of such small size,
So clear, so shallow that, although he had weak eyes,
The hungry cormorant now easily could find them.
The fishes learned, to their great cost,
That trusting kindly predators is never wise,
Though in this case they would have lost
Perhaps no less, whichever way they had themselves
Decided, since the human beast
Would have no doubt crammed down at least
As many of them in his gullet. Men or wolves,
It's all the same to the one who's eaten, for what
Is the difference in the end? A gut is a gut is a gut,
In my opinion, and whether sooner or later, the sequel
To being ingested in one proves all flesh is equal.

X. 3

The Treasure-burier and His Crony

A scrimping, penny–pinching, man amassed
A hoard that grew so sizeable at last
That he decided he had need
Of someone he could trust to guard it for him. Greed
And her companion, ignorance, led him to make,
In choosing a trustee, a ruinous mistake.
He reasoned: "If I keep it here
Inside my house it will so tempt me that I fear
I'll spend it, making me a thief
Who robs himself." Did I hear right? A thief! My friend,
I pity you. It is self–robbery to spend
Upon your own enjoyment? Why, that is past belief!
Goods we may never use are goods forever wasted;
Indeed, they cause us harm. Do you wish to reserve
Your riches for an age when pleasures can't be tasted?
Wealth takes hard effort both to get and to preserve,
Which makes its value less. Although he could have found
Trustworthy individuals prepared to serve

And keep his money safe, he chose, instead, the ground.
And with a crony whom he asked to help him hide it,
He dug a hole and put it in. Then, some days on,
When he returned to check, he found his treasure gone –
There was the hole they'd dug but nothing now inside it.
Correctly guessing who the culprit was, he ran
And told his helper, "Get your shovel out again.
I have more money yet to bury and I plan
To add it to that other lot." At which the man
Sneaked off and put the money back, expecting when
Its owner had departed he would grab it all.
But having grown too wise to fall
Into the same old error, now the owner took
And kept his wealth at home, deciding to employ it
On present pleasures, not inter it but enjoy it.
And having lost all he had buried, the poor crook
Was shocked: he had been hoisted on his own petard!
Deceiving deceivers is never hard.

X. 4

The Wolf and the Shepherds

A wolf, filled with humanity
(If in this world such things can be),
Considering his cruelty,
Which he engaged in only by necessity,
Once musingly soliloquised:
"I am much hated. And by whom?
By all. We wolves are universally despised.
The villagers, with dogs and hunters seek our doom
In mobs that sweep so loudly through the countryside
That Jupiter's ears must ring. Which is why we have fled
From England's shores, each with a price upon his head.
There, not the pettiest squireen
Fails to post signs upon the green
Condemning all our kind to die,

Nor does one little brat dare cry
But that its mother warns, "Hush, dearie, go to sleep
Or the bad wolf will hear you." Such is the price I pay
For finishing off some mangy ass or half-dead sheep
Or vicious-tempered dog, attempting to allay
My hunger pangs. Henceforth let me not eat
Things that had breath in them; let me abstain from meat
And starve to death on grass and leaves. Could it
Be worse than being hated universally?"
Saying these words, what should he see
But shepherds, cooking on a slowly turning spit
A fresh-killed lamb. "Incredible!" he said. "I'd be
Ashamed to spill his innocent blood. Yet there they sit,
His guardians, feasting on his flesh, they and their dogs;
And I, wolf that I am, should I
Be tied by finer scruples? No, by all the gods!
I'd be ridiculous. When Willy lamb trips by
I'll need no spit above a fire
For him or the dam he suckles or his great-horned sire."
That wolf was right of course. Are we not plainly told
To see all things as prey with which to set our table,
The animals included, while, much as we are able,
We limit them to fruits, as in the age of gold?
Have they no hooks to hang great stew pots on the fire?
Oh, shepherds, shepherds, all that the wolf does wrong
Is to be not so strong
As mighty you. Must he live like some fasting friar?

X. 5

The Spider and the Swallow

"Oh, Jupiter, who from your pregnant brain
By some obstetrical legerdemain
Gave birth to Pallas, my old foe,
For once in your life, just once, would you please show
A bit of sympathy when I complain?

Procne the swallow is stealing every bite
I try to take. She caracols in flight,
She skims the water and the air
And whisks away my flies just as they light.
They are *my* flies, I say, not hers to share.
Damned bird! I'd have my web filled, but for her,
For all my threads are strong and tight!"
Speaking with such wild insolence,
Arachne, now a spider but a woman once,
Complained to Jupiter
As if all flies were hers by special right.
But keen upon her prey, despite the spider's cries,
Philomela's sister harvested the skies,
Pitilessly joyful as she captured flies
To feed her ravenous brood, from whose wide–open beaks
Came nursery noises, formless calls, demanding shrieks.
Arachne, starving, shrank to feet and head,
A weaver out of work. And then her web was torn!
The swallow, swooping past to snatch a fly, instead
Snagged spiderweb and spider, swinging on a thread,
Up, up, into the sky, airborne!

Jupiter anciently decided
That at the feast of life the guests would be divided.
At Table One, the strong, the vigilant, the deft
Eat first. At Table Two, the weak get what is left.

X. 6

The Partridge and the Cocks

A partridge hen was put to feed
Among a certain group of cocks,
A rude, forever quarrelsome, ungallant breed.
Although she might have hoped her sex
And natural kindliness that all are due
Would bring the cocks – so amorous for the other gender –

263

To treat her kindly and defend her.
They treated her with all the manners of the zoo.
They showed the alien female not the least respect,
But beat her with their wings and with their beaks
      they pecked.
"They must all hate me!" she first thought,
But soon perceiving how ferociously they fought,
Spurring each other's sides in never-ending war,
She grew resigned. Said she, "It is the way they are.
One cannot blame them, only weep that they exist!
When God made all the beings on creation's list
He did not limit them to models of one kind.
Cocks have their nature, partridges have theirs.
If I had power to choose, as I have not,
I'd live among a gentler lot.
The master here decrees a different scheme of things.
He captures us with subtle snares,
Puts us to dwell with cocks and clips our wings.
Man is the only cause of our despairs."

X. 7

The Dog Whose Ears Were Cropped

"Why me? What have I done
To be attacked by my own master?
Mutilated! What disaster!
How will I appear in front of everyone?
Oh, king of animals or, should I say, dictator!
If someone did the same to *you* . . . !"
So whined Growler, a pitbull pup. But the man with shears,
Unmoved by pitiful cries, calmly went on to do
As he intended, and cropped the puppy's ears.
Now, Growler felt he'd lost, but with the passing years
He saw he'd gained. For as he grew and got in fights,
Urged by his nature to wreak havoc on his peers,
He would have had to straggle homeward many nights,

With these bits altered by a hundred bites –
For vicious dogs end up with mangled ears.
The less that's sticking out for others to get sight of,
The less there is for them to take a bite of.
Witness, Master Growler, around his neck a band
Of spikes like a metallic wreath,
His head as smooth and earless as my hand:
A wolf would not know where to sink his teeth.

X. 8

The Shepherd and the King

Two demons grip our lives, demanding each its share.
They've driven reason out, robbed of dominion there.
I have not found one heart not subject to their will.
If I am asked to tell their names and high position,
Why, one of them is Love, the other is Ambition.
The first has wide domain, the second wider still,
For even within love it's hidden.
But that I'll speak to later, now I'll put in rhyme
The tale of how a shepherd by a king was bidden
To join his court – oh, years ago, in olden time.
The king observed a flock that filled the countryside,
Browsing in peace and health, the young and old alike,
And by the shepherd's care immensely multiplied.
The king was pleased to see what pains the shepherd took.
"I find you fit," he said, "to be the people's guide.
So leave your sheep to graze, come shepherd men instead.
Henceforth as highest judge you'll weigh the bad and good."
And soon with scales in hand he stood.
Although he'd seen no more of men than hermits do –
His flock, his mastiff dogs and wolves were all he knew –
He had good sense and quickly learned to play his part.
In brief, he made a brilliant start.
His hermit neighbor came in wonderment to call.
"Am I awake," he asked, "or dreaming? Is this you?

You great? A favorite? Be wary what you do!
It's slippery near a throne. At one misstep you'll fall.
But even worse is what may happen if you fail,
Many once illustrious have perished in some jail.
You cannot see the trap in which you'll fall hereafter.
I speak as friend. Fear all." But he was met with laughter.
And so the hermit persevered,
"The court has dulled your wits already, as I feared.
You're like that blind man who, one winter, it is told,
Happened to grasp a serpent, paralyzed with cold.
It felt like leather to his touch. Oh, lucky day!
He'd lost his belt, this strap would keep his pants from falling.
As he thanked heaven, a passerby cried out, "Appalling!
Ye gods! Oh, throw that frightful, deadly thing away!
That is a snake!" "A strap!" "A snake! A snake, I say!"
"Why is tormenting me apparently your pleasure?"
"You mean you plan to keep this treasure?"
"Why not? The belt I lost was worn. This new one's nice.
You speak from envy, wish me harm."
Unwilling to accept advice,
The blind man paid a mortal price,
For soon the snake revived and bit him on the arm.
And I predict you will be tried
By circumstances bitterer than death, by far."
"Than death? I can't imagine. Tell me what they are."
"A thousand wounding things," the hermit prophesied.
And so it proved. All happened as he specified.
Swarms of court intriguers, spreading packs of lies,
Whispered everywhere with such effect
That soon the judge was tarnished in the monarch's eyes,
His competence in doubt, his honesty suspect.
Now plots were laid, well-paid accusers swore his guilt.
"He swindled us," they charged. "He built
A palace with our wealth." "Show me," the king insisted.
But all he saw bespoke a quiet moderation,
A desert's bareness, not one touch of ostentation:
Of only that his wealth consisted.
Well, then, he hoarded stolen jewels, gleaming rocks,

A coffer heaped with them, secured with ten strong locks.
But when the king threw back the cover of the box
The slanderers saw what seemed a joke.
For, there inside the chest lay only rags, not riches –
A little cap, a well-worn pack and threadbare britches,
The things a shepherd wears, his crook and weathered cloak
And, I would guess, the pipes he plays.
"You simple treasures," he said, "relics of happier days,
Who never set tongues wagging with false, envious stories,
I take you up again. Let us be gone. These glories,
These rich palaces, were dreams, phantasmagories.
Oh, Sire, if I've offended, accept my true contrition.
As I climbed up, I knew my fall was sure to come.
I loved the heights too well – but then, who hasn't some
Slight tincture of ambition?"

X. 9

The Fishes and the Shepherd Who Played the Flute

Beside a brook that ran along
The border of a flowery glade
Where warm spring zephyrs softly strayed,
The shepherd Thyrsis sang a song,
Then played upon his pipes in aid
Of the young shepherdess, Annette,
His voice and instrument entwined in a duet
That would have moved the dead to hear it.
Annette meanwhile sat by the brook
And fished with a well-baited hook,
But sat in vain, for not a single fish came near it.
The shepherd, having won caresses
By singing to coy shepherdesses,
Thought that the fish likewise would throng
To hear him sing, but he thought wrong.

He sang to them: "Oh, finny citizens who swarm
Beneath these ripples, leave your nymph below and see
This one above who has a thousand times her charm.
There is no need for you to flee
The prisons she will keep you in, for only we
Poor men are made the victims of her cruelty.
Fine fishponds clearer than the purest crystal wait
For you to swim in them. And if some find the bait
They bite proves fatal, who could wish a sweeter fate
Than dying by Annette's white hand?
But from an audience as deaf as dumb, no grand
Response ensued. And Thyrsis, finding his honeyed words
Were wasted, scattered on the winds like birds,
Got a strong net and flung it, hauling in a mess
Of fish, which he spilled at the feet of his fair shepherdess.

Oh, you who shepherd humans, not just flocks of sheep,
You kings who think by reason to command
The spirits of a foreign nation,
This never is the way to keep
A people in your subjugation.
But use your nets to hold them and, at length,
They'll do as you demand.
It only takes sufficient strength.

X. 10

The Two Parrots, the King, and His Son

Two cockatoos, a father and his son,
Enjoyed a regal diet, sharing bread
Two demi–gods, a son and father, fed
This pair of birds, a favorite each one.
Their symmetry of ages made a bond
Of special warmth, the fathers greatly fond
Of one another, and the sons, despite
The light impulsiveness of youth, both quite

As close in all they did, from day till night.
This was high honor for the younger parrot, since
The human father was a king, his son a prince.
By temperament, that shaping gift of fate, the child
Loved birds. Besides his parrot he was much beguiled
By his pet sparrow, a joyful creature, pert and bright.
This rival pair, the sparrow and the cockatoo,
One day were playing, as young creatures often do,
When, suddenly, play turned to fight.
The sparrow, not considering
The parrot's beak, joined battle bravely,
But took such blows that, injured gravely,
Near dead and with a trailing wing,
He seemed beyond recovering –
At which the prince, enraged, impetuously killed
The little cockatoo. His father heard
The noise of it and desperately called his son,
But called in vain: the deed already had been done,
He was on Charon's barge. The talking bird
Was silenced now, his voice forever stilled.
The father, to repay his son's demise,
Flew at the prince and instantly tore out his eyes,
Then, seeking refuge, fled into a towering pine
Where he could savor his revenge, safe and secure.
The king himself soon came and, trying to allure
The parrot down, he said to him, "Old friend of mine,
Come home to me. What good does it do either one
To cling to hatred, vengeance and despair? Let's leave
Such things outside the door. For, deeply as I grieve,
I must in truth admit my son
Was the aggressor. No! Not he!
Fate, not my son, was guilty of the blow that took
Your son away. It was not he but destiny
Wrote one son's death, the other's blinding, in that book
That holds all time. So let's together turn the page
And give each other comfort. Come back to your cage."
"Sire king," replied the cockatoo,
"Can I take what you say as true

After the outrage done to you?
The fault is destiny's, you claim, not mine,
But is such language only masking your design
To tempt me back? Whatever you intend, I know
That whether fate or Providence rules earth below,
It's written here above that, perched atop this pine,
Or in some wood where I may hide,
I can live out my days allotted, a safe distance
From rage that threatens my existence,
But that to you seems justified.
Kings have an appetite for vengeance, for they live
Like gods on earth. You will forgive
My deed, you say, and I'll believe you. Even so,
I think henceforth it will be wise
For me to keep away from both your hands and eyes.
So do not waste your time, friend King, just go –
Take yourself elsewhere. It's too late
To talk about my coming back. To separate
Can end not only love but hate."

X. 11

The Lioness and the She-bear

When hunters killed her cub a lioness
Let out such awful roarings of maternal grief
That all the forest, in distress
At so much noise, began to long for some relief.
Yet neither night's soft darkness nor its other powers
Of healing had the least effect
Upon this queen. Throughout the hours,
All night, all day, her ullulations went unchecked,
Till not one creature in the forest slept a wink.
At last the she–bear said, "I think,
My dear old friend, you need
To hear some words of frank advice. Is it not true
That all those children who have made their passage through

Your teeth had mothers, too?" "They did," the queen agreed.
"Well, if their mothers, mourning them, left us in peace,
Is that not possible for you?"
"You're asking this of me? Of me? My cries should cease?
But it's my child I've lost! For me, there's no release.
I'll mourn in my old age!" "But who compels you to?"
"Why, Destiny. I am the object of her hate."
From every mouth one hears it: "I am cursed by fate."

This is addressed to you, you hapless human clods
Whose overdone self–pity is all I deprecate.
If those who see themselves as victimised by fate
Remembered Hecuba, they'd thank their kindly gods.

                                                                    X. 12

The Two Adventurers and the Talisman

The road to glory is no highway strewn with flowers:
Just think of Hercules's ordeals,
God though he was, with few to rival his great powers
Portrayed in myth, still fewer history reveals.
Yet, of those few, one man, whose tale will now be told,
Once went to seek his fortune in the realms of gold,
A cohort at his side. One day,
Proceeding on their quest, they came upon a pole
Hung with this talisman, inscribed upon a scroll:

"Whoever you may be, adventuring this way,
If you wish to behold a sight
Not ever seen before by any wandering knight,
You need but cross the boiling torrent
You find before you; then carry the stone elephant
That rests upon its farther bank right to the top
Of that sky-piercing mountain, all without a stop
To catch your breath before you stand upon its peak."

The second cavalier by now was feeling weak
From nosebleed. "If that churning current is as fast
As it looks deep," he said, "assuming we get past,
Why then are we to lug that elephant with us?
This enterprise is stupid! It's ridiculous!
Maybe the mage who wrote that message by some sleight
Might carry it four steps, but to that distant height?
And in one breath? No mortal man could do that trick –
Unless of course the elephant was very small,
A pygmy figurine, like on a walking stick.
But such a deed would bring one no acclaim at all.
I say this message is intended as a trap,
A riddle with no answer, foolish childish pap.
So you can have your elephant, but I'll depart."
The cautious thinker left, the bold adventurer dived,
Eyes shut, into the current, swam with all his heart
And, fighting his way amidst huge turbulence, survived
To reach the other shore, where, as he stepped, he found
The elephant, as promised, standing on its ground.
He seized it, climbed with it, not resting, to the height,
Where he beheld a wondrous sight:
A wide parade ground by an open gate. He strode
Through it into a city. The elephant began
To trumpet loudly; crowds poured out into the road,
All grimly armed, a sight that every other man
Who'd climbed to this high place had fled.
Yet this one, rather than retreat, instead
Stood there and faced them, ready with his final breath
To make that mob pay dearly for a hero's death.
At once, to his amazement, shouts from every side
Hailed him as king, in place of one who'd long since died.
Like Sixtus, when he first refused the papal ring,
He modestly demurred. "My friends," he said at length,
"I fear your crown may be a burden past my strength."
(Is it so awful, really, being pope or king?)
They soon found his reluctance did not mean a thing.

Blind fortune follows where bold daring blindly leads.
Sometimes a man proves wiser if he simply acts,
Not taking all the time that cautious wisdom needs
To sift and weigh together all the daunting facts.

X. 13

Discourse

TO MONSIEUR THE DUKE DE LA ROCHEFOUCAULD

On numberless occasions, seeing man behave
No differently than animals,
I've often thought this king for whom the others slave
Is not a bit less fallible
Than are his subjects, and that nature
Has put in every living creature
Some portion of an essence from which each draws its spirit:
I mean that spirit of the body, physical,
Molded of matter. Now I will show it.

An hour when hunters wait, perhaps when waning light
Shoots its last arrows down into the western sea,
Or when the rising sun will soon dispel the night
But the full day is yet to be,
At such a time I'll climb a tree beside a heath
And, there, like a new Jove on that Olympus, I
Will fire a shot, like thunder booming from the sky
To blast a rabbit browsing unawares beneath.
Immediately all his companions flee en masse,
Who, moments earlier, eyes wary, ears alert,
Frisked gaily in the heather, banqueting on grass,
With sprigs of thyme for their dessert.
But now, in panic at the sound
My weapon makes, they disappear
Into their city underground –

Where, once in safety, they forget the danger; fear
Soon fades. I watch the rabbits re-emerge, a band
Of revelers, gayer than ever, cupped within my hand.
And are not human beings much of this same sort?
Driven off course by raging gales,
They scarcely limp into some port
Than once again they hoist their sails,
Defying storms and reefs, for lands
Far off, true rabbits in the palms of Fortune's hands.
Here is another instance showing what I mean,
A commonplace example everyone has seen:
When dogs out of their neighborhood go past a yard
They don't belong in, all the ones confined inside,
Their heads as one preoccupied
With getting their next lunch, regard
Them as intruders and all at once begin
A barking, snapping, snarling, splendid choral din
As they escort them down the fence
To its far end and they've gone hence.
So heads of state and fawning courtiers who surround them,
As well as leaders in all trades and all professions,
Preoccupied with power, status and possessions,
Like dogs will savage those not in their packs and
        hound them
As standard practice. Charming women, authors, too,
Do just the same. Woe to the writer who is new!
But to cut up the pie amongst as few
As can be managed – that's just business, I'm afraid;
It's how the game is always played.
I could cite scores of such examples in support,
Of this, but the best works are those kept short,
As I've been taught by masters of this art. What's more,
To treat such subjects with the best effect one ought
To leave one's readers with some things for further thought:
This discourse endeth now, therefore.

All that is solid in my work I owe to you,
Whose modesty is equaled only by

His greatness, you, who cannot hear a word of praise,
However mildly said or doubtlessly deserved,
Without embarrassment, who has at last
Reluctantly allowed some homage to your name
To figure in these pages, defending them against
Disfigurement by time and by the censor's hand,
A name known to the ages and to all the nations
As one that honors France, a nation that has bred
Great names in greater number than any other nation,
Permit me now at least to say to all the world
That it is you from whom I've drawn my inspiration.

X. 14

The Merchant, the Noble, the Shepherd, and the Prince

Four seekers for a brave new world,
Escaping shipwreck, by the waves were hurled
Near-naked on the shore of a far distant land:
A merchant, a proud noble, a shepherd and a prince,
And now, like Belisarius, once in the command
Of Roman armies but a wandering beggar since
His fall from favor with the emperor, they too
Seemed now compelled to beg if they were to survive.
The tale of how, by various chances, this odd crew,
So different in their births, had happened to arrive
Just there, just then, upon that spot,
Is tedious to tell, so tell it I will not.
Suffice it that they had and that, beside a spring,
The castaways assembled, each considering
Their situation. The prince began to yammer on
Bad things that happen to great men. "Best to avoid
Such talk," the shepherd said. "Instead of being drawn
Into bemoaning our bad luck let's be employed
In working all together for the common good.

What use complaining? Can it cure
What ails a man? No, it cannot and never could.
Let's get to work! That is the only road that's sure
To bring us to our goal." A shepherd said such things!
A shepherd? Yes, why not? Did God give only kings
The power to reason? Do inborn limitations keep
All shepherds, as they keep all sheep,
From thinking? His fellow castaways upon the strand
Of that vast wilderness, America, agreed
To follow his advice. The merchant said that he'd
Give lessons in arithmetic, for which he planned
To charge a fee, so much per month. The prince replied,
"I will teach statecraft." Then the noble, "I take pride
In knowing heraldry, and to promote that knowledge
I plan to start the first New World heraldic college."
Halfway to India they were, yet still preoccupied
With arrant nonsense of that ilk! The shepherd said,
"Your plans sound fine, my friends, but still
A month has thirty days, so must we wait until
This one is past before we get our bellies fed?
The pictures that you paint are fine,
But, come tomorrow, will we dine?
We're starving now, so can you say
Just how these lovely schemes will bring us food today?
That is the point, you understand:
In our hard circumstance mere knowledge does no good.
For that it takes my working hand."
That said, the shepherd marched into the wood
And broke off limbs for firewood, which he sold to pay
For food for them that day and in the days ahead,
Preventing slow starvation from taking them away
To demonstrate their talents down among the dead.

The point I'm making in this tale
Is that, with little learning, men find ways to live
And that, of all the gifts that nature has to give,
The hand is our best helper and soonest of avail.

X. 15

276

Book Eleven

The Lion

Great Sultan Leopard, it is said,
By seizing chattels from the dead,
Had pastures filled with oxen, deer parks richly stocked,
And grassy leas where fat sheep flocked.
And then, across the forest, in a bordering nation,
A lion cub was born. The leopard duly sent
The sort of trite congratulation
That rulers send by custom, not the least bit meant,
Then asked the fox, his chief adviser, to provide
His cold-eyed politician's views on the event.
"You fear this cub is dangerous,"
He told the old campaigner, "but since his father died
What danger can he be to us?
This orphan rather might be pitied now, for he
Has threats enough at home to keep him occupied
And must give thanks to destiny
If he can manage to retain
What power he has, much less embark on a campaign
Of foreign conquest." Shaking his head, the fox replied,
"I feel scant pity for such little orphans, Sire,
For one must in the end decide
Either to cultivate their friendship or conspire
To have them killed before their teeth and claws emerge
And they can do us harm. I urge
You not to wait, for I have cast
His horoscope and there I see a war projected
In which his friends will be protected
And he to them will prove a lion unsurpassed.
Try to be one of his allies,
Or, failing that, take steps to weaken him." This wise
Advice was wasted on deaf ears –
The sultan slept, as did his subjects, for some years,
Until the lion cub became a lion. Then,

When bells began to toll to warn the countryside
Of his approach, the fox was sent for once again
To counsel some defense. He sighed,
"Why bother yourselves trying? You've too long delayed.
Now, if a thousand fighters came to give us aid,
It would not be enough. Besides, the more there are
The more they cost, for troops at war
Eat sheep as much as lions do. I say, appease
This one, who can, unaided, with consummate ease,
Defeat all these allies who live at our expense –
The lion himself has three that cost him not three cents:
His strength, his courage and his vigilance.
Throw him a sheep at once; if one does not suffice,
Throw him another and, as well, some of your best
And fattest cattle, hoping thus to save the rest."
Once more the sultan scorned advice
And he and his allies won nothing but disaster
As he they feared became their master.

To keep a lion friendly one must pay the price
Of seeing his great power growing ever vaster.

XI. 1

The Gods Wanting to Instruct a Son of Jupiter

FOR MONSEIGNEUR THE DUKE OF MAINE

Jupiter had a son who, owing to the line
Of his illustrious descent,
Possessed a soul that was divine.
No child as yet knows love, but this young god's intent
From his first years was to discover
The pleasing ways that make a lover,
For he in his young self combined
An amorous spirit and a mind
Beyond his years, which time on its swift wings, alas!

Too soon bears off, as seasons pass.
The goddess Flora, charming in her manner, eyes
Agleam with laughter, was the first to captivate
The young Olympian's heart. Love's panoply of sighs,
Of tears, of pleasing eloquence: in short, each trait
Love can inspire he had in full. And yet a son
Of Jupiter must have far other gifts than one
Sired by some lesser god. The craft of sweet seduction
He seemed to know untaught, as if from memory,
He practiced it so perfectly.
But Jupiter, desiring him to have instruction
In higher matters, called the other gods. "I've prided
Myself," he said, "that till this moment, unassisted,
I've ruled the universe. But now I have decided
You newer gods will be enlisted
In other tasks that I want done.
I'm speaking of that precious child we see below:
My blood runs in his veins. He is indeed my son
And will in time be worshipped. Yet he needs to know
All that there is to know before he can be lauded
As an immortal." At his words, the gods applauded.
The boy was eager to know all. And so, to start,
Mars said he personally would teach the boy that art
By which a host of heroes had
Brought honor to Olympus and enlarged its sway.
The blond Apollo answered, "I will make the lad
A poet, teaching him to play
The lyre." "Oh, very fine, but what I plan to do,"
Said Hercules in his lion skin, "Is teach him to subdue
His passions, overcome the monstrous beasts of sin
And poisonous temptation which, though slain, begin
At once to live again and grow
Like hydras in our hearts. From me, the foe
Of spineless self–indulgence, he will learn to tread
Those paths, less frequented, by which the virtues lead
To honors and to fame." Then Cupid said he'd show
Him everything he'd need to know.

⚜

281

And Love was right. What can't be done
When spirit and the wish to please are joined in one?

XI. 2

𝔗𝔥𝔢 𝔉𝔞𝔯𝔪𝔢𝔯, 𝔱𝔥𝔢 𝔇𝔬𝔤, 𝔞𝔫𝔡 𝔱𝔥𝔢 𝔉𝔬𝔵

Wolves and foxes make bad neighbors. Should I decide
To build myself a house I'd never choose a site
These two inhabited. One of the latter spied
On a farmer's hens at every moment, day and night,
But juicy as they looked, he yet could never quite
Decide to go on the attack:
First, hunger drew him on, then danger drove him back,
For which he blamed the man the hens belonged to. "Hey,"
He said, "Can this clod keep on mocking me this way
And think that I won't make him pay?
I start to make my move, I stop, I start, I work
Myself into a sweat, while he, that redneck jerk,
Sits happily at home, quite effortlessly coining
Good money raising hens and capons he will sell,
Plus hanging some up to cure as well,
While I, thief that I am, past master of purloining,
If I steal one old cock, I'm overjoyed. Oh, why
Did Jupiter decree that I must be a fox?
On all the powers of Olympus and the Styx
I swear this oath: I'm going to get that lousy guy!"
For his revenge he chose a night when all the farm
Slept as if drugged and wrapped in fog,
The owner of the place, his farmhands and his dog,
His hens and chicks and capons, under the same charm.
The farmer's failure then to lock the henhouse tight
Soon proved a costly oversight,
For in the dark, unseen, the thief slipped through the gate
And savagely proceeded to depopulate
That undefended city. Dawn
Revealed the carnage done that night,

282

A scene from which the sun, in horror at the sight,
Might almost have turned back, withdrawn
Beneath the sea once more. Just such a scene resulted
When Agamemnon, son of Atreus, insulted
Apollo, whose hot anger left the Trojan plain
Strewn with the lifeless bodies of Greek warriors slain
Within a single night. Another dire event
Of bloody chaos followed when crazed Ajax slew
Whole flocks of sheep and goats he saw around his tent,
Supposing that they were Ulysses and his crew,
Whose treachery, in his maddened eyes,
Had let his rival rob him of his rightful prize.
The fox, another Ajax, at killing hens the best,
Made off with all he could and massacred the rest.
At which, with no recourse except to shift the blame
On some poor underling (just as it's always done),
The owner yelled, "Damn dog, I ought to drown you! Shame!
Why didn't you bark to warn me at the time he came?"
"But, boss, why wasn't it up to you? You were the one
Who could have stopped him. If you went off to bed before
You had made sure to lock the door,
Can you, the master, tell your dog, who has no stake
Or interest in the outcome, he should have stayed awake?"
That dog's remarks were very sound
And would indeed have seemed profound
If posted on some sage's blog,
But being just a simple dog
He went unheard and quickly found
His master knew the verb, 'to flog.'

Thus you – whoever you are – paterfamilias
(An honor I do not aspire to), if as you sleep
You trust another's eyes to keep
Your household safe, your error may prove serious.
Be last to go to bed, see that the bolt is thrown.
With much to lose, trust no one's eyes except your own.

XI. 3

The Dream of an Inhabitant of the Mughal Empire

In the Mughal dominions, in some bygone year,
A subject dreamed he saw a powerful vizier
Among the blessed in Paradise
Enjoying bliss as endless as beyond all price.
He dreamed again and now he saw instead,
In yet another country, in torment on a bed
Of flames, a pious hermit in whose every limb
There was such pain the damned might well have pitied him.
He woke. These visions left him shaken.
Minos, the judge of souls, for once appeared mistaken.
He asked a seer to interpret, for it seemed
There must be some significance to what he'd dreamed.
The wise one told him, "Cease your wonderment.
This is a vision that the gods have sent.
In earthly life, it seems that the vizier had wanted
A hermit's solitude; the hermit's days were haunted
By the desire to move among the great viziers."

If I might dare to add my comments to the seer's,
It would be to extol the virtues of seclusion,
Which gives its lovers gifts in full, unforced profusion,
Pure gifts from Heaven that bloom about their feet.
Oh, solitude, where I find hidden charms replete,
If I might stay forever in your secret glade,
Away from the loud world, at ease in your cool shade,
Then while I lingered, timeless, in the shadows there,
The muses, those nine sisters, could be all my care,
As, far from courts and towns, they taught me from the skies
To understand those motions, hidden from our eyes,
Of those bright wanderers, their names and essences
That shape our selves and fates with all their differences.
But since I was not born for such ambitious schemes,
Let me at least find gentle pleasures by those streams

And in my verses paint the flowers by their sides.
The tapestry that fate is weaving for me hides
No warp of shining golden thread,
But if, in sleep, above my head,
No paradisal scenes are spread, then must my sleep
Yield any less delightful dreams, or be less deep
Because of that? To spare simplicity I vow
Renewed devotion, so when the moment comes to bow
And take my leave, my life will have been free of fret
And I shall die without regret.

XI. 4

The Lion, the Ape, and the Two Asses

Concerned that to rule well he should
Avoid the bad and seek the good,
The lion asked the ape, a famed authority
From academe, to school him in morality.
The gist of the first lesson his instructor gave
Was this: "Great King, to govern wisely, every prince
Must in his rulership evince
A zeal that puts the welfare of the state above
That tendency we term self-love,
For from that source, that seed, there grow
The other faults one sees in creatures here below.
To rid oneself completely of this sentiment
Is not one day's accomplishment:
Indeed, it is immensely hard
To curb in any way the power of self-regard,
And to succeed in this you must
Not let your august person be identified
In any way with actions foolish or unjust."
"Examples, please," the king replied.
"The two things need to be defined."
The teacher said, "Each social rank – I have in mind
My own, as well – each occupation,

Each segment of the population,
Believes itself to be the best
And feels itself above the rest,
Dismissing them as ignorant
Or vulgarly impertinent,
And similar cheap labels thoughtlessly applied.
And yet, contrarily, self–love leads us to praise
In sky–high terms all those with whom we are allied,
For it's a splendid way to raise
Ourselves to the same level. Many a reputation,
I have no doubt, is purely based on affectation,
Intrigue and the fine knack of putting on an air
Of consequence, a gift the ignorant seem to share
More than the wise. The other day
I watched two asses ambling side by side together
Along the highroad, trading compliments with each other.
Each one in turn would take the trowel up and lay
The praise on thick. I heard one say,
'Milord, do you not find the human animal
Supposedly so perfect, foolish and unjust
In using our name, Ass, so ancient, so august,
As a rude epithet for any he deems dull
Of wit or ignorant? Have you not heard
How with another little word
He constantly defames us, saying
Our speech and conversation are but mindless braying?
Humans are pleased to think that they
Rank far above us, but that's nonsense, for, indeed,
It's you who truly speaks, their orators who bray,
So, let them hush. But now, no more about that breed.
I understand you and you me, and that is all
That needs be said. As to the heavenly sounds that fall
Upon one's ears when you are singing, Philomel,
The nightingale, would need voice lessons to produce so
Glorious a tone. You would outdo Caruso!'
The other jackass said: 'Milord, your words portray
My image of yourself.' These dunces, not content
With mutual backscratching, went

To the big city, where they reasoned that if they
Would each extol the other, each would by this scheme
Reflect upon himself the public's fond esteem.
I know of many, nowadays,
Not just the lowly asses but the powers–that–be
Whom heaven has seen fit to raise
Above them by a fine degree,
Who'd call each other not 'my lord' but 'majesty'
If they so dared. But I disclose
More than I should of them, perhaps, and must suppose
His Majesty will keep the secret. He desired
That I tell how self–love makes fools of mortal creatures.
When I discuss injustice, more time will be required."
So spoke the ape. I don't know what, if anything,
He said about that second subject – it has features
That might make even the most authoritative teachers
Reluctant to discuss it with a sharp–toothed king.

XI. 5

The Wolf and the Fox

How is it that the fox, in Aesop's estimation,
Hasn't a rival when it comes to trickery?
I've tried to understand but lack an explanation –
Why isn't the wolf behaving just as cannily
When he defends his life or tries
To take another's? Personally,
I'd say he is and moreso, and if that defies
My master, I dare say I yet may prove I'm right –
Although, admittedly, in this first case I cite,
The fox wins all the honors. Out for a stroll one night,
He peers into a well and in its depths he sees
The moon's reflection, round and white,
And looking to his eyes like a delicious cheese.
Wound on a pole above the well, a rope suspends
Two buckets, set so one will rise as one descends.

Then, like a famished dog impatient for his supper,
The quick brown fox leaps in the upper,
Which instantly begins to fall
Till it hits bottom, where he finds no cheese at all.
Could he have made a fatal error?
Freed from illusion, pained, in terror,
He sees the only way to reemerge will be
To find another victim, just as starved as he,
To take his place and raise him out of misery.
Two days go by and not a soul comes near the place,
While passing time in two nights space
As usual shrinks the silver face
Of earth's companion from a circle, luminescent,
Into a much more meager crescent.
By now Sir Fox is in despair,
When, luckily, friend Wolf slinks past,
Appearing too caved-in to last.
The fox calls, "Pal, I'd like to share
A treat with you that's sure to please!
You see this object? It's a most exquisite cheese
That shaggy Faunus made with milk from the cow, Io.
If Jupiter fell ill, he would regain his brio
The moment that he tasted such elysian food.
Although I've eaten all but this small crescent, you'd
Find it enough to satisfy
Your hunger. So, step in that bucket there which I
Expressly left above to give you a nice ride."
However artfully the fox had modified
The truth, the wolf was stupid not to know he'd lied.
He got into the bucket, which, by his weight descending,
Propelled the bucket upward on the other side,
From which the fox emerged in a triumphal ending!
Don't sneer at the wolf, for we are equally naive,
And when we meet a clever liar
We are as ready to believe
The words we dread or else desire.

                                                    XI. 6

288

The Peasant from the Danube

Do not judge others by their looks – to men or mice
That is an old cliché but still is good advice.
In fact, a mouse's big mistake
In this regard once served me as a means to make
That argument, while, now, recasting it, I'll base
My proof upon a man, a peasant with a face
As homely as Socrates's or Aesop's, an old cuss
Who lived far up the Danube – Marcus Aurelius
Portrayed him faithfully for us.
It is well known how the first two appeared,
So let me briefly sketch the third: more like a bear
Than like a man; a bush of beard
Grew on his chin; his eyes seemed hidden in the hair
Of matted brows; he had a scowling, hostile glare,
A crooked nose, lips grossly thick; his shaggy coat,
Of leather from a long–haired goat,
Was belted in with spiny furze. This man, so dressed,
Had left behind his native home
Beside the Danube to go west,
As envoy from the lands along its length, to Rome,
When nowhere on the earth lay safely past the reach
Of its vast greed. Arriving there, he made this speech:
"You, Romans, who, with your great senate, wait to hear
What I will say, to all the gods whom men revere
I pray for inspiration. May those immortals guide
My tongue so not a word I speak needs be called back;
Without their aid mens's minds are only occupied
By ill and unjust thoughts, which we must put aside
Or else we break their laws. Our torment on the rack
Of Roman greed is less a witness to your might
Than evidence that we have erred in heaven's sight.
But, Rome, beware! Beware! The gods in future may
Bring home to you the anguish that is ours today,
And having, in full justice, given us the swords
You used to conquer us as cruel overlords,

Let us make you our slaves in turn.
Why are we yours, can someone tell me? Let me learn
Why Rome is worth a hundred nations. Please rehearse
The reasons for your right to rule the universe.
What brings you to disrupt lives simple as our own?
We plow our fields in peace and after they are sown
Employ our hands in tasks of other useful kinds.
What have you taught us? We have minds,
We Teutons, and we are, like you,
Endowed with courage. If our greed
And violence had also equaled yours, we too
Might have turned conquerors. Indeed,
We might have conquered you but yet known how to use
Humanely those great powers your governors abuse
In ways that strain imagination.
The gods majestically enshrined
Upon your altars surely find
Your cruelties a profanation,
For you must know that those immortals are not blind,
And in your brutal actions their offended eyes
See only things that they despise:
Atrocities that are to them a desecration
Both of their temples and their worship; rage to acquire
More power and wealth that grows to a consuming fire.
Nothing contents the Romans who invade our lands.
The crops from our rich earth, the works of our skilled hands
Are not enough to sate their greed,
So call them home. We will not plow our fields to feed
Their hunger; we will flee our villages to find
Safe refuge in the mountains; we will leave behind
Our dearest mates to live in solitude, with wild
And frightful bears our only neighbors, each man sworn
Not to beget another child
To populate a land of slaves in Rome's support.
As for our children who are now already born,
We pray to see their lives immediately cut short:
Your praetors force us to such criminality,
So call them home. With their instruction, we will learn

Nothing but vice and laxity,
And, having learned them, we will turn
Corrupt and venal as you are –
For I have seen no evidence in Rome thus far
That you are honest men. Have I no bribes in hand?
No favors to dispense? Then I must understand
That I cannot expect your courts to help my cause.
It seems that the chief justice administering your laws
Is otherwise engaged. Which brings me to a close.
My speech has been a bit too tactless, I suppose,
And you condemn to death all those
Offending you with their complaints." He fell prostrate.
All Rome was much astonished, admired his courage, sense,
And the inspiring eloquence
This untaught savage had the gift to demonstrate.
They made him a patrician, which was, the crowd believed,
The only punishment his noble speech deserved.
New praetors were appointed and the Senate moved
That this man's speech to them should be the model hence
For all petitioners. But that such eloquence
Was often heard in Rome there is scant evidence.

XI. 7

The Old Man and the Three Young Ones

An octogenarian, planting saplings,
Amazed three teenage boys, smart alecks, local striplings.
"To build at your age would be dumb, but planting trees,"
They said, "that's crazy! What is the point in starting these
With so much labor? Before you pick one fruit you'll be
Old as Methuselah!" He'd lost it, plain to see.
"Why dedicate your life to working on a scheme
You won't live to complete? You've no time left to dream
Of big ambitious things you hope someday to do.
So dwell upon your past; make short range plans, not long.
The future is for us, not you!"

The old man answered, "But you're wrong!
You cannot claim the future yours,
For making things takes time and nothing made endures.
Your lives and mine are all in the pale hands of Fate,
And none of us has long to wait.
Which one of us will be the last to see this great
Blue dome above us? Can you say with not one doubt
You have one second more before your time runs out?
Descendants not yet born will thank me for the shade
My trees will give them. Truly, must the wise be faced
By obstacles that block their selfless efforts, made
For others' future joys? For that is the fruit I taste
Today, this present moment. And tomorrow, too,
And some days more perhaps, perhaps more days than you.
For I may yet, before I'm done,
Above your graves some mornings watch the rising sun.
Time proved him right. One lad was drowned
Soon after his ship left harbor, bound
For North America. Another, having ascended
High in the army's ranks, had his enlistment ended
By a shot he never heard. The third
Fell from a tree he climbed to cut a twig to graft.
The old man, mourning, carved upon their marble shaft
This tale I've told, as it occurred.

XI. 8

The Mice and the Hoot-Owl

If you have some new marvel to communicate,
Perhaps it's best to realise
That when you say to people, "Listen, this is great!"
Your marvel may not seem so special in their eyes.
But yet the tale that follows may be one to view
As an exception: I find it quite phenomenal
In its account, and in its essence like a fable
That also happens to be true.

Because it was so old, a hollow pine was felled,
A hoot owl's ancient castle, a gloomy, dark retreat
Where that grim bird, Fate's augur, had in secret dwelled.
Within the trunk, in chambers carved by time, were found,
With other tenants, swarms of mice, all lacking feet,
But nonetheless well–nourished, sleekly fat and round.
The owl had kept them fed with little piles of wheat
He put amongst them, having previously removed
Their little legs with his sharp beak – which surely proved
The bird made use of reason just as much as men.
The first mice he had captured soon escaped again,
But the smart fellow, pondering the problem, thought
Of the solution: simply maim the mice he caught
And he could dine upon them any time he chose –
Today, he would eat these and then, tomorrow, those.
To eat them all at once, he clearly understood,
Would be impossible and, for his health, not good.
With foresight equaling our own, he then contrived
To bring them grain so they survived.
Could a Cartesian have obstinately seen
That owl as only clockworks, merely a machine?
What spring could have produced the thought
Of thus disabling all those creatures he had caught?
If thought was not what he displayed,
Then what thought is is Greek to me.
Here are the arguments he made:
"These critters, when I've caught them, flee,
So I should eat them instantly.
But eating them all is totally
Impossible, so don't I need
To keep them for a while? Agreed.
And while I do, I'll have to feed
Them while, somehow, preventing them from fleeing.
But how? Cut off their legs!" Would any human being
Have in the end done better? In what way did his thought
Not evidence the logic Aristotle taught?

This is not a fable: the tale it tells, however extraordinary and near-incredible it may seem, actually happened. I have perhaps somewhat overstated the foresight of the owl – I do not pretend to have established for a fact that animals reason exactly as described here, but such exaggerations are allowed in poetry, particularly in the branch of it that has served my purposes.

XI. 9

Epilogue

Thus end my muse's wanderings
By that pure stream whose current springs
From Helicon's high crown of snow.
Into the language of the gods she has translated
The endless dialogues of creatures here below
In voices nature lends them, ever variegated.
As the interpreter for peoples so diverse
I've turned them into actors, each with a role to play.
But since all that exists within this universe
Speaks with more eloquence than all my lines display,
Should any being find my verses need correction,
Should this, my work, not prove a perfect paradigm,
Still, I have marked a path that leads in a direction
That others yet may follow in the coming time.
Those the nine muses favor will achieve the goal,
Teach many lessons I undoubtedly left out,
And with a dedication never less than whole.
Nor will they lack great subjects on which to expand:
For while my muse was with small matters occupied
Louis was conquering Europe and with his mighty hand
Completing noble projects heretofore untried
By monarchs of the past. Given such deeds to rhyme,
Those the nine muses favor will conquer death and time.

Book Twelve

Dedication

TO MONSEIGNEUR THE DUKE OF BURGUNDY

Prince, uniquely in the care of the Immortals,
Suffer my wafting incense to perfume your portals.
If I seem tardy with these presents from my muse,
My years and my fatigues must serve as my excuse.
My spirit dwindles, even as yours upwards springs –
Yours does not walk, it runs, it seems to go on wings!
That pattern for your virtues, your heroic sire,
Upon the field of Mars has blazoned his in fire,
And having once brought Victory home upon his blade
Let none complain of him that with a giant's stride
He does not lead his troops in glorious parade:
Some deity (our sovereign King!) calls him aside
Who triumphed on the Rhine in but a month's campaign.
For then the times required audacity and speed,
When now a rapid pace might prove too rash indeed.
But hush to this – for Love and Laughter, nymphs the twain,
Care little for long speeches, that is very plain,
And such divinities must now compose your court.
They will attend you always, though a sterner sort
In time will come to stand in yet a higher place:
Wisdom and Justice then will regulate and guide.
Consult this latter pair to help you judge a case
In which the Greeks sound sense defied
And, failing to show caution, were seduced
By charms that left them utterly reduced
From man's condition – and to beasts transmogrified.

Ulysses and His Shipmates

Storm–driven, helpless, fearing all that fate might bring,
Ulysses and his men, for ten years wandering,
At last were cast upon the shore
Whose realm the sun god's daughter ruled,
Fair Circe the enchantress, schooled
In every twist of mystic lore.
She made them up a potion to entice their thirst,
A delicate but deadly brew
That robbed them of their reason first
And then their human forms – for, as they drank, they grew
New bodies and new faces. Presto! They were changed
To beasts of every stripe. They ranged
From towering elephants to tiny moles,
With lions and bears, et cetera, between these poles.
Yet one man wisely spurned the drink:
Ulysses, who knew what to think
Of such deceptions. And as he perfectly combined
Heroic bearing and resourceful mind
With smoothly artful speech, his charmer met a charm
As potent as her own to alter and disarm.
Now, since a goddess makes no secret of her feelings,
She soon confessed she was aflame,
While our Ulysses was too cool in all his dealings
Not to have pressed his winning game.
He begged her if she loved him to release his crew.
"I will, my sweet," she said. "But would they wish me to?
Go ask them first. Let them agree before I do."
Ulysses shouted, "Shipmates! She who poisoned you
Can also cure. Dear friends, you can be men again!
I offer you the choice. Is this your wish? Why, then
At once you're free, your old humanity restored."
The lion pondered, then he roared,
"I am a fool! Is that your thesis?
That I'd renounce my gifts to be as I began?
Now I have teeth and claws to tear my foes to pieces.

I'm king! Why be Ulysses' loyal little man?
You'd have me be a soldier, marching in the rear.
Change is a word I will not hear!"
Ulysses tried the bear. He said, "It's sad, old bruin,
That one who looked so handsome now looks such a ruin."
"Looks how?" replied the bear in his gruff tone.
"What are we really saying here, ex-brother?
How do I look? The way a bear should look! Just who
Informed you that one form is better than another?
I'll leave it to my she-bear's eyes to see me true.
If you dislike my looks, bug off and leave me be.
I'm happy, have no cares at all, and I am free!
I tell you flatly, loud and clear,
Change is a word I will not hear."
Rejected yet again, now Ulysses tried
To get the wolf to change, but was again denied.
"Comrade," the Grecian said, "it seems a paradox
That till the echoes ring the shepherdess laments
How as a carnivore you decimate her flocks,
When as a man you would have sprung to her defense.
Your life was once exemplary.
Now leave these woods and choose to be
The thing you were when you began –
Not cruel wolf but kindly man."
"Does one exist?" asked Wolf. "If so, where can he be?
You call me carnivore. And what, my friend, of thee?
Have you not butchered many, even more than I,
Of those same sheep whose loss the villagers decry?
When I was human, did I spill
Any drop of blood the less?
For nothing but a word you kill
Not one but all, with unremitting savageness.
Are you not wolves to one another? All in all,
Considering the facts as fairly as I can,
I think a wolf to be less beastly than a man.
And so, strange though it may appear,
Change is a word I will not hear."
Ulysses summoned all, small, middle-sized and great,

To be his men again, each to his epic fate,
But each one in his turn refused.
Their liberties, the woods, their pressing appetites –
All these were their supreme delights.
The thought of heroism left them unenthused.
Each one felt liberated, doing as he craved,
When all in fact were self–enslaved.

Prince, it was my wish to find
A theme that might amuse but yet instruct your mind.
Ah, what a lovely gift for you!
But finding it was not an easy thing to do –
Until at last Ulysses' shipmates came to view.
Here in this lowly world live myriads of their kind –
Such men for whom I say you must
Show your contempt and your disgust.

XII. 1

The Cat and the Two Sparrows

To Monseigneur the Duke of Burgundy

A cat and a tame sparrow, nearly the same age,
Had spent their lives together, each a family pet,
The kitten's basket always by the young bird's cage.
The pesky sparrow often would torment the cat,
Forever pecking at him, while, with his sharp claws
Kept scrupulously sheathed, the cat would merely fend
His small companion off and use his nimble paws
To bat the other one away,
The two of them like fencers, duelling in play
That always spared the smaller friend.
And though the bird with his sharp bill
Continued pecking, harder still,
The cat refused to be disturbed
And, using wise discretion, kept his temper curbed –

For friends must never let emotions go so far
That playful games turn into war.
From having been together since each started life
They lived in peace by habit and avoided strife.
But when a second sparrow flew
From trees outside the house to visit them, the stage
Now held three characters: the noisy clown, the sage,
And this new interloper. Soon, a quarrel grew
Between the birds, in which the cat of course took part.
"This stranger," he exclaimed, "does he suppose that he
Can come in here like this and start
Attacking my best friend and pay no penalty?
Can this rude sparrow from another neighborhood
Think he can beat up this from ours? I'll not betray
My friend, on a cat's honor!" Joining in the fray,
He killed and ate the stranger. "Sparrows do taste good!"
He mused. And, having thought the implications through,
He killed and ate the other too.

What moral is implied? For, lacking one, a fable
Is not a finished work. Vague possibilities
For this one come to mind, but still I am unable
To sum them up succinctly. Prince, your abilities
So far exceed my own you will see instantly
What my muse and her sisters have left dark to me.

XII. 2

The Miser and the Ape

A man amassed a hoard. It's known, those so obsessed
Will often come to be possessed.
Pistoles and ducats, minted gold of every kind,
Consumed him wholly – yet such hoarded wealth I find
Also quite worthless. To keep his treasure well–secured
Our man lived on an island, on all sides immured
By waves, which, like a wall, kept prowling thieves away.

And there, with pleasure he considered great,
But that I would consider small, both night and day
He strove to count, to calculate,
To tally up his fortune. And each time, having finished,
He started once again to calculate and count,
For, always, he found errors, and the net amount
Seemed often to have been diminished.
His pet, a gangling ape – in my opinion wiser
Than his peculiar master, the compulsive miser –
Would sometimes on an impulse throw
Gold pieces out the window to the sea below:
For since the miser locked the place when he was gone,
He saw no risk in leaving heaps of coins upon
The counter if he left the job,
Which meant that if the ape was taken by the notion
That it would be great fun to lob
Some shiny things into the ocean,
Nothing prevented him. When I attempt to weigh
The pleasures of the two, I find it hard to say
To which of them I'd give the prize,
The human or the ape. One philosophic set,
Whose reasoning would take too long to summarize,
Would choose the simian. At any rate, the pet,
On nothing but pure mischief bent,
One day grabbed coins in fistfuls from the pile and sent
Them skipping briskly, one by one, across the waves:
Rose nobles, ducatoons,
Jacobuses, doubloons,
These bits of metal that our human species craves
Beyond all else. And if he had not heard the miser's key
Inserted in the lock, the ape would soon have pitched
Them all, down to the last gold ducat, in the sea,
Which has by many, many shipwrecks been enriched.

God has seen fit to keep from harm a lot
Of wealthy types who do no better with what they've got.

XII. 3

The Two She-goats

As long as she-goats have existed
They have in every age persisted
In roaming freely. Thus, they seek out places where
All evidence of man is rare,
And if there is some region where no roads are found
Or well-worn trails, but jagged peaks and cliffs abound,
That's where these ladies go to stroll along the edges
Of precipices and high ledges,
For nothing can deter them when they wish to climb.
Once, two of these capricious dames,
Both bearing high-born goatish names,
Decided simultaneously that it was time
To leave the lower fields and seek some distant ridge.
Along the way, by chance, they met at a small bridge
That ran above a rapids: a single plank so thin
Two weasels passing on it would have fallen in.
Still worse, the fearful height and wildly rushing waters
Should surely have unnerved these Amazonian daughters.
But no: despite the danger, neither of them shrank
From confrontation.
One put a hoof upon the plank
And then, so did the other. It was a situation
That, somehow, puts me much in mind
Of when our king, great Louis, met
Philip the Fourth of Spain, and the two signed
A treaty on an island in a river. Yet,
The difference in this instance was that those
Two goats were not, as were the kings, inclined
Toward peace and, step by step, advanced till, nose
To nose, our head-strong wanderers stood, mid-way,
With neither willing to give way.
(As the story goes, one was by family related
To that unrivaled she-goat once donated
By Polyphemus to Galatea, and the other

To the she–goat Amaltheus, who suckled Jupiter.)
Since neither would retreat both fell into the water.

Hardly the first example of chance's
Influence on earthly circumstances.

XII. 4

To Monseigneur the Duke of Burgundy

WHO ASKED M. DE LA FONTAINE TO WRITE A FABLE TO BE
CALLED "THE CAT AND THE MOUSE"

How shall I please a prince to whom the goddess, Fame,
Will in my writings build a temple in his name?
Shall I compose a fable which – this point is vital –
Must have "The Cat and the Mouse" as title?

And should I in the tale I'll write depict a beauty
Whose looks conceal, beneath their surface, cruelty?
Who toys with all the hearts her many charms entice,
As cats have always done with mice?

Or shall my subject be Dame Fortune's fickle deeds?
There could be nothing better suited to his needs
Than to be shown how Fortune, often, in a trice,
Turns on her friends, as cats on mice.

And shall my tale portray a king of such appeal
To Fortune that for him alone she keeps her wheel
From turning as, beset on every side by foes,
He plays with them so cleverly the strongest feel
Like mice beneath a cat's quick blows?

But, gradually, I see that nothing will suffice
Except a tale that's short, for, if I am not wrong,
My effort will be spoiled if I go on too long –

For then the prince would see my muse's wise advice
As his fair game, as cats see mice.

The Old Cat and the Young Mouse

A young and unsophisticated mouse imagined he
Could get an ancient cat to show him clemency,
And he began reciting reasons to the beast:
"Sir, you should let me live," said he.
"For how expensive can it be
To feed a mouse as small as me?
Is any in this house the least
Deprived by me of nourishment?
For me, one grain of wheat's a feast,
One walnut and I'm corpulent.
But now I am so thin that you had better wait
And let your children eat me at some future date."
The other said: "You dare to speak to me like that?
You might as well address the deaf. You ask a cat,
Especially an old one, to show mercy? Not
In a million years! By ancient feline law, now die!
And when you pass through Hades's gates
See if you can persuade the Fates.
Meanwhile, my children will find other foods to try."
That's what he told the captive mouse. The moral I
Intend my fable to express
Is this: youth sees such reasonableness
In its demands of age it confidently expects them
Fulfilled at once, but age is pitiless
And rejects them.

XII. 5

The Ailing Stag

A stag fell ill, and stags from all the nation quickly
Ran to assist him, weak and sickly
Upon his bed of grass, to nurse him or to try
Consoling him at least, a rude and pushy crowd.
"Good sirs!" he said, "Please let me die,
For if fate is at last allowed
To send me off you'll end this bogus lamentation."
But no one heard. All stayed, dispensing consolation
Till it pleased God to let them go –
But not before each took a cheering cup or so,
Which in the stags' case meant carousing,
Not by imbibing but by browsing
On all the bushes near the spot
Without the slightest invitation,
Till it was like a desert, bare of vegetation.
And since the ailing stag had not
One meager bite left in the pot
He had to fast and shortly perished of starvation.

Those doctors called to treat your body or your soul
Will often leave you in the hole.
What things have come to nowadays!
One may protest, but still one pays.

XII. 6

The Bat, the Bush, and the Duck

Convinced, all three, that they would have small luck
Prospering in their country, the bush, the bat and the duck
Turned merchants, paying equal shares
Into a partnership to sell assorted wares
In distant lands. They set up bank accounts,
Employed a sales staff, chartered agents

Known for their carefulness and their intelligence,
Kept ledgers showing the amounts
Received or spent. And things went perfectly
Until their ship, bound through a region
Of narrow straits, uncharted reefs and dangers legion,
Sank with their goods in the dark storehouse of the sea.
Our trio wept in vain about their plight,
Or, rather, kept their lips sealed tight,
For even the smallest merchant knows
His losses are the thing that he must not disclose
If he's to keep his credit sound.
The loss that, purely through bad luck, these three
Had suffered was past fixing. The news soon got around
And there they were, sans cash or credit or resources,
Each one compelled to wear the cap of bankruptcy.
No lenders opened up their purses.
The interest payments due that they could not afford.
Court summonses, the sheriff and a clamoring horde
Of creditors who pounded on
Their doors each day before the dawn:
Such matters kept them occupied
With finding ways to make all parties satisfied.
The bush snagged every passer-by. "Good sirs," it moaned,
"Oh, tell me, please, where is that merchandise I owned?
In what deep trench beneath its waves
Is the ocean hiding it from me?"
The duck kept diving, searching for it, fruitlessly.
The bat, afraid of being seen by daylight, hid in caves
Where no one went, trailed by the sheriff constantly.

I know of many a debtor who is neither bat
Nor bush nor diving duck, nor tangled in affairs
Of just this sort, but simply a great aristocrat
Who has to come and go by his back stairs.

XII. 7

367

The Dispute between the Dogs and the Cats
and
The One between the Cats and the Mice

Discord has reigned forever in the universe.
Examples proving this are countlessly diverse,
For in our world this goddess has many a devotee –
The elements themselves would be
The first on any list: one is amazed to see
How they unite in matter so contrarily.
And yet, what myriads more there are
Than these four kings, engaged in an eternal war!

In some past age, a multitude of dogs and cats
Lived in a spacious residence
Where the decrees of law and stringent governance
Prevented all domestic spats.
The master of the house took care to regulate
The things all did, the meals they ate,
And took his strap to any he thought prone to fight,
Till all behaved like cousins, kissingly polite.
This state of near–fraternal peace and unity
Inspired the whole community.
But then it ended. An action hardly consequential –
A soup bowl given one, an extra bone presented
To someone's favored pet – was seen as preferential,
An outrage, furiously resented.
I have read chroniclers who blame the whole affair
On one who gave his whelping bitch a larger share.
Whatever it was, an altercation
Began and grew into a blazing confrontation
Between the cats' side and the dogs'. A regulation
Someone proposed aroused such yowling indignation
Among the cats that there was general consternation.
The lawyer for the cats said his advice
Was to consult the book of laws. But on investigation

The volume proved to have been eaten by the mice.
There followed a fresh round of litigation,
For many guileful cats had waited
All of their lives to find so good a provocation
To treat the mice as vermin, their whole population
Fit to be stalked, pounced on and exterminated.
The master of the house gave them his approbation.
Returning to my theme, I have not seen one creature,
One animal, one being, under earth's broad sky
Without its enemy: such is the law of nature.
It is a waste of time to seek for reasons why –
God's works are good, his purposes I cannot know.
But what I do know is that conflicts often grow
From venomed words. Even at sixty years
You've learned so little, humans, that you need to go
To school again and sit while graybeards bend your ears.

XII. 8

The Wolf and the Fox

Why does no mortal happily
Accept his lot? Those men who yearn
To lead the soldier's life in turn
Are eyed by soldiers enviously.

A fox once eagerly desired
To be a wolf, or so it's said.
Hey, has no wolf perhaps aspired,
Just once, to be a sheep instead?

I marvel that a prince of eight
Could with a moment's thought propose
A fable that my gray-haired pate
Would have long struggled to create
In verse less telling than his prose.

369

Indeed, no poet's lines could phrase
His quick ideas half so neatly,
Nor yet express them so completely,
Thus further adding to his praise.

To play a simple pipe of reeds
Is the one talent I can show
But soon the time will come, I know,
To trumpet his heroic deeds.

I am no prophet, darkly wise,
Yet I see written in the skies
That in the coming years his glories
Will call for Homers, more than one,
To chronicle the epic stories
Of all he'll do – though there are none
Among our present poets able
To do so yet. But, that aside, let's have our fable.

The fox says to the wolf, "Dear friend, my daily diet
Is just too boring. An old cock or scrawny hen
Is all I ever get. Chicken! I'm sickened by it.
But you eat better with less risk to you, since when
You hunt you roam abroad, while I must always go
Near people's houses. Comrade! Bro!
Teach me your trade, those skills you know.
Make me the first of all my foxy race to keep
His larder stocked with nice fat sheep:
You will not find this fox to be a thankless one."
"I'll do it," says the wolf. "One of my pack just died.
Let's go and skin the carcass. You can wear his hide."
The fox agrees. Then, with the skinning done,
The wolf says, "For decoying mastiffs from their flocks
We do the following things. Take note."
Clad in the wolfskin now, the fox
Tries learning his teacher's rules by rote.
Repeating them over and over. After a shaky start,
At last he knows them all by heart.

Then, having passed the course, he gets his chance to be
The hero of his dreams, for now, what does he see
But a great flock of sheep approaching. Instantly,
The new wolf rushes on them, spreading panic wide,
Just as Patroclus, in Achilles' armor, terrified
The Trojans once, and old men, wives and matrons fled
For refuge to the temple. But now the sheep themselves
Imagine they see fifty wolves,
And shepherd, dogs and flock, in dread,
Flee to the village, leaving one sheep to satisfy him.
The robber seizes her, but then, somewhere close by him
He hears a crowing cock and right away he's off
To catch it, this false disciple, first taking time to doff
His scholar's robe so he can run yet faster,
Forgetting the sheep, his lessons and his wolfish master.

Why try to be what we are not?
Pretending we can do so is a mere illusion,
For we will always, like a shot,
Revert to our true selves upon the first occasion.

Your matchless spirit, Prince, inspired
My muse to write this fable. All is drawn from you:
The plot, the dialogue required,
And, certainly, the moral too.

XII. 9

The Crawfish and Her Daughter

Shrewd souls, like crawfish, sometimes turn their backs
Towards where they aim to go; the skillful sailor tacks
Away from port to get there; or in some enterprise
That must be hidden, safe from enemy detection,
The strategist looks elsewhere with such eager eyes
He sends his foes all galloping in that direction.
My subject's small, but one may learn of greatness by it:

There is a certain hero to whom I could apply it,
A conqueror who alone, without the least fatigue
Could easily defeat a hundred–headed league.
What he plans not to do, and what he'll do in fact
His enemies can't know – until they are attacked!
He keeps his goal concealed; it is in vain they seek.
Together, they make puny efforts at delay:
But then his strength bursts forth and all are swept away.
Against one Jupiter, a hundred gods are weak.
Allied with Destiny, LOUIS would be able
To best the universe – but let us have our fable.

One day old Mother Crawfish nattered at her daughter,
"Dear God, the way you walk! Why can't you do it proper?"
"Mother!" said the daughter. "I walk like you exactly!
Can I walk any different than my whole family?
You want me to go frontwise, with you so screwed around?"

And, clearly, what she said was sound.
For from our families our characters arise.
The rule is universal, having application
To both the good and bad, the foolish and the wise
And many who are neither. As to my observation
About concealing one's intended destination
By turning one's back, why, that applies
In warfare – elsewhere, use it with discrimination.

XII. 10

The Eagle and the Magpie

The eagle, queen of the air, once landed on a lea
Where chance had also brought the magpie, Marjorie,
A pair of birds as different as two birds could be
In outlook, language, spirit and, as one might see,
In feather.

372

The magpie was afraid, but having recently
Dined well, the eagle reassured her, saying, "We
Should fly companionably together,
For if ennui plagues Jupiter my master, he
Who rules the universe, the same holds true of me,
His servant. So amuse me; say some funny thing."
At once the loudmouth magpie started chattering
Non-stop, on this, on that, on everything.
That man described by Horace, an old public crier
Who walked the fields dispensing news, both good and dire,
Could not have known one half the gossip the pied bird
Began to babble, telling the eagle she would fly
Around the land and bring back tales of all she heard.
God knows, she'd make a perfect spy.
Her offer failed to please. The eagle said, "Goodbye,
My dear, don't fly with me. Stay here. My court
Does not need gossips of your chattering sort.
Such characters are dreadful." The magpie, though not shy,
Could think of nothing to reply.

Consorting with the gods is not so glamorous
As it might seem and often proves calamitous
For mortals. Tattlers, spies and types whose kindly faces
Hide treacherous hearts make their environs odious.
Though, like the magpie, all frequenting such high places
Must wear the colors of two parishes.

XII. 11

The Kite, the King, and the Hunter

TO HIS MOST SERENE HIGHNESS MONSEIGNUER
THE PRINCE DE CONTI

The gods, being kind, want kings, their earthly regents,
To be the same. Of powers given to them, lenience

373

Is the most beautiful, and sweeter yet than vengeance.
Prince, clearly you agree, known as you are for cooling
Hot anger in your heart before its flames can rise.
Achilles, who had no capacity for ruling
Wrath in his own, is for this reason in our eyes
A hero less than you: that epithet applies
To none but those who do, as in the age of gold,
A hundred acts of good in this imperfect world.
Few men are born to greatness in our modern days –
If leaders merely do no harm they win high praise.
But, far from following such examples,
You by a thousand generous acts will merit temples
Where with his lyre Apollo will acclaim your deeds.
I know that you are much awaited by the gods
In their great palace, where a hundred years of life
In its surroundings surely will be time enough.
But in your house, soon married to a noble wife,
A hundred years will be too short a time to measure
The long continuation of your wedded pleasure,
Which the god Hymen will accord you mutually.
For you and your fair princess can deserve no less:
In proof of which I need but cite her loveliness;
And cite as well those gifts that heaven so lavishly
Has given you both, which ornament your youthfulness
With qualities the two of you alone possess.
To the proud Bourbon lineage she brings the leaven
Of matchless grace and spirit: heaven,
Benignly watching from above,
Gave her twin talents, whose effect
Is, first of all, to win respect,
And, equally, to garner love.
The joys you are to know are not for me to say,
So, I will hush and then portray
The doings of a bird of prey.

For years a kite had lived, unthreatened, on its nest
Until a hunter, in a quest
For some fine gift to please his king,

Decided the rare bird would be the perfect thing:
For, as a thing is rarer, its value surely grows.
Thus, catching it alive, he brought it to the court,
Presented it, and – if there's truth in the report –
Watched as it clamped its talons on the monarch's nose.
Oh, no! The monarch's nose? – His very own. Quite so.
Was he without his crown? His scepter? Or his mace?
It would have made small difference whether he was or no:
It treated the king's nose like one on any face.
The shock ensuing, the huge uproar, the distress
Within the court, words lack the power to express.
But yet the king sat mute – for to evince
Excitability does not become a prince.
The bird stayed put where it had landed,
Refusing to move. Its master called it, he commanded,
Held out his fist, a bloody lure, inflicted pain:
It did not budge one inch; his efforts were in vain.
The insolent beast was patently prepared to stay
Until the sun came up next day.
Despite the deafening noise, apparently it chose
To make its nest that night upon the sacred nose.
Attempting to dislodge it had made it stubborner yet,
But, when at last it flew, the monarch ordered, "Let
The kite go free, also the man, who was intent
On pleasing me. Each followed his own natural bent,
The one, an untamed kite, the other, a man bred
For life in the deep woods. And as for me, whose head
Is burdened with a crown, I know
How kings must act: both are absolved. I let them go."
The courtiers felt astonished, thrilled and elevated
By such an act – which they would not have imitated,
For very few, not even kings, take as their own
This model of forgiveness. The hunter here portrayed
Did well to have survived, though the mistake he made,
In common with the kite, was failing to have known
That it is perilous to come too near a throne,
His education having been
Only from forest creatures: is that so great a sin?

This tale is from Bidpai, a Hindu from those lands
Along the Ganges, where no human stains his hands
With other creatures' blood, and even kings obey
This teaching. "How can it be surely known," they say
"That at the siege of Troy this splendid bird of prey
Was not a warrior? It could have been that then
He was a king or one of those heroic men.
And what he was before he could become again.
For, like Pythagoras, we think that we exchange
Forms with the animals: at first perhaps a kite,
But then a pigeon; human now, but due to change
Into a bird that with its feathered kind takes flight."

He told another tale of king and man and bird;
I tell it now: same elements, differently stirred.

A certain falconer, once having caught a kite –
A feat accomplished scarcely once a century –
Thought that so rare a gift would certainly delight
His king: it was the highest peak of falconry.
With burning eagerness he mingled with the crowd
Around the throne, like someone all his life allowed
To be there, certain that his gift
Would surely make his fortune, lift
Him up among the ranks of those
Most favored souls, when, suddenly,
The bird, still wild, ferociously
Cramped its steel talons viciously upon his nose.
The poor man howled, the courtiers fell
To loud guffawing and, as well,
The king. Who wouldn't have? I swear
I would myself have given an empire to be there.
Can a pope laugh? I would not care
To state with certainty one can,
But any king who cannot on occasion dare
To laugh out loud is in my eyes a poorer man.
For laughing is a godly pleasure – Jupiter,

Despite his dark, forbidding brow, is given to laughter,
As are the other gods. Once, watching Vulcan hobble
As he brought drink to Jove, that whole immortal throng
Burst into laughter well–nigh inextinguishable,
Or so the old myth goes. Were the gods right, or wrong?
On that I'll change the subject, with good reason,
But since we're speaking here of moral rules,
What do these stories teach us? Just that in every season
Merciful kings are fewer than hunters who are fools.

XII. 12

The Fox, the Flies, and the Hedgehog

A fox, an old and sly one, canny, worldly wise,
Wounded by hunters, fallen helpless in the mud,
His tracks marked by a trail of blood,
Attracted those winged parasites that we call flies.
He held the gods to blame. Why should he be a victim?
Why had fate chosen so unfairly to afflict him,
Consigning him for flies to eat?
"What, me? Attacking me, undoubtedly the brightest
Of all the forest's creatures? Since when are foxes meat?
And is my tail no use against them? Not the slightest!
It is a useless burden in this situation.
Go! May the gods destroy your pestilential nation!
Eat someone of a lower class than I!"
A hedgehog from the woods nearby –
He's new to my fables – thought to try
And save him from the buzzing cloud
That circled him, an avidly bloodthirsty crowd.
He said, "I'll throw my quills and spear them by the dozen
And soon relieve your torment, cousin."
"Friend, do not do that," said the fox, "because this group
Is all but satiated and, if they leave, a troop
Whose appetite is far more ravenous will swoop

In swarming hundreds down upon me
And pitilessly feast as they go crawling on me."

From low official to high magistrate,
We find no dearth of hungry eaters here below.
This was a tale that Aristotle long ago
Applied to humankind. One sees in every state –
Our own especially – that as men's bellies grow
Full to satiety their appetites abate.

XII. 13

Love and Folly

That small boy, Cupid – Love – conceals a mystery.
His arrows and his quiver, his torch, his infancy
Are emblems not to be deciphered in a day.
Thus, all I aim at here is telling in my way
How this blind child, a god, became deprived of sight.
As to the question, whether such an evil could
At the same time effect some good,
I leave it to a lover to decide what's right.

Before he had yet lost his eyes,
Love with Folly once contested
With eager spirit for some prize.
A squabble started: who had won it? Love suggested
They call the other gods as an impartial jury,
But Folly, never patient, in a sudden fury,
Instead struck Love such a tremendous blow it left
Him blind from that day on, bereft
Of any ray of light to guide
Him on his way, at which the goddess Venus cried
For vengeance: one need only say
She was a woman and a mother to convey
Her cries of rage. Great Jupiter and Nemesis
Felt their ears ringing, and, as well,

Those gods who sit below as judges down in Hell –
In short, all of that crew. She charged, with bitterness,
That the assault had left her son, save with a cane,
Tied to one spot. For such a monstrous crime no pain
Was punishment enough. This debt must be repaid!
Then, having thought it through and weighed
The interests of the public and the plaintiff, too,
The court in session high above
Judged that the only thing to do
Was to make Folly, henceforth, lead the way for Love.

XII. 14

The Crow, the Gazelle, the Tortoise, and the Rat

To Madame de La Sablière

Though I might labor till the end of days
To make, in verse, a temple in your praise,
My work would stand unfinished, for each part,
As I would have been conscious from the start,
Would needs have been made worthy of this art
The gods invented and that goddess's name
Who would be worshipped there. Upon the frame
Of its great door I would have carved in stone,
THIS PALACE IS THE GODDESS IRIS'S OWN –
Not hers who in the skies is Juno's aide
But hers who here on earth would be obeyed
Not just by Juno but by Jupiter,
Each proud to serve as her mere messenger.
Depicted on the vaulted ceiling, crowds
Of gods and goddesses among the clouds
That swathe Olympus would perform the rite
Of her apotheosis: reverently
They would enthrone her, canopied in light.

And on the walls one would, in fresco, see
Her life at every stage illuminated –
A pleasing tale, not one unduly weighted
With those untoward and terrible events
That when they happen topple governments.
Deep in the temple, in its holiest space,
Would be her portrait, with her smiling face,
Her beauty, her fair attributes, that art
Of pleasing, effortless upon her part,
That wins from all such homage. I would direct
That in the scene the portraitist must show,
Adoring at her feet, the world's elect,
Its heroes and its demigods and even
The gods themselves, at times forsaking heaven
To worship at her altar. And I would show
The radiance in her eyes made by the glow
From the rich treasures in her mind – although
That would not be an easy thing to render,
Because that heart, both infinitely tender
And keenly passionate, unmasks to friends
And friends alone; because that spirit, born
Deep in the firmament, most subtly blends
Man's beauty with those graces that adorn
The woman, in ways not easily expressed.
Oh, Iris, who can charm the wariest,
Who knows the art of pleasing perfectly,
And whom to know is to love equally
With one's own self (that is, without a trace
Of *amorousness*, a word that has no place
Within your court, so let it now be banned),
Allow my muse someday to help my hand
Give shape to this crude sketch. To lend it grace,
I'll use it now, unfinished, as the base
For a new fable in which friendship brings
Such rich rewards that, when you come to hear it,
Its simple tale may entertain your spirit
A little while at least. It seems that kings

Are scarcely bound by friendship: as we see,
Unloving monarchs aren't your cup of tea,
But rather common souls prepared to give
Their lives in order that their friends might live.
Few humans I have seen have been so good.
Four animals who lived within a wood
In true community now demonstrate
A mutual love our kind should imitate.
The rat and the gazelle, the tortoise and the crow
Lived in a close-knit group, a sweet society,
And, looking for security,
They settled in a spot that humans would not know.
What optimists! No place exists, no matter where,
Beneath the sea, across the desert, in the air,
That man will not at last invade to set his snares.
One day, as the gazelle was frisking, unawares,
Upon the plain, a hunting hound, that instrument
Of man's barbaric pleasure, having caught her scent
Upon the grass, began to chase her and, in fear,
She fled. When evening came and she did not appear
To share their meal, the rat said, "Why are we just three?
Has the gazelle forgotten us?" "If only I
Had wings, as crows do, I would fly
Right now," the tortoise cried, "to see
Where our swift-footed friend might be
And what mischance has kept her from our company.
I know her heart: she'd never voluntarily
Abandon us." At once, at his top speed, the crow
Flew off to search for her and when he saw, below,
The poor gazelle, caught in a net, painfully trying
To free herself, instead of wasting time by flying
Down to her side at once and plying
Her, like some obstinate school master,
With silly questions as to how and why and when
She'd fallen into this disaster,
The bird, with better judgement, instantly again
Returned to tell the rest the news.

When they had heard, then shared their views
As to their course of action, they
Decided that the crow and rat should both pell mell
Rush to the aid of the gazelle.
"The tortoise," said the crow, "should stay
At home, for by the time she makes it there,
Our little mountain goat will be in rigor mortis."
His words were scarcely said before the quicker pair
Were off, while in the rear, determinedly, the tortoise
Came crawling after, grousing, "Drat these legs! Oh, why
Are they such little stumps? It's so unfair that I
Am burdened with my house!" The rat, named Nibbleknot,
And aptly named, meanwhile arrived upon the spot,
Gnawed at the net and set their dear companion free.
What joy they felt! But when the hunter now appeared
And asked, in fury, "Who has robbed me of my prey?"
The three friends quickly disappeared,
The rat into a hole, the crow into a tree,
And the gazelle into the wood. Half-crazed that he
Found no one near for him to blame,
The man now saw the tortoise as she slowly came
To help her friend. "What can have bothered me?" he said,
His rage in check, "Here's something I can eat instead,"
He dumped her in his sack. The tortoise would have bled
To save them all, had not the crow flown fast to tell
This latest news to the gazelle.
Pretending to be lame, she hobbled past the man,
Who dropped the heavy sack and ran
In hot pursuit, which gave the rat the time to cut
With his sharp teeth the knotted cord that held it shut
And so set free this other sister in the group,
Who otherwise would have been boiled for turtle soup.

Such was the tale that Bidpai told,
Yet with Apollo in the least inspiring me
I would, to please you, set it in an epic mold
And make it long, an Iliad or Odyssey.

While everyone would be essential to the plot,
The role of hero would be played by Nibbleknot,
While Princess Carryhouse's pleading urgency
Would bring Sir Crow to take the part
Of spy, then serve as messenger, and the gazelle
Would use her wits to draw the hunter from the dell,
Permitting Nibbleknot to thwart
His cruel plans. So each one's call
Would be to act and work to benefit them all.
And which deserves most praise? I'd say, the selfless heart.

XII. 15

The Forest and the Woodcutter

A woodcutter's axe handle broke or was mislaid,
Which spared the forest further cutting by his blade
Until he got a new one. So he humbly prayed
To the great trees surrounding him
That they should give him just one limb,
One smallish stick, for then, he said,
He once again could earn his bread.
He would employ his axe elsewhere, of course he would:
These ancient firs and oaks would stand as they had stood
For many ages, leaving all who saw them charmed.
The forest innocently gave. The liar stropped
His blade, set it on its new helve and then, rearmed,
Attacked the noblest trees and dropped
Them, stripped of their branches, to the ground.
The forest made a keening sound.
Its gift, so generously made,
Had been with treachery repaid.

So goes society and its contentious factions,
Where doers of good are punished for their benefactions.
I'm tired of preaching on it; but seeing such outrages

Inflicted upon forests that for many ages
Have given shade and refuge, who does not feel disgust?
But I protest in vain. Those things I most revile,
Ingratitude, abuse of trust,
Have never yet gone out of style.

XII. 16

The Fox, the Wolf, and the Horse

A fox, quite young, but innocent not in the least,
Saw the first horse of his short life's experience.
He called a wolf he knew, his peer for ignorance:
"Come quickly, friend! Some unknown beast
Is in our meadow, calmly grazing.
So big! So beautiful! I am enraptured, gazing."
"But is he stronger than we are?" the wolf replied
With scornful laughter. "Portray this wonder if you will."
"If I could paint or if in school I'd learned the skill
Of using words, I'd do it, since it would provide
A foretaste of your joy at seeing him. But, hey!
Come view him in the flesh. Dame Fortune may
Have sent us prey we both might find delicious."
They went. The grazing horse, at sight
Of such a raffish pair, was instantly suspicious
And on the verge of taking flight.
"Milord," the fox began, "your humble servants. Might
We learn your noble name?" The horse, a brainy steed,
Said, "Sirs, my blacksmith has inscribed my apellation
Upon my shoe, there for the literate to read."
The fox deplored his total lack of education:
"My parents lived down in a hole, in constant need,
And never could afford to pay for my tuition.
The wolf's were rich, however. It was their ambition
To give him proper schooling. He knows how to read."
The wolf, puffed up with flattery,

324

Approached the horse to demonstrate how well he read,
But by his purblind vanity
Lost four of his back teeth instead
When the horse let fly behind him with a well-shod hoof
And galloped off. Half-dazed and streaming blood, the wolf
Lay prostrate, weakened so that he could scarcely groan.
The fox addressed him, "Friend, I've heard an ancient saw,
Which that big animal just printed on your jaw:
'The wise are wary in approaching things unknown.'"

XII. 17

The Fox and the Turkeys

To halt a fox's depredations,
A flock of turkeys made a tree their citadel,
But when the sly one saw how they stood sentinel,
On constant watch, at battle stations,
He cried, "Do they imagine they can get away
With mocking me, that they alone need not obey
My long-established law? By all the gods, not so!"
He made good on his threat. The moon that night, aglow,
Seemed to be favoring the turkey cocks,
But Reynard, who had many a time
Laid siege to well-defended flocks,
Reached in the bag of tricks well-known to every fox:
First he would grip the tree trunk as if about to climb
Straight up to get them, next fall down
And seem to die, then spring to life, resuscitated.
The Harlequin, that madcap clown,
Could never have impersonated
So many characters. He did such things as raise
His tail aloft and make it blaze
With glints of moonlight, plus myriads of other tricks.
Bedazzled, tired, afraid to sleep, all strained to fix
Unblinking eyes upon him till, exhausted, they

Began to tumble, senseless – half of them, at least –
Out of the tree. The fox hauled each in turn away
And stored them in his larder for a future feast.

To dwell on dangers till our minds grow paralyzed
Can make it likelier our fears are realized.

XII. 18

The Ape

In Paris once they gave a wife
To a baboon. As husbands go
He was an ape and very rough.
He beat her up a lot and so
She got way down, poor dame, and finally she died.
Their son put on a crazy show,
Made frightful noises, howled and cried;
The husband laughed – his wife was dead.
By then he had a brand–new bride
For him to beat up on instead.
And he was always drunk, stumbling from bar to bar.

Don't look for any good from imitative types,
But as between baboons and literary apes
The species Author is the worse by far.

XII. 19

The Scythian Philosopher

A dour philosopher, a Scythian born and bred,
Proposing to moderate the joyless life he led,
Traveled to Greece, where, as he went from place to place,

He met an ancient man, the likeness of a sage
Described by Virgil, a man grown regal in his age
As any king, and with an air of tranquil grace
And deep contentment almost godlike. He took
Great pleasure in the beauty of his garden. There
The Scythian found him walking, holding a pruning hook
To tend his trees, culling their fruit to have them bear
Only their best, and limbing, shaping, cutting away,
And so amending nature that it would repay
The husbandry he lent at a usurious rate.
The Scythian was amazed. Why was the Grecian bent
On such destruction? Could it be wise to mutilate
Poor growing things? "Give me this harmful implement!
Leave them to time's sharp sickle blade –
Soon all will stand within the shade
By its dark stream." "I've only cut," the sage explained,
"What was superfluous, unproductive,
And with that gone the rest have gained."
The Scythian found his words instructive.
Once home again in his harsh land,
He took a pruning hook in hand
And went about advising all to be destructive.
He roamed his orchard, lopping branches for no reason,
Regardless of their beauty or the growing season
Or waxing moon or waning, till all was purified.
His orchard withered and it died.
This Scyth evokes the puritan lacking
The tiniest leavening of doubt,
Who maims the human soul by hacking
Its desires and passions out.
Guilty or innocent, all pleasures
Are purged by the same sweeping measures.
I cannot bear such people – they deprive
Our hearts of that vitality that each so treasures.
They kill us while we are alive.

XII. 20

The Elephant and Jupiter's Ape

In some past age Rhinoceros and Elephant,
To settle which of them should be crowned emperor,
Agreed to fight each other in a tournament.
But on the day of the event a messenger
Brought news: a monkey from the court of Jupiter
Had just appeared up in the sky
With a caduceus, the staff of Mercury,
Gripped in his paw. The elephant immediately
Concluded that this creature, Giles by name, was sent
By Jupiter as envoy, bent
On seeking out His Greatness – or so goes the story.
So with much pride in his own glory
He waited, none too patiently, for the descent
Of Master Giles, whom he found rather dilatory
In offering his credentials. But when at last
Giles came before His Excellency –
Who had prepared himself, with pleased expectancy,
To hear Jove's message – no word passed
The envoy's lips. The elephant's presumption,
That all the gods were partisans in his dispute,
Was based upon the rash assumption
That those who rule the firmament
Care whether one is either fly or elephant.
And since the messenger stayed mute
He found himself reduced to speaking on his own.
"My cousin Jupiter," he said, "from your high throne,
Surrounded by your court, you are about to see
A splendid combat in the lists."
"What combat?" asked the monkey, frowning solemnly.
The elephant replied, "You did not know that we
Are to-the-death antagonists,
That upstart, the rhinoceros and I?
For, since he claims he is of nobler stock than me,
The Elephantidae and the Rhinoceri
Are now at war, two kingdoms very widely famed,

328

As you undoubtedly must know." Said Giles, "I prize
This knowledge greatly. In our vast region of the skies
We have not heard a word of this." Amazed, ashamed,
The elephant inquired, "Then what has brought you here?"
"I am to portion out a single blade of grass
Between two nests of ants. Whatever comes to pass
Eventually will have a claim on our attention.
But your great war has not yet happened to appear
Before the council of the gods. In their eyes all,
However great, however small,
Are of identical dimension."

XII. 21

A Fool and a Wise Man

A witless fool kept throwing rocks at an old sage,
Who turned on him at last and said, "Good pard,
You've done a splendid job. Accept this coin as wage,
For efforts such as yours deserve a fine reward.
But you should be much richer, having worked so hard.
You see that fellow passing? He has means to pay.
Send him your gifts: he will reward you right away."
Enticed by the gold coin, he did as he was told
And threw rocks at this second man,
But this time when he did he was not paid in gold.
With iron bars and cudgels, the man's footservants ran
And worked him over briskly, back and side and head
And left him lying as for dead.

In royal courts such fools amuse
The king, who laughs as they abuse
The vulnerable. But if one lacks
The strength to punish their attacks,
There yet can be a good solution:
Set them on someone with full means for retribution.

XII. 22

The English Fox

To Madame Harvey

Goodheartedness in you accompanies good sense,
With scores of other virtues, too many to cite here:
Nobility of soul, an inborn confidence
That lets you move in any sphere,
An easy sense of humor, frank and unconstrained,
And a great gift for friendships, faithfully maintained
In spite of Jupiter and the late stormy weather.
For all of these a solemn ode would be your due,
But such pomposities have small appeal for you,
So I will simply patch together
A few words favoring your state:
You love it. To think profoundly is a trait
The English have, arising from a temperament
Which spurs them to investigate
A multitude of subjects and experiences
And thus expand the empire of the sciences.
My saying this is no mere wooer's compliment,
Because you English lead us all in intellectual powers –
And even your English hunting hounds
Have keener noses than have ours.
Your foxes are craftier too: my grounds
For saying so are based upon the clever trick
One found to save himself, a stratagem as slick
As any history discloses.
The rascal, fleeing for his life, just yards ahead
Of hounds pursuing him (the ones with the keen noses),
Came to a gibbet where, in various stiff poses,
A row of outlaw animals was hanging, dead:
Badgers, foxes, owls, all thieves by reputation,
Left there to rot, to edify the population.
With his last bit of strength, the fox climbed up and swung
Among his fellow thieves, as if he had been hung.
(I picture Hannibal, hard pressed and near defeat,

Decoying the Roman captains in the wrong direction,
Certain they had him, then seizing the moment to retreat,
Like a wise fox evading enemy detection.)
The pack of hounds, arriving where
The fox had led them, filled the air
With furious barking till their master ordered them
To end the chase – for though they howled and bayed as if
They wanted to get at the stiff
Lineup above their heads, the fox's stratagem
Had fooled the man completely. "This guy has found
A foxhole he can hide in, safely under ground,"
He said. "My dogs are just excited now to see
This crowd of honest gentry on the gallows tree.
Well, he will get there yet." He did, to his regret.
He felt quite safe. The basset hounds beneath him baying
Could never reach him, gently swaying
With his dead peers. And if another day he met
With the same pack of dogs he saw no reason why
The trick would not work twice. But it did not, poor guy.
Next day it failed him and he left his bones to dry
With all the others. The truth is, a new situation
Requires a new method, but the fox for his salvation
Had thought of only one, though not from being shy
Of intellect, of course, for one cannot deny
That all the English have a good sufficiency
Of mental powers – yet often a deficiency
In love of life, with a result too often dire.
As I've implied, it would require
A labor quite beyond my strength
To sing your talents, for my lyre
Does best with odes of modest length.
And songs and verses seldom please
One's own or any other nation
When drenched with perfumed flatteries.
Your king once made the observation
That one plain word of love outweighs
Four pages filled with flowery praise.
So please accept this modest gift my ancient muse

Has fashioned in her final days,
A trifling thing, one that she rues
For all its imperfections. Still,
Could you not share the loving homage it conveys
With one who warms your English climate's chill
With voyagers she brings from Cythera? I mean,
Of course, Mancini, in the realm of love true queen.

XII. 23

Daphnis and Alcimadura

IN IMITATION OF THEOCRITUS
TO MADAME DE LA MÉSANGÈRE

Most winning daughter of a mother who alone
Is courted by a thousand hearts, and with your own
Crowd of admirers all intent
On pleasing you – and not a few among them bent
On offering you their love – I cannot help but mete
To each of you a share of that fine incense I
Obtain from Mount Parnassus, high
Upon its slopes, and with my secret art make sweet.
So, I commence my song of praise . . .
But then I halt: it would require
A strength beyond me now. My lyre
Takes more than I can give these days
And I must use my voice with care,
For it grows weak and I have little time to spare.
Then let me simply praise that true and tender heart,
Those noble sentiments, that grace, that intellect
In which you have no peers of either sex, apart
From her whose talents yours so perfectly reflect.
But yet take care your roses may
Be not so set with thorns that they
Let none approach or Love may say

The same to you. For this small deity
Can punish those rejecting him, as you will see.

Long since, a youthful temptress came
To grief, defying Eros' great hegemony.
Alcimadura was her name.
Both wild and proud, she frequented the woods
And meadows, dancing on the grass alone,
Obeying no laws but her own
Capriciousness and rivaling her sisterhood's
Most beautiful, while yet surpassing all the rest
In cruelty. And even as she spurned all pleas
Her face was still the loveliest.
What could she not have done had she desired to please!
The shepherd Daphnis, handsome, young and nobly born,
Had the bad luck to fall in love with her, but scorn
Was his reward. Her heartlessness was absolute:
No pity, not one glance, one word, would she bestow
Upon him till, discouraged by his vain pursuit,
He only wished to die. And so,
In hopeless desperation, he hastened to the door
Of this inhuman creature, where his words of woe
Were lost upon the wind. He waited,
Ignored, as she and her fair sisters celebrated
Her birthday, the flowers of her beauty matching those
From blossoming meadows and garden rows
They picked for her. "I wanted you to see me die,"
He shouted, "but it seems that I
Am just too hateful in your eyes
For even that, and so it comes as no surprise
That you would now deny me this last mortal grace.
I've told my father when I die that he must place
My grazing land, my flock of sheep, my sheepdog, too,
Before your feet: those things of mine your heart refused.
All else I own is to be sold, the money used
To found a temple on whose altar all will view
Your image, wreathed with flowers, fresh each day.

333

And near that temple I will lie
Beneath a simple stone, with words on it that say:

Daphnis died for love. Pause here, you who pass by,
Shed tears for him on knowing he
Died of Alcimadura's heartless cruelty."

Then, having said these words, he felt death drawing nigh.
He would have said yet more, but was cut short by pain.
Next moment from the door in all her finery
The ingrate stepped, triumphant. Though it was urged
        that she
Should pause to weep for Daphnis, the urging was in vain.
She sneered at Eros' power with complete contempt.
And that same evening, imagining herself exempt
From all the laws of love, she danced among a crowd
Around the blind god's statue, which by the whim of fate
Came tumbling down on her and crushed her with its weight.
At which a voice came from a cloud
And said these words that Echo spread throughout the air:
Let all now love: she who refused it is no more.
Soon Daphnis' spirit, standing now on death's dark shore,
Shook in amazement as it saw hers coming there.
All Erebos now heard as his fair murderer
Begged Daphnis to forgive, but he was deaf to her,
As Ajax to Ulysses, Dido to her abandoner.

XII. 24

The Judge, the Physician, and the Hermit

Three saintly souls, each as determined as the rest
To lead a life of conscience, equally possessed
By the same spirit, the same final vision, chose
Three different paths to follow: for, as the saying goes,
All roads lead to Rome, and they believed that they
Would meet again at last though each went his own way.

One, touched by the delays, the upsets, the frustration
Of court proceedings, offered all his arbitration,
Pro bono, having no concern for worldly gain.
Since laws came into being, our imperfect strain
Has by its own offenses condemned itself to spend
Half of its life in court – three fourths! – perhaps the whole!
Our peacemaker felt certain that his work would mend
This rotten state of things. The next saint for his role
Chose that of the physician, a choice that I must praise,
Because of all professions the best one, to my mind,
Is that which eases pain. Since patients in those days
Were just like patients now, it was hard work. They whined,
Self-pitying, resentful: "It's not fair! He tends
To him, to her, to them, because they are his friends.
While they get special treatment we are all neglected."
But these complaints were minor next to those directed
At the well-meaning expert in conciliation.
No one was satisfied. On hearing his summation
Both sides would shout accusingly,
"He's tipped the scales! Conspiracy!"
Disgusted by such talk, the judge sought the physician.
Both having only met complaints and opposition,
The two, distressed, each forced to give up his ambition,
Fled to the wilderness, where each of them might bring
Himself to tell those silences the pain he felt.
And there beneath a rocky crag the third saint dwelt,
Next to a pure, upwelling spring,
A place untouched by storms, unnoticed by the sun.
They asked their friend to give them counsel. "Everyone,"
He said, "depends at last upon himself alone,
For by whom can one's needs be any better known?
To gain self-knowledge is the primal task assigned
By nature's majesty to all of humankind.
But can you do so in your hectic public spaces?
It is not possible, except in tranquil places.
To seek this knowledge elsewhere is gross fallacy.
Stir up the water. Can you see your faces?
Stir up yourselves, what selves may you then see?

The spring is muddied, thickly roiled,
Its crystal made opaque, its clarity now spoiled:
One cannot see oneself, however hard one tries.
My brothers (said the saint), stay here.
In solitude your clouded vision will grow clear
And you will see yourselves at last with your own eyes.
Thus spoke the hermit. And they heard
And followed, both of them, his salutary word.
But this is not to argue that under all conditions
Such practical pursuits must always be abjured.
For death exists, suits must be tried and sickness cured.
We need both lawyers and physicians.
Thank heaven we have them. Both of those professions
Deserve, I say, abundant honors and possessions.
But yet the self gets lost in these communal needs.
Oh, you, whose lives are occupied by public deeds,
Who judge, who lead, who legislate,
Who live exposed to rough and real events, to hate
That brings you down and the corruption of success,
You do not see yourselves, you see no one at all.
For if a happy moment comes when, free from stress,
You start such meditations, some flatterer comes to call.

Here ends the final lesson of these many pages.
May it prove useful, centuries on from now.
I offer it to kings, I proffer it to sages:
What better way to take my bow?

XII. 25

Acknowledgments

Besides, in spirit, my grandmother, Anna Giesecke, whose legacy of books and learning unexpectedly gave me both the means and the excuse to begin, I most especially thank my wife, Heather Davidson Hill, for the candor and loving patience with which she has listened to my readings of a plethora of translations in progress over the years. David and Franny Mitchell and Bill and Peggy Braden also lent me their invaluable ears in our travels on several continents. Other friends, the Bergens and the Hubbards, it is too late to thank, except in memory. Stephen Anderson, knowing the fables *à l'origine*, has given me wise advice on fine points, as has Marcel Gutwirth, whose comments on several fables helped greatly in my efforts to understand and convey La Fontaine's subtleties.

Richard Wilbur has done me the great kindness of reading samples of my work over the years and giving me the confidence to continue. Though I have never met John Hollander, I will always be grateful for his recommendation that allowed my translation of the great fable, "Ulysses and His Shipmates," to be published in *Raritan Quarterly Review* when Richard Poirier was its editor. More recently, Richard Seaver, Arcade Publishing's president and editor in chief, has with great politesse put up with my frequent impulse to fly off in several directions, thus keeping this book on course in its long journey into print. Thank you, Dick.

Notes

The world of Aesop's fables is a magical one, set in a golden age when the animals, nowadays mute, could still speak and Zeus ruled over the gods on Mount Olympus and sometimes hurled thunder-bolts down to warn his unruly, exasperating subjects, the animals – including the human animal – that he was angry at them for their misbehavior. As this is not a scholarly edition of the fables but one meant for the so-called general reader, for whom too many explanatory notes may be a hindrance rather than a help, I have decided against providing fable-by-fable end notes. That said, the following may nevertheless prove helpful.

Acheron	the river souls must cross to enter Hades (see entry)
Aeolus	god of the winds
Aesop	legendary Greek author of the fables
Ajax	Greek warrior in the siege of Troy, driven violently mad when not he but Ulysses was awarded the armor once worn by the great Achilles
Alecto	one of the three Furies (see entry)
Amphitrite	sea goddess, wife of Poseidon
Apollo	the divine archer, god of medicine and music and inspirer of oracles
Apple	the golden fruit inscribed, "for the most beautiful," with which Discord fomented the bitter quarrel among Hera/Juno, Aphrodite/Venus and Athena/Minerva on Mount Olympus, leading ultimately to the Trojan War on earth below
Arachne	a woman who foolishly dared to challenge Athena to a weaving contest and in punishment was changed by the angry goddess into a spider

Areopagus	high court of justice of Athens
Arion	a poet, perhaps a real one, of the 8th century B.C., purportedly saved and carried ashore by a friendly dolphin after a ship's crew had robbed him and thrown him overboard to drown
Athena	goddess of wisdom, jealously proud of her skill as a weaver, born from Zeus's forehead fully grown and clad in armor. Also Pallas Athena.
Atropos	one of the three Fates (see entry)
Aurora	goddess of the dawn
Bidpai	an apocryphal Hindu storyteller, source of many of La Fontaine's fables in Books VII–XII. Pilpay in French texts.
Boreas	the north wind
Cassandra	seeress, daughter of Priam, king of Troy and his queen, Hecuba. Inspired by Apollo, she constantly prophesied the city's doom but was fated not to be believed until too late
Castor & Pollux	twin demigods, living as stars in their Zodiacal constellation, Gemini
Calliope	muse of epic poetry
Cerberus	three–headed guard dog stationed at the gate to Hades, allowing all to enter, none to return
Charon	the old boatman who ferries the souls of the dead across the river Acheron
Circe	enchantress, daughter of Helios, the sun god, and ruler of the island of Aeaea. When Ulysses (Odysseus) and his crew land on its shore, Ulysses alone refuses the potion she offers them and as the others thirstily drink it they are turned into animals.
Cupid	see Eros
Discord	goddess of strife, the Greek Eris, eternally provoking quarrels and wars among both families and nations. See Apple

Empedocles	ancient philosopher who, unable to comprehend the wonders of Mt. Etna, threw himself into it
Eros	Venus's blind son; sometime husband of Psyche and, like goddess Discord, a great disturber of the peace among men and beasts. Also Amor, Love, or Cupid.
Fame	spirit who spreads rumors, true or false, around the world
Fates	the "spinning sisters," Clotho, Lachesis and Atropos, who respectively weave, spin and cut the thread of each human life
Faunus	minor Roman god of the woods, goat-footed and goat-horned like Pan in Greek myth
Fortune	the fickle goddess whose ever-turning wheel determines the outcomes of life. Also Destiny and Chance.
Furies	the Greek Eumenides, Alecto, Tisiphone and Megaera, female spirits with snakes for hair, they dwell in Hades, from where they may be sent up to earth by Jupiter to punish human crimes
Ganymede	a beautiful young boy, seized and carried up to Olympus by Jupiter's eagle, to serve as cupbearer to the king of the gods
Genghis Caligula Jaws	my translation of Rodilardus, the name of the cat in "The Congress of the Rats" II.2. Borrowed from Rabelais, "Rodilardus" is a latinical pun on the obsolete French word "rongelard," implying, more or less, "gluttonous bacon eater," but, since it has to be explained with a note, no longer very amusing for a present-day, English-speaking reader.
Hades	king of the world of the dead, itself called Hades. Also Pluto.
Helen	most beautiful of women, wife of the Greek, King Menelaus. Her abduction by Paris, son of King

Priam of Troy, instigated by Venus, brought on the Trojan war.

Hercules   demigod of superhuman strength, one of Jupiter's many children by mortal women

Hydra   nine-headed monster that sprouted two new heads for each one cut off

Hymettos   mountain in Attica, celebrated among poets and from which the Greeks collected excellent honey

Io   in Ovid's *Metamorphoses*, a young priestess of Juno hotly courted by Jupiter but changed by him into a white heifer to keep Juno from catching them in flagrante.

Iris   goddess of the rainbow

Juno   vengefully jealous wife of Jupiter, the original womanizer. Also Hera.

Jupiter   ruler of both lesser deities and earthly beings, sometimes hurling thunderbolts down from Mount Olympus at his unruly subjects, the animals (including the human animal), to warn them of his anger at their incessant demands on his fatherly patience. Also Jove and Zeus.

Mars   god of war

Mercury   Jupiter's wing-footed messenger, known for his slyness

Minerva   the Roman goddess of wisdom. See Athena.

Morpheus   god of sleep

Mt. Olympus   the peak inhabited by Jupiter and his quarrelsome family of lesser gods

Parnassus   the mountain next to Olympus, sacred to the muses of poetry and art

Phaedrus   early Roman fabulist, one of La Fontaine's main sources of Aesopic fables

Phaethon   Helios's inexperienced son, who tried to drive his father's sun chariot across the sky one day but nearly set the earth ablaze when he could

	not keep the winged horses at the right altitude, forcing Jupiter to stop him with a thunderbolt
Phoenix	Arabian bird that after centuries of life consumes itself in fire yet always re-emerges from its black ashes, immortal, its feathers dazzlingly beautiful once more
Phrygian	epithet for Aesop, in legend a slave of the king of Phrygia, in Asia Minor
Scylla and Charybdis	sea monsters, the one a dangerous rock, the other a horrible whirlpool. Those attempting to sail the narrow passage between them must face the dilemma of avoiding the rock without being sucked down by the whirlpool
Simonides	Greek poet of the 6th century, B.C., said to have been the first to compose odes on commission, i.e., for pay. Only a line or two of his works are now extant
Styx	a river in Hades on which the gods swore their solemn oaths
Tethys	a sea goddess, daughter of the ancient Titans, Uranus and Gaia
Venus	Roman equivalent of Greek Aphrodite, goddess of beauty
Vulcan	the lame god who forges Jupiter's thunderbolts in his volcano smithy
Xanthus	river dyed red by the blood of the gods, in a furious battle between the pro-Achilles and pro-Hector deities in the Trojan War, provoked by Discord, spurred on by Eros (see entry)
Zephyr	the warm, gentle west wind of springtime

Contemporaries to whom Fontaine dedicated fables

Dauphin	Louis XIV's first legitimate son and dedicatee of books I–VI, 1668
Duke de La Rochefoucauld	author of *Maxims*
Duke of Burgundy	the dauphin's son, Louis's grandson
Duke of Maine	a son of Louis by his mistress, Madame de Montespan
Madame de La Mésangère	daughter of Madame de la Sablière
Madame de La Sablière	La Fontaine's beloved and brilliant patroness, from 1672 until her death in 1693
Madame de Montespan	Louis XIV's mistress, to whom La Fontaine dedicated his second collection of fables, VII–XI, in 1678, when Madame de Maintenon supplanted her
Madame Harvey	Ann Montague, widow of Sir Daniel Harvey, Charles II's ambassador to Constantinople; sister of the Duke of Montague, Charles II's sometime envoy to the French court
Mademoiselle de Sévigné	once perhaps considered a possible candidate to succeed Louis XIV's mistress, Louise de la Vallière.
Mademoiselle de Sillery	La Rochefoucauld's niece
M.D.M.	"Monsieur de Maucroix," La Fontaine's close friend and correspondent, from their first meeting at the Faculty of Law in 1637, to the poet's last days, in 1695
M.L.C.D.B.	Count of Brienne, an ill-starred nobleman who collaborated with La Fontaine on a volume of religious poetry

Monsieur de Barillon	Louis XIV's ambassador to the court of Charles II

For further reading, one of the great original sources is of course Ovid's wonderful *Metamorphoses*, while Edith Hamilton's *Mythology* remains an indispensable modern introduction to all the major and minor actors in classical myth. Antonia Fraser's *Love and Louis XIV* is fascinating on the intrigues of Louis XIV's court that provided the social backdrop for the satire of the fables. Marc Fumaroli's *The Poet and the King* offers a nuanced account of the cultural and literary influences that shaped La Fontaine's poetic career. Fumaroli's edition of La Fontaine's original work, *La Fontaine: Fables*, along with its copious notes, served as my principal source for this translation.

Index of Titles